MARXISM AND EDUCATION

This series assumes the ongoing relevance of Marx's contributions to critical social analysis and aims to encourage continuation of the development of the legacy of Marxist traditions in and for education. The remit for the substantive focus of scholarship and analysis appearing in the series extends from the global to the local in relation to dynamics of capitalism and encompasses historical and contemporary developments in political economy of education as well as forms of critique and resistances to capitalist social relations. The series announces a new beginning and proceeds in a spirit of openness and dialogue within and between Marxism and education, and between Marxism and its various critics. The essential feature of the work of the series is that Marxism and Marxist frameworks are to be taken seriously, not as formulaic knowledge and unassailable methodology but critically as inspirational resources for renewal of research and understanding, and as support for action in and upon structures and processes of education and their relations to society. The series is dedicated to the realization of positive human potentialities as education and thus, with Marx, to our education as educators.

Series Editor: *Anthony Green*

Renewing Dialogues in Marxism and Education: Openings
Edited by Anthony Green, Glenn Rikowski, and Helen Raduntz

Critical Race Theory and Education: A Marxist Response
Mike Cole

Revolutionizing Pedagogy: Education for Social Justice Within and Beyond Global Neo-Liberalism
Edited by Sheila Macrine, Peter McLaren, and Dave Hill

Marxism and Education beyond Identity: Sexuality and Schooling
Faith Agostinone-Wilson

Blair's Educational Legacy: Thirteen Years of New Labour
Edited by Anthony Green

Racism and Education in the U.K. and the U.S.: Towards a Socialist Alternative
Mike Cole

Marxism and Education: Renewing the Dialogue, Pedagogy, and Culture
Edited by Peter E. Jones

Education and Social Change in Latin America

Edited by

Sara C. Motta and Mike Cole

First published in 2013 by
PALGRAVE MACMILLAN®
in the United States—a division of St. Martin's Press LLC,
175 Fifth Avenue, New York, NY 10010.

Where this book is distributed in the UK, Europe and the rest of the world,
this is by Palgrave Macmillan, a division of Macmillan Publishers Limited,
registered in England, company number 785998, of Houndmills,
Basingstoke, Hampshire RG21 6XS.

Palgrave Macmillan is the global academic imprint of the above companies
and has companies and representatives throughout the world.

Palgrave® and Macmillan® are registered trademarks in the United States,
the United Kingdom, Europe and other countries.

ISBN: 978–1–137–38067–8

Library of Congress Cataloging-in-Publication Data

Education and social change in Latin America / edited by
Sara C. Motta and Mike Cole.
    pages cm.—(Marxism and education)
    Includes index.
    ISBN 978–1–137–38067–8 (alk. paper)
    1. Education—Social aspects—Latin America. 2. Social change—
Latin America. 3. Social movements—Latin America, I. Motta, Sara C.,
1973– II. Cole, Mike.

LC191.8.L37E379 2013
306.43—dc23   2013026023

A catalogue record of the book is available from the British Library.

Design by Newgen Knowledge Works (P) Ltd., Chennai, India.

First edition: December 2013

.

We dedicate this book to the memory of Hugo Chávez, who once described Venezuela as "a giant school" and to the countless—often invisibilised and undervalued- popular educators, educational visionaries and communities in struggle who give birth to and tenderly nurture the pedagogical innovations, emancipatory horizons and revolutionary educational practices that are at the heart of the reinvention of 21st Century Socialism in Latin America, and beyond.

Contents

Part III   Education and Pedagogy
from Below

Illustrations

Figures

Tables

Series Editor's Preface

La lucha continua no terminará fácilmente! The struggle will continue. It will not be easily concluded!

Che Guevara, 1967[1]

Let's make no mistake these are *interesting times.* Global capitalism is currently undergoing its deepest crisis since the 1930s. An international capitalist plutocracy has emerged and become entrenched, consolidating since the late 1970s, even more decisively so in the 2000s and its power and exclusivity grows exponentially. Today is therefore interesting too for democratic socialist renewal and inevitably for Marxism as itself a diverse body of reasoning and indispensable educative resources and inspiration for progressive *social change.* So long as there is capitalism there will be Marxism. We may thus preface this book remarking that the systemic economic and social problems of global capital are again becoming ever more widely appreciated (in the full senses of the term), analyzed, exposed and demystified *from below* in the development of politics for viable socialist alternatives. Political economy in contemporary neoliberal forms is challenged and historical materialist dialectics move on *with* Marxism and *as* education for making *really useful knowledge.*[2] Capitalism, despite its most evident power and multidimensional penetration through ravenous *commodification of everything,* reveals itself as structurally deeply flawed, wounded, stumbling perhaps, though hardly less strong. However, it is no longer beyond challenge as *the* modernizing *TINA.*[3] Slogans such as the longstanding, perhaps timelessly meaningful in modernity, "Community not commodity" and more recently topical and equally pertinent Occupy Movement's, "We are the 99%," or on another note, the complementary situationist radical gastronomy of "Eat the rich" or more specifically "Eat the bankers,"[4] spark activist political and analytical imagination for countering injustices of punitive austerity meted out to the victims of capital's immanent capacity for destruction and collapse. Contradictions abound. Other ways and means of producing a humane world are necessary and available, indeed, have been available for some time for moving with ingenuity toward social renewal within ecologically sensitive and sensible boundaries of a humanizing nature for feasible growth and prosperity.

Arguably, no region is more vibrant in these terms as Latin America is today. Indeed, to many observers a veritable *pink tide* flows with inspiration, learning and popular Left leaning empowerment[5] to engage, and develop our passages through varieties of mid-twentieth century New Left Marxism toward realizing possibilities of contemporary democratic socialism. In this broad context, I have approached the task of presenting this Preface by aiming to set the central theme of this book in relation to the Series; to the global economic crisis; and ongoing general issues in Marxism for popular education and socialism. I have also aimed to not preempt specific substantive themes and topics in the main chapters or repeat introductions, or indeed, to single out any specific contributions by suggesting they are especially noteworthy, except for the moment of poetic art, which is especially pertinent and timely. Each contribution is informative and engaging and the collection of chapters constitutes an integrated whole, the first with focused contemporary Latin American specificity on education and fits splendidly well with the spirit of the Series.

However, it is impossible do justice in full measure to the range of problematics and substantive topics that the present conjuncture realizes and my remarks in this respect will be superficially indicative at best. Most importantly, is it impossible to pay any detailed attention to US economic regional and military dominance over Latin America, to the subtle and/or gross transformations, emergent during the twentieth century in the Monroe Doctrine and ideological re-imaginings of 'Manifest Destiny,' and for the 'Washington Consensus' and *Pax Americana* today. Nor can we examine the ramifications of the *global financial system* itself, where for instance despite indications of emergent pluricentrism, it serves to articulate and underpin US Federal Reserve capacities for deploying the US dollar as the reserve currency for co-optation of baseline 'market sentiment,' 'confidence' and 'credibility' on a global scale, and as a means of disciplining flows of monetary volumes and values in the global politics of emerging 'credit' transactions. The US military/industrial/financial mega-state is, in effect, the global trend regulator for corporate taxation, as well, setting standards for corporate compliance in terms most favorable for the international capitalist class in relation to their own subaltern, neo-comprador national contexts of accumulation and avoidance/ evasion in paying their fair dues. Only brief mention can be made of the interconnected impacts on the economies of emergent nation states, through IMF and World Bank mechanisms, etc., along with their own susceptibility to potentially ruinous competitive deflationary undercutting among each other racing to the bottom in support of their own capitalist economies.

In turn each of these mechanisms organically tend to reinforce US corporate global 'private' interests in the names of 'freedom,' creativity and modernizing for 'progress.' Thus we see that language colludes in the global class struggle, providing vocabulary for mediating and legitimating processes of non-productively shifting around huge tranches of unemployed capital for acquisitions, mergers and asset stripping often into reinflating commodity bubbles of various kinds, as well as working more productively into the dynamics of the 'real' economy; not least, investing in all manner of capitalizing possibilities for profit generation on 'well-being' and social regulation, in privatizing health care, welfare, education services and prisons, too, as 'modernization.'

Together these items provide some indication of the systemic background to the focus of the present book. In turn they should be set alongside patterns of relations among the emerging world powers in capitalization, especially those of China apparently rosy in its prosperous state capitalist global future while locked in a financial/ political clinch of immense proportions with the US economy, but also India and Brazil, and more specifically with the Latin American members of the BRICS.[6] We may note in this frame that they have gathered into formal recognition of their constituting a newly emergent collective force and potential authority consolidating for inter-regional cooperation through the CELAC Santiago Declaration (January, 2013).[7] While probably doing little to significantly undermine systemic neoliberal *capitalism*, as such, the global order in economic production, distribution and exchange (the reverse, most likely), this is significant not least for possibly checking US global and more specifically its Latin American regional hegemony.

We can therefore refocus and recognize national and international movements and consider policies in Latin America as being distinctively at the forefront of practical resistance to neoliberal demands on the poor, working classes and precarious. There we see political forms and movements that effectively set their faces, bodies and energies against years of successful dominant global capital class formation, *in and for itself*, and can detect in effect Latin America's shifting toward mounting clear opposition to *practices of the global war of position from above.*[8] Latin America thus demonstrates resistance to the growing empowerment of the international ruling class's continued building on its subaltern national ruling classes' deep histories of effectively appropriating unmerited benefits through their state's fiscal and monetary regulations, corruption and direct capital accumulation, modernized feudalism and repression. Progressive moments in Latin American nationalism and internationalism provide critical models, in effect educative *texts* for working to hold back dominant class free-riding on emergent capital-in-collectivity and empowerment through its voraciously enclosing by capitalization each possible element that constitutes the *productive commons*, rendering these into private property to make yet more private property and items of consumer interests and identities. Challenging the power bases of debt repayment hegemony, for instance, and opposing strangulation of redistribution policies supportive of extending social equity, democratic citizenship and popular social progress *in order to reinspire the local, national and regional commons* have once more become realities in Latin America. Much debated, the symbolically reinvigorated spirits and historical reputations of Simon Bolivar (despite Marx's trashing Bolivar's reputation, perhaps) and José Carlos Mariátegui live on in continuing productive tensions[9] while doing effective service, with Gramsci and Freire, along with our contemporary countless others; all organic activist/intellectuals in *educating the educators in, with and about their own conditions for changing the future* (Marx, 1845).

Finally in this opening context, we should bear witness in celebration and with deep regret to the passing of Hugo Chávez and the contributions, not without ambiguities, of his life and leadership in material and symbolic forms. His legacies are currently being debated, fought for, with and over at each level of political practices, not least concerning popular and more formal education. His was a life in struggle that has been outstanding, inspirational for Latin America and beyond, amply demonstrating that *it is not going to be concluded easily and there is a very long way to go!*

However, this arresting title and its subtitle—*What If Latin America Ruled the World?: How the South Will Take the North into the 22nd Century*—and elaborated contents of Oscar Guardiola Rivera's recent book does vigorous preface duty for us as backdrop for this book.[10] He offers an indepth historical review with engaging synthesis of *American*, north and southern hemispheres' potential in global transformation, a narrative en route to humanitarian renewal drawing creatively on key elements of Marxist methodology, ontologically and epistemologically for substantive descriptive analyses. It is thus deeply serious in its dynamic penetrating account and notable in its playful forms, too. With Guardiola-Rivera we might reflect, for instance, on the United States' own increasingly significant Latina/o population and that if combined with Mexico the most populous in the world in this regard. We should reflect that while demographics, language and cultural forms are significant, are *necessary* certainly, alone they are *insufficient* as decisive currency or *determinate* mediators in progressive social transformation.

In historical terms we might pause to note specific ironies springing to mind, while glimpsing the geo-historical twist of Iberia's current fate; once the fifteenth-century European instigator of globalization but today fully implicated in the economic and financial insecurity of the European Union, itself regional victim as one of the PIGS,[11] reminding us with Marx that "all that is solid melts into air, all that is holy is profaned."[12] Thus, Iberia's young generations of 'over-educated poor' are now trammeled in *austerity*, in effect blame worthy and useless (quite literally, it seems) as redundant elements of labor power in neoliberal capital logic terms[13] and implicated moreover in the serious risk of triggering further destabilization of the global economy by tilting Europe yet further, possibly toppling into ever-widening ripples in financial melt down.

Yet more irony for Iberia, when considering how it did so much to establish the pre-conditions for mercantile capital's systemic existence, through pillage, piracy, slaving, colonialism and eventual imperialism while trading at an advantage, whereas now it serves as a site for reinvigorated class struggle by *educating a new generation of potential grave-diggers* for the dominant world of capital it once served to inaugurate. Thus, we might note more specifically, as scholar activists, that Spanish silver funded the material conditions of historical possibility of Marx's and Engels' own lives and work as leading participants in the emergent nineteenth-century international labor movement, activists and theorists of finance and productive capital's emergence, its immanent structures and its potential demise. The specter Marx and Engels identified continues to hunt down the vampire of globalized political economy.[14] Moreover, perhaps more than just another straw in the wind, we should also note that at the moment of this writing there is rioting across Sweden, thereby bringing the scandal of confusion to liberal hopes by tainting the aura of progressive Scandinavian social democracy, now continuing to shift into the neoliberal gear it once seemed to be so effectively able to resist, while modeling for the starring role in mediating contradictions of capital in humanity and with evident humility and decency. At the other end of the 'European' social, cultural and geographical spectrum, perhaps, current manifestations of 'Islamic neoliberalism' is arguably provoking a Turkish 'Occupy' movement into life resisting authoritarian repression. Furthermore, while simultaneously demonstrating the contradictions within itself, Europe's political institutions are themselves at a loss to cope while struggling to devise democratic mechanisms for moving forward; in fact not so unlike the constitutional chaos in congressional gridlock for the current Obama administration in the United States. Thus, democracy itself is in crisis. With Hegel and Marx we might reflect idiomatically in transgression: "What comes around goes around."

In this broad and dynamic context, *Education and Social Change in Latin America* is a timely, pertinent, groundbreaking, challenging and most welcome contribution-in-collectivity to the Marxism and Education Series. In broad terms it marks a sharply focused moment in recognition and celebration of the achievements of Latin American radical popular education practices for emergent socialist progressive movements. It is deeply historical as well as dynamically contemporary in form and content; combining vibrant materialist analysis with graphic description and delicate moments of truth in creative cultural, indeed *practical* forms. It dramatizes and instantiates integrated scientific, philosophical and moral imagination in play for the restless work of *generating socialist theory and research as educative*, pedagogic (and andragogic) *practices*. Its primary focus is action, *praxis* in forming regenerative pathways toward better futures for freedom and equity.

All this sits well with the aims and spirit of the Marxism and Education Series, of course, where it is about openly renewing dialogues for generating materialist immanent and ideology critique and opposition to *political economy* in all its 'liberal' and potentially fascist manifestations, *both* romantic and bureaucratic. Thus, this book reports on themes that are analytically *transgressive*, working across long familiar dichotomies as themselves powerful 'boundaries,' borders constituted in tension. They are moments for realizing *both/ands* in what appear to be irreconcilable *either/ors;* sites in ambiguity for new contexts to be deconstructed, challenged, *struggled with and within* to rearticulate and realize constructive *praxis, and always with respect as appropriately due.* Thus, several dualist themes are indicative as interconnected areas of contention for realizing pedagogies of Marxist critique and devising socialist strategies and collective identities in empowerment in social transformation: *public/private, state/civil society, leaders/followers, schooling/education, educators/ educated, personal/political, ethics/politics, abstracted professionalized expertise/grounded demotic practices,...dual power/unitary power, reform/revolution,...with armed struggle/nonviolent resistance rejecting armed struggle.*

Across and systematically connecting each focus much remains open for continued discussion regarding longstanding dimensions of contention on relations, for instance, between Marxism and anarchism on the one hand, and Left social democracy on the other, as well as the progressive potential in religious and faith-related practices and alternative cosmologies, and including legality and human rights discourses serving as tools, topics and resources in progressive struggles. Simultaneously each moment is indicative of ongoing meta-theoretical themes in ontology and epistemology, methodologically vital for under-laboring our understandings of social class for Marxism, and for conceptualizing political relations in each identity-forming moment of social segmentation in movements for socialist regeneration. Each of these themes remain critically *open*, just as they do in the necessarily uncompleted and restlessly productive 'totality' of Marx's own writing, analyses and practices, and material historical legacy; *in struggle...to be remade for our own real time.*

In these terms the contributions to the book are realist and realistic, historical materialist in contextualizing what we may regard as specificities of the breaking wave of Latin American ways of enacting the golden threads of Marx's own pivotal work, the perspectives elaborated and critically distilled originally while ever to be 'completed' as practices for articulating confluences in the European Enlightenment *Rationalist* with the *Romantic* traditions and thus synthesized for specific understanding and moments in struggle, material *practices* for real situations. Especially so perhaps when we reaffirm with Marxism in what we might regard as the brilliant critical *articulation of reason and romance, technique and joy* that put the *social relations of capitalist production at stake.* Importantly then, these analyses are intimately connecting in/as *science and* in/ as *humanity* for the central theme of Marx's critique of political economy, namely that capital is not simply thing-like, and 'objective' (though it has these characteristics, emergent in structuration, of course) but "a definite social relation between men, that assumes, in their eyes, the fantastic form of a relation between things." Thus such art and science is concerned with addressing social relations specifically where they are *fetishised as commodities.*[15] Emergent here are glimpses of the role of moments of 'magic' echoing, for the context of this book, Latin American specified versions of reality in 'illusion.' The time/spaces of *solitudes* are *evocative of* critical analysis of reality in all manner of *sublime* instances, of science/art as praxis challenging representational forms in service of *ideology critique of/as* class struggle. Thus, with Marquez and with Marx we can appreciate the notion of recognizing the integrative practical wisdom of the person who "repeated until his dying day that there was no one with more common sense, no stone cutter more obstinate, no manager *more lucid or dangerous*, than a poet" (Garcia Marquez, *Love in the Time of Cholera*).[16] Continuously implied, therefore, is the *complementarity* of scientific and artistic practices for humanely changing our world. And that herein are vital modalities in *educating the educators, critiquing and negating oppression and structures of social relations in inequity and creating inversions in fatalist TINA representational practices.* Such de/reconstructing of social reality thereby serves in *regenerating ourselves, individually and collectively,* and reminding us of those 'men' (individualized collectives/collective individuals in Marx on *capital*, above) captured in fantastical, fetishized social forms, as *selves.* Moreover, invoking and seizing the *instantiating critical moments of opportunity for opening, for negating constraints and thus reconstituting communities of knowledge and resistance for material collective well-being.*[17]

In these chapters we can recognize that social, cultural and economic inertias, pitfalls and false starts abound by which neoliberalism can reenter, often subtly, disguised as 'progressive' individualized forms, in 'liberty' fitted for comfortably controlling the marginalized in 'freedom' and in fact reproducing their marginality, precarity and worse. Notable here, 'meritocracy' as *the* high-powered modernist ideology of control *par excellence*, the beguiling and continuously updated untruth that social mobility contingent on formal educational provision is *the* primary systemic mechanism that will settle the future in conviviality and social justice.[18] It is evident that contemporary patterns of widening inequalities of wealth and income, as well as the full armory of social capitalizing opportunities this entails for the well positioned, gives the direct lie to messages of benign possibilities of liberal equities arising simply by *trickle down*, let alone social structural opening via *merit*. The underlying message abstracted here is that success in achieving progressive social change requires strategic transformations that run culturally and structurally deep in order to secure the future of yet more humane practices where we can look forward to recognizing and dealing with necessary freedoms *and* in the future problems emergent on horizons of democratic socialism, itself. The aim must be to create contemporary forms of participatory democracy, 'state' forms that prefigure and support forward movement dispersing existing inevitable reactionary state and cultural mechanisms.[19]

By the same token such realism asserts that there is very little room for swift, fluent and immediately decisive transformations in the context of current 'democratic' forms despite some distinct strides and quickening of pace being made, especially within Latin America. As these chapters ably document, regenerating productive alliances and social movements, formulating policy and moving to collective practices through which we recognize that benign cycles of transformative learning in organization are always in context, always marked by contingency in specificity. They are always emergent, structurations in complexity, uncertain, risky moments in struggle. Thus progressive movement is inevitably constrained, not least by the state of politics, and by the politics of the state, involving the competing strengths and interests of the urban and rural working poor, along with those of indigenous groups, of labor movement alliances and divisions, as well as liberal progressive professionals, middle classes and, of course, by fully self-affirming capitalist ruling class elites and all the obvious and disguised powers and institutional arrangements they can muster in reaction, often effectively populist in their form. Furthermore, complexities of progressive capital generating practices arise in relation to gendered and ethnic social dynamics themselves not least in the context of economic power elites and apologetics of dominant class formations, both national and international. It will not be easy. Rarely do *wars of maneuver* from below succeed in direct confrontation alone, while *war of position*[20] requires patient building in united fronts with passive resistance as well as cultural criticality, with leaning against the pressures as well as strategic actions potentially striking in exuberant confrontation across and against long horizons of reaction and inevitable setbacks. Poignant contemporary case in point is, perhaps, where once again we watch intently, reflect upon and try to relearn difficult lessons in relation to the currently stalling Arab Springs, or as mentioned earlier, we cannot but anticipate with caution for progressive renewal in Turkey today (May/June, 2013), and with alarm more generally the ongoing intractable and ever heating cauldron of the Middle East.

To sum up our preface, capitalism is real and very well entrenched in a variety of forms across Latin America. It is historically constituted while emergent in complexity, uneven, variable, plural and arguably just now coming into its turbo-modernizing own. It is being challenged, nationally, regionally and locally, in all its manifestations whether direct, indirect and/or ambiguous across myriad ideological dimensions. Importantly, for *Marxism as education* and the practical scholarship that is *really useful knowledge*[21] some of its challenges come in the guise of recognizing modernized forms of *premodern popular capital formation* in small-scale networking and traditional cultural forms of security in communal trust practices that are deeply embedded in histories of local-level survival, which may be reinvented in forms of petite capitalisms. Arguably, these are *nascent socialist practices*, for instance, in peer-to-peer microfinancing, credit unions and other microforms of cooperation. Nevertheless realism dictates that, in these practices, there is always potential for ambiguity in their resourceful but possibly inward looking identity boundary forming nature; narrowly self-serving for survival *in exclusivity*, as well as potentially so in acquiescence to wider and ever present powers of repression and exploitation of master/slave relations. In dual-power terms all such forms are emergent on culturally embedded historical arrangements in mutuality, vital 'social capital' to be deployed for contemporary building communities of survival and resistance to corporate capital and its states. These are delicate issues then, and there is no easy and obvious formula. In this context technology most especially as materialized ingenuities of knowledge practices, whether in communications and progressive networking or in all manner of forces of material production in relation to eco-security, for instance, *remains double-edged* (if not triple, quadruple, etc.), as sources of social facility that underpin potential opportunities for success in humane transformation and also available to be deployed and deeply implicated in exploitation, contexts of social disciplining and displacement, along with repressive surveillance and control as well.

This book assembles ample evidence, reasoning in multidimensional cogent analysis of potential for continuous expanding movement, in hope and expectation for struggles in socialist transformation; *movements from below*, toward reinforcing upward spirals of socialist structures, morale and reinvigorating spirits of 'magical' conviviality *as educative practices*. Fun too, for and in ongoing progressive struggles in Latin America today! There is no doubting however: "La lucha continua no terminará fácilmente!"

Anthony Green
July 2013

Notes

1. Che Guevara in a letter to Fidel Castro on leaving Cuba in 1967 to continue the struggle in Bolivia.
2. See R. Johnson (1979), "Really Useful Knowledge: Radical Education and Working Class Culture," in Clark, Critcher and Johnson (eds.), *Working Class Culture: Studies in History and Theory*, London: Hutchinson.
3. TINA: There is no alternative. Often attributed to Margaret Thatcher signaling her advocacy of economic liberalism with individualism in domestic familial forms.
4. "Eat the rich" is a slogan I first saw written on the railway bridge, Main Street, Northampton, Massachusetts, in 1978. "Eat the Bankers" associated with Professor Christopher Knight, Marxist situationist activist for Financial Fools' Day/G20 Meeting in London, May 1, 2009.
5. Referring to leftist, politically 'pink' rather than 'red,' Latin and South American states in terms of recent experiences of relations with the United States, internal democratic reforms with inclusivity and empowerment from below, plus economic redistribution. See for discussion and recent literature P. Kirby (2010), "Probing the Significance of Latin America's 'Pink Tide,'" *European Review of Latin America and the Caribbean Studies* 89(Oct.): pp. 127–133; and G. Prevost et al. (2012), *Social Movements and Leftist Government in Latin America: Confrontation or Co-optation*, London: Zed Books.
6. BRICS: shorthand for emergent association of states in cooperation and potential global influence, namely B (Brazil), R (Russia), I (India), C (China), S (South Africa).
7. Find at http://www.gobiernodechile.cl/media/2013/01/Declaration-of-Santiago-engl.pdf.
8. War of maneuver/position from above: while I am taking these terms from Gramsci on class struggle, where he drew on military strategic and tactical thinking in making the broad distinctions between maneuver as movement for immediate and direct assault on the state for outright victory, distinguishing this from war of position, which refers to struggles that are relatively long drawn out (siege-like, perhaps) and potentially immensely complex involving cultural forms in relation to state institutional apparatuses (including ethics and identity politics, along with monetary and fiscal policy, employment, religion, welfare, education, legality, etc.) as terrains and modes of struggles for influence and legitimacy for domination in hegemonic leadership, rather than armed struggles to win dominance through establishing monopoly of power of force, though this too, is always in play, lurking, threatening where and if possible and deemed likely to be effective. Thus class war of position from above, that is, by the (global) ruling class refers to the complex of mechanisms that bear

down on any aspects of political economy within any sovereign state that supports the interests, with continued and expanding hegemony of both internal and external subaltern positions, and global capitalist plutocratic elite 'state' power. Excellent contemporary case in point is the emergent powers in combination with the tax avoidance possibilities available to international corporations using legitimate facilities of tax havens freeing capital from responsibilities to the nation state's context of production. The Holy Grail being Apple's capacity to pay tax where and almost if it chooses thus avoiding/evading huge volumes of such foregone revenue in line with their legal obligations to shareholders. Or, all the forms of elite exclusive access to elite educational institutions at any level. All this in relation to the simultaneous effects of articulating with the class politics of securing a beneficial position through 'legitimate' means: (i) application of labor regulations hampering organized labor's attempts to maneuver their collective power in unions to weaken effective collective bargaining; with class media identity politics of (ii) demonizing of labor leadership, and class media identity politics through (iii) vilification of welfare recipients/glorification of entrepreneurial responsibility in 'creating jobs,' etc., in those state jurisdictions. See for effective introduction to war of position: P. Thomas (2009), *The Gramscian Moment: Philosophy, Hegemony and Marxism*, Leiden/Boston: Brill, pp. 141–150.

9. Simon Bolivar, eighteenth- or nineteenth-century influence, and progressive, contemporary inspiration in ambiguity, e.g. hostile biography by Marx (in *The New American Cyclopaedia*, Vol. III, 1858, Marx-Engels Internet Archive); Bolivarianism, however, identifies elements of progressive forms in today's terms, especially so in the interpretations associated with Hugo Chávez's stellar political career; and interesting for prefiguring earlier twentieth-century politics of collectivist democratic struggles in relation to José Carlos Mariátegui's (1894–1930) perspectives on the role of indigenous peoples in liberation struggle and progressive modernism. Also interesting for recognizing the dialogical 'openness' of Marxism, especially so when set alongside the range of positions Marx himself took in relation to Russian pre-capitalist collectivist forms and nascent communism, for instance (see Anderson, 2010), and illustrating the critical theme that Marx writings as a totality are not a fully finished form to be appropriated as dogma, but a developing corpus across the real materiality of his biography in authorship to be dialogued with; including addressing the abstraction that historical materialism is a theory of staged historical sequences into the future. This brings us full circle here therefore, and is important to contemporary struggles in Latin America for identifying modernist progressivism in relation to indigenous cultures and Mariátegui's 'Gramscianism,' see

José Carlos Mariátegui's (1928) *Siete Ensayos de Interpretación de la Realidad Peruana*, Lima, 1984, and Roxanne Dunbar-Ortiz reviewing Marc Beckers' (2009), "Indians and Leftists in the Making of Ecuador's Modern Indigenous Movement," *Monthly Review* 61(04).

10. Oscar Guardiola_Rivera (2010), *What If Latin America Ruled the World?: How the South Will Take the North into the 22nd Century*, London: Bloomsbury.

11. PIGS: P (Portugal), I (Italy), G (Greece), S (Spain).

12. K. Marx and F, Engels (1848), *The Manifesto of the Communist Party*, section 1, para. 18, available at http://www.marxists.org/archive/marx/works/1848/communist-manifesto/ch01.htm#060.

13. In late May/early June, 2013, unemployment rates are reported by BBC (May 31, 2013) sourced at Eurostat:

	Total %	Youth % (under 25s)
Portugal:	17.8	42.5
Italy:	12	40.5
Greece:	27	62.5
Spain:	26.8	56.4

14. See D. McNally (2011), *Monsters of the Market: Zombies, Vampires and Global Capitalism*, Leiden: Brill, pp. 113/114, 171–173.

15. See K. Marx (1867), *Capital*, I, London: Penguin (1976), pp. 163–164.

16. With Gabriel Garcia Marquez this complex moment in/as solitude works by depiction in depth ontology, with dialectical multi-leveled, poly-scalar textuality and is materialist in this relational form (not unlike Marx representations in historical materialist 'irony,' perhaps; see fn 17, too). It is ruthlessly challenging while delicately poised between reification and hypocrisy, for practices of surviving embedded histories of 'One Hundred Years' of oppression, realizing solitude without and within. It echoes too Franz Fanon's life and work, perhaps a foil for posing existential problems for radical practices, namely who can come through untainted, and how, except through varieties of self-knowledge in social alchemy of potential self deception? Thus it refers to 'magical' practices of managing the negations, the unreal in the being and nothingness of 'fetishized' social relations achieved (or acquiesced to) only by embracing insanities of either super controlled rationality or 'privacy' in breakdown? See for dramatic depiction of Fanon's problematic in the text (or better still a performance) of Cheryl Churchill's 1972 play *The Hospital at the Time of Revolution*. For an attempt to review and throw light on this kind of theme in Marx's own biography see Mary Gabriel (2011), *Love and Capital: Karl and*

Jenny Marx and the Birth of a Revolution, New York: Littlebrown; and Dienst (2011), *The Bonds of Debt: Borrowing against the Common Good*, London: Verso, pp 137–153.

17. See discussion of critical tropes for dialectical methods and engagement across Marx's analyses by Humphrey McQueen (2005), "Reading the 'unreadable' Marx" written for "Marx Myths and Legends," http://marxmyths.org/humphrey-mcqueen/article.htm.

18. See Michael Young's (1958) classic text in critical irony, *The Rise of the Meritocracy*. There is plenty of contemporary evidence to indicate that social mobility has stalled and that neoliberalism has put paid to the mythology on all fronts despite liberal 'soft' right-wing media working overtime on repairing the myth; or recent treatment by S. Themelis (2013), *Social Change and Education in Greece: A Study in Class Struggle Dynamics*, New York: Palgrave. See for Latin America: "Special Report: Gini back in the bottle," in the *Economist* (October 13, 2012), and Luis F. Lopez-Calva and Nora Lustig (2010), *Explaining the Decline in Inequality in Latin America: Technological Change, Educational Upgrading and Democracy*, Brookings Institute, http://www.brookings.edu/~/media/press/books/2010/declininginequalityinlatinamerica/declininginequalityinlatinamerica_chapter.pdf.

19. See for discussion George Ciccariello-Maher (2009), *Dual Power in the Venezuelan Revolution*, http://kasamaproject.org/international/1106–38venezuela-a-different-kind-of-power.

20. See n 8.

21. See n 2.

References

Anderson, K. (2010), *Marx at the Margins: On Nationalism, Ethnicity and Non-Western Societies*, Chicago: University of Chicago Press.

CELAC (2013), Declaration of Santiago at the First CELAC Summit, http://www.gobiernodechile.cl/media/2013/01/Declaration-of-Santiago-engl.pdf

Ciccariello-Maher, G. (2009), *Dual Power in the Venezuelan Revolution*, http://kasamaproject.org/international/1106–38venezuela-a-different-kind-of-power.

Dienst, R. (2011), *The Bonds of Debt: Borrowing against the Common Good*, London: Verso.

Dunbar-Ortiz, R. (2009), "Indians and Leftists in the Making of Ecuador's Modern Indigenous Movement," *Monthly Review* 61(04).

Economist (2012), *Latin America: "Special Report: Gini Back in the Bottle"* (October 13).

Gabriel, M. (2011), *Love and Capital: Karl and Jenny Marx and the Birth of a Revolution*, New York: Littlebrown.

Garcia-Marquez, G. (1989), *Love in the Time of Cholera*, London: Penguin Books.

Garcia-Marquez, G. (2003), *One Hundred Years of Solitude*, New York: Harper Collins.

Guardiola-Rivera, O. (2010), *What If Latin America Ruled the World?: How the South Will Take the North into the 22nd Century*, London: Bloomsbury.

Johnson, R. (1979), "'Really Useful Knowledge': Radical Education and Working Class Culture," in Clark, Critcher and Johnson (eds.), *Working Class Culture: Studies in History and Theory*, London: Hutchinson.

Kirby, P. (2010) "Probing the Significance of Latin America's 'Pink Tide,'" *European Review of Latin America and the Caribbean Studies* 89(Oct): pp. 127–133.

Lopez-Calva, L. and Lustig, N. (2010), "Explaining the Decline in Inequality in Latin America: Technological Change, Educational Upgrading and Democracy," Brookings Institute, http://www.brookings.edu/~/media/press/books/2010/declininginequalityinlatinamerica/declininginequalityinlatinamerica_chapter.pdf.

Mariátegui, L. (1928), *Siete Ensayos de Interpretación de la Realidad Peruana*, Lima.

Marx, K. (1845), *Theses on Feuerbach*, http://www.marxists.org/archive/marx/works/1845/theses/theses.htm.

Marx, K. (1858), in *The New American Cyclopaedia*, Vol. III, 1858, Marx-Engels Internet Archive, http://www.marxists.org/archive/marx/works/1858/01/bolivar.htm.

Marx, K. (1867), *Capital*, I, pp. 72–73; London: Penguin (1976), pp. 163–164.

Marx, K. and Engels, F. (1848), The Manifesto of the Communist Party, section 1, para. 18, http://www.marxists.org/archive/marx/works/1848/communist-manifesto/ch01.htm#060.

McNally, D. (2011), *Monsters of the Market: Zombies, Vampires and Global Capitalism*, Leiden: Brill.

McQueen, H. (2005), "Reading the 'unreadable' Marx," written for "Marx Myths and Legends," http://marxmyths.org/humphrey-mcqueen/article.htm.

Prevost, G. et al. (2012), *Social Movements and Leftist Government in Latin America: Confrontation or Co-optation*, London: Zed Books.

Themelis, S. (2013), *Social Change and Education in Greece: Study in Class Struggle Dynamics*, New York: Palgrave.

Thomas, P. (2009), *The Gramscian Moment: Philosophy, Hegemony and Marxism*, Leiden/Boston: Brill.

Young, M. (1958), *The Rise of the Meritocracy, 1870–2033: An Essay on Education and Inequality*. London: Thames & Hudson.

Acknowledgments

The editors would like to thank all the participants in the Education and Social Change in the Americas workshop held at the Centre for the Study of Global and Social Justice (CSGSJ) in Nottingham in June 2011 as part of the Marxism and Education Renewing Dialogues (MERD) series, where the seeds for this edited collection were planted. We would also like to express our gratitude to all the authors of this volume who have worked with us to bring the project to fruition, the people at Palgrave Macmillan, particularly Sarah Nathan and Scarlet Neath for their precision, support and commitment, and to Anthony Green, editor of the Education and Marxism Series, for his belief in the project since its inception.

Introduction: Exploring the Role of Education and the Pedagogical in Pathways to Twenty-First-Century Socialism in Latin America

Sara C. Motta

The horizons of political imagination and practice in Latin America are expanding as witnessed by the election to power of governments to the Left such as Chávez in Venezuela, Morales in Bolivia, Correa in Ecuador and Ortega in Nicaragua and the emergence of a plethora of popular social movements that are contesting and creating alternatives to neoliberal capitalism. In the praxis of this reinvention of emancipatory popular politics the role of education and the pedagogical are central (see also Motta, 2014a, b, c). We are using "pedagogical" in its wide sense here to refer not just to teaching methods but also to an articulation of educational aims and processes in social, ethical and affective as well as cognitive terms.

Struggles over education policy are concrete sites of contestation over development models, cosmologies, and alternatives to capitalism. Educational policy and practice is a space where new forms of mass intellectuality and engaged critical scholarship connected to the realities of marginalized and excluded communities are emerging, and movements are developing both informal and formal pedagogies of everyday life, which expand the practice of social and political change. They also create multiple pedagogical innovations that forge alternatives in the here and now. Arguably the politics of knowledge—who controls the production of knowledge, what is considered knowledge, how that knowledge is produced and who that knowledge is for—is a central political problematic in the struggle for alternatives to capitalism in the twenty-first century.

Situating this politics of knowledge within its philosophical context is an important task in our engagement with, and ability to learn from, these struggles for social and political alternatives. For it enables the framing of these processes through the lens of a distinctly Latin American philosophical tradition. This tradition, as Jon Mansell in chapter 1 in this volume argues, speaks from the position of exteriority/margins and in opposition to the epistemological politics of capitalism and colonialism. He develops this analysis through a contextual situating of Paulo Freire's *Pedagogy of the Oppressed* suggesting that this enables us to better understand the centrality of the ethical and the embodied as foundations of liberatory pedagogical practice.

We can therefore read the emergence and development of traditions of popular education, the praxis of critical scholars such as Freire, and the everyday pedagogical construction enacted by educators, movements and communities in struggle as paradigmatic of the forging of a distinct Latin American tradition. It is in the praxis of new popular forces be they social movements or leftist governments that a theoretical and philosophical renovation and revolution is unfolding (see Mignolo for a similar analysis in relation to Zapatismo, 2002). This is a praxis in which those historically silenced and spoken over by dominant articulations of theory, political power and political categorization appear on the historical and political stage as political subjects. Their praxis therefore presents a profound assertion of the ways in which the creation of alternatives to capitalist coloniality is deeply pedagogical and how these pedagogies enable the uniting of education with everyday life, theory with practice, the private with public and the mind with the body.

This philosophical situating of the key thematic of this collection also indicates the importance of historiography in our understanding and analysis of the role of education in processes of social transformation in the region. As it is argued in chapter 8 of this volume, it is important to make a distinction between education as a liberatory process on the one hand and schooling to reproduce and ideologically sustain compliant workers, on the other. The former describes the actualities of educational practice in the countries under discussion in this book; the latter the realities of practice in the capitalist heartlands. Liam Kane in chapter 2 in this volume engages with history through opening a dialogue between popular education as practiced in Latin America and Marxism of the twentieth century. He therefore creates a bridge between those on the exteriority of Latin America and those on the exteriority in the West who produced critical theorizations out of their experiences of revolutionary and popular struggle. Kane's contribution foregrounds the importance to not essentialize the political and pedagogical praxis of Latin American popular politics but rather create a double and reciprocal reading of Marxism through popular education and popular education through Marxism. In this, he spotlights the tensions and the resonances between these traditions and suggests ways forward through which Marxism might learn from popular education.

Of particular salience is a questioning of the need for intellectual vanguards and rather a focus on the collective construction of knowledge by the oppressed and excluded in relation to their lived experience; the need to open from a monological and universalistic conceptualization of revolutionary strategy and revolutionary subjects toward engagement with multiplicity and plurality in strategies and subjects; and the importance to not only focus on the content of theory for social transformation but also the way that that theory is produced. As Mignolo continues: "Thus it is not about thinking 'theories' that help us to understand 'reality,' but to find theory in and through reality."

Such analysis raises important questions in relation to the differences between twentieth-century socialism (20 cs) and twenty-first-century socialism (21 cs) and the political categories that are relevant and able to engage meaningfully with such struggles.

At this point, it is important to make a distinction between 20 cs and 21 cs.

Twentieth-century socialism tended to have the following features:

- (White, male) organized working class,
- Top-down control as Stalinism became entrenched,
- Atheism (except some varieties of Christian social democratic socialism),
- Lack of ecological awareness,
- A general belief that the end justifies the means. (Cole and Motta, 2011)

Twenty-first-century socialism, on the other hand is characterized by:

- Women of color playing a central role,
- The involvement of the informal economy,
- Genuine attempts at participatory democracy,
- A central focus on the spiritual, in particular, in Latin America, Roman Catholic liberation theology and indigenous religions,
- Ecological awareness,
- Central processes viewed as ends as well as means. (Cole and Motta, 2011)

As Enrique Dussel (2008, p. xvi) argues in relation to these new forms of popular politics: "These movements and events represent signs of hope, in the face of which we must begin to create a new theory. This new theory cannot merely respond to the presuppositions of the last five hundred years of capitalist and colonialist modernity. It cannot set out from bourgeois postulates or from those of real 'socialism.'"

In chapter 3 I open a dialogue between the Open Marxist tradition and the pedagogical and epistemological praxis of social movements, including the CTUs (Venezuela), MST (Brazil), autonomous piqueteros (Argentina), Universidad de la Tierra (Mexico) and the Escuela Política de Mujeres Pazíficas (Colombia) as a means of engaging with these questions. In using the Open Marxist framework she seeks to bring visibility to the role of the pedagogical in the politics of knowledge of movements, the construction of integral liberation through the development of affective and embodied pedagogies, the importance of place in the emergence and formation of alternatives, and the openness and plurality at the heart of the reinvention of pathways toward 21 cs. In so doing she foreground how this differs from 20 cs, in a similar way to Kane's (in chapter 2 in this volume), but also rereads Open Marxism through the pedagogical praxis of movements. This rereading is an act of critical reflection from within and a way to suggest processes of epistemological decolonization of this theoretical tradition, which still often produces theory outside and above movements reproducing elements of the politics of coloniality in its practice.

From this philosophical, historiographical and theoretical grounding the book moves to the concrete educational and pedagogical practices, struggles, and experiences of Left governments and social movements. These contributions enable us to identify and systematize key questions and problematics in the struggle to construct an educational and pedagogical praxis, which enable the flourishing of popular alternatives to neoliberal capitalism.

Education Struggles and/in Left Governments

Multiscalar Nature of Counter-Hegemonic Education Struggles

Particularly important in the analysis of Left governments offered in this volume is that an analysis and evaluation of education struggles and policy cannot be adequately addressed if: (i) education struggles are disconnected analytically from an understanding of their relationship with broader counter-hegemonic struggles; and (ii) political economy analysis of such counter-hegemonic struggle remains at the level of the nation-state. Rather as Mieke Lopes Cardozo, Thomas Muhr, Lenin Valencia Arroyo and Mike Cole demonstrate in their contributions to this volume, an analysis of the limitations and potentials for the development of alternative and popular educational strategies, policies and practices can only be understood by analyzing the dialectical relationships between popular movements and governments, and by situating this analysis within the broader class dynamics of the state and international class coalitions.

Thomas Muhr (chapter 4) accordingly shows how the development of an innovative educational program in Nicaragua is not only the result of the election to power of a Left leaning government but also the favorable regional conjuncture within which this election occurred. Through the creation and consolidation of ALBA, conditions have been fostered for the successful design and legalization of educational policy that seeks to democratize and expand access and transform curricula in a way that enables learning which aims to foster the self-liberation of Nicaragua's popular classes. However, Muhr ends with a question about how such constitutional and policy commitments will be put into practice, suggesting further research is needed into the relationships and balance of power among popular movements, the Nicaraguan government and the Nicaraguan state.

Similarly, Mieke Lopes Cardozo (chapter 5) combines a neo-Gramscian analysis with a postcolonial theorization to foreground the importance of fostering the conditions for the creation of popular organic intellectuality in the creation of counter-hegemonic alternatives and of ensuring that this is embedded within a decolonizing educational philosophy and practice. She uses this to evaluate the Morales government's commitment to a decolonizing educational policy and its prospects for realization particularly in relation to Normales—teacher training institutes that produce the country's teachers. She demonstrates how there are struggles over the meaning of decolonizing and indigenous epistemologies within popular movements resulting in ambiguous support for the reform program. She also importantly highlights the difference between a government and the state, demonstrating the conservative nature of the educational institutions of the Bolivian state and therefore the barriers to realization of this policy program represented by Bolivia's teachers and the institutions that produce them. Lopes Cardozo also notes that there is a sense that promises of change and development are not being met.

However, she concludes, this does not fully take into account the discursive shift of Bolivia's new education reform, which incorporates elements of cultural recognition and political representation.

Lenin Valencia Arroyo (chapter 6) in his analysis of the development of two indigenous universities in Peru and Ecuador demonstrates how the prospects for realizing the decolonizing potential of educational policy are achieved when popular movements are organized and participants are active in shaping and giving meaningful content to its implementation and development. Thus in the case of the Peruvian Intercultural University of the Amazon (UNIA) in which only formal participation of indigenous groups and movements occurred, the decolonizing and radical potential of the university project has not been realized. Rather popular demands and energies have been co-opted and displaced. While the Ecuadorian Intercultural University of Nationalities and Indigenous People of Ecuador—"Amawtay Wasi" (UINPI)—is the direct result of organizations linked to indigenous social movements in Ecuador. It is therefore part of a broader counter-hegemonic struggle in which the correlation of forces and levels of articulation of indigenous communities resulted in the implementation of decolonizing curricula, critical pedagogies and development of engaged (multiscalar) critical scholarship that presents a challenge to elements of the colonial capitalist structure and practice of Ecuadorian educational institutions.

Francisco Dominguez' contribution (chapter 7) demonstrates that when there is a favorable conjuncture of social forces that are able to both occupy the state and articulate with movements in society then a radical rupturing with the logics of capitalist coloniality in the national level educational system can occur. This involves not only occupying the bourgeois educational institutions of the state but also creating new parallel, decentralized and democratized educational institutions, curricula and practices and ensuring the democratization of educational material. In the Venezuelan case, the democratization of educational institutions via initiatives such as Infocentres, the redevelopment of curricula, the development of education missions, changes to the constitution and democratization of access to educational materials and information is fostering the self–education of the masses. This is resulting in a historically and political significant intellectual transformation that is becoming the engine of agency that is bringing to reality the Bolivarian Revolution.

Mike Cole (chapter 8) also stresses the importance of parallelism. He argues that while the revolutionary inspiration of Chávez is pivotal, often the official socialist statements from political figures, such as Chávez, and official state documentation on education are not put into practice in the formal education system. He examines revolutionary socialist practice in an alternative school, arguing that it is here that anticapitalist critical pedagogy is a reality. The processes at the school involve a lived critique of capitalist society, both educationally and socially, the forefronting of social justice, and socially productive labor with revolutionary socialism at the core. All this is in direct opposition to schooling to produce obedient workers. In tandem with the 2013–2019 Socialist Plan, the cofounder of the school, Miguel Cortez, concludes by stressing the importance of democratizing history—of the centrality of local history to bridge the gaps between generations. For the development of participatory democracy and 21 cs, the barrios need to be organized, and a discourse has to be constructed. The students at the alternative school in Barrio Pueblo Neuvo are actively involved in this construction, thus providing an exemplar for the resolution of the major contradiction between the progressive policies of the government and schooling as practiced in Venezuelan schools.

Education and Pedagogy from Below: "Changing not only the Content of the Conversation but the Terms of the Conversation"

As Mignolo argues (2009), developing alternatives to colonial capitalism involves not only changing the content of the conversation, or producing new emancipatory knowledges, but also changing the terms of the conversation, so transforming the way we produce such emancipatory knowledges. This involves shifting our focus to the subjects of knowledge construction and reconceptualizing the nature of intellectual production in a way that overcomes the epistemological politics of capitalist coloniality in which the letter and word become the anchor of knowledge that entails a divorcing of the word from the world. This has historically posited a particular type of knowledge (the written and conceptual), particular form of knowledge creation (abstract, individualized and often masculinized) and particular content of knowledge as the pinnacle of epistemological development.

Such a questioning in practice is being actively developed by social movements and collectives across the continent. Collective processes of knowledge production, building on traditions and histories of popular education, are important ways in which movements and communities are developing their own theoretical and strategic readings of the world. Such readings begin from the lived experiences and oppressed bodies of the excluded and enable not only deeper understanding but also the development of tools to change their conditions. This involves bringing dignity and agency to those otherwise written over by dominant intellectual and political discourses, challenging the divisions between thinkers and doers and mind and body, which characterizes capitalist coloniality.

As Jennifer Martinez (chapter 9) demonstrates in relation to the Comités de Tierra Urbana in Venezuela, the methodology developed is used in preparation for all national meetings. It aims to forge without eradicating difference and the placedness of individual CTUs, the development of CTU strategy across scales and spatialities. Such a collective process of systematization and theorization is produced through facilitating individual and collective reflection on the lived practise and struggles of CTUs. It is resulting in communities becoming agents in their self-liberation through the democratization and transformation of their conditions of everyday life.

Or as Ivette Hernandez (chapter 10) demonstrates in relation to the development of strategies, projects and objectives by the Penguins Student movement in Chile, this has been based on an open, plural and creative process. It has involved the reoccupation of spaces in schools and publics and their organization along lines of horizontality and participation. This has fostered the time and space necessary to develop critical analysis of their struggles for a democratization of education on the basis of a dialogue between multiple knowledges; reflection on lived experience, critical theorization produced in textual forms and visual materials, for example, produced by other collectives. It has resulted in the flourishing of a plurality of perspectives and analysis of the education system in Chile, the limits of neoliberal democracy and the strategies and objectives of the student movement.

Ana Margarida Esteves' contribution (chapter 11) on the pedagogies of the Solidarity Economy movement demonstrates how the use of critical pedagogy in workshops about political economy and gender enable the female participants to reread their experiences of multiple oppressions. This is facilitated with the use of pedagogical materials developed by the movement out of previous pedagogical experiences and collective reflections and used as a means to give critical depth to women's experiences, struggles, and agency. One result is to provide participants with the technical skills and critical understanding of how to set up a cooperative; however these pedagogical processes also enable a politicization of the private sphere. This challenges the dualisms between the public and private of colonial patriarchal capitalism and results in women transforming conditions of gender oppression in their communities and lives. These transformatory processes have led participants to seek and access further educational opportunities in which, as Ana argues, they become world travelers who are able to bridge epistemological worlds and so deepen their capacity to transform their individual and communities' conditions of exclusion.

Pedagogies of Possibility: Creating Movements and Political Subjectivities

However there is another area in which the pedagogical plays an important role. This is in the (re)construction of sociabilities, political subjectivities and collectivities, so in the very creation of movements themselves, out of the ashes of destruction neoliberal capitalism wrought in communities' lives. The pedagogical is here not merely understood as practices and methodologies that enable the creation of collective readings of the world that can shape political strategy and analysis. Rather the pedagogical becomes an essential part in the coming into being of popular political subjectivities and organizations. Here pedagogies of reoccupying and re-creating space as well as affective pedagogical processes become central.

As Jennifer Martinez (chapter 9) demonstrates in the case of the CTUs, the very act of coming together and sharing space, time, and experiences in a way in which all have the right to speak is a pedagogical process that creates solidarities, collectivities, affinities, and shared histories of co-construction. It offers moments of self-reflection, which often do not result in immediate outcomes or decisions but rather create alternate temporalities from those of the constant demands of political organizing. This fosters conditions for deeper collective understanding and connection within individual CTUs but also between multiple CTUs across space. These are the implicit pedagogical processes from which sustainable movements in struggle and new relationships built on trust, reciprocity and respect are built. However, as she also notes there are tensions in maintaining the sustainability of these processes and space due to contradictions with the increasing bureaucratization of the state and resulting uneven and politicized access to resources.

Ivette Hernandez (chapter 10) demonstrates similar pedagogical processes in the Penguins movement. These helped create the conditions of possibility for the emergence of a new popular and plural political actor on the previously depoliticized and disarticulated terrain of Chilean democracy. In particular, the logics of reoccupying commodified and disciplined school spaces, public buildings and open spaces and challenging the way those spaces were created through horizontal forms of organizing and relating created the conditions for a weaving together of previously atomized students into a web of new relationships, ways of relating and commitments. This fostered the opening of political imaginaries and development of collective horizons of understanding out of which new, popular political subjectivities emerged, which not only challenged the marketization of Chilean education system but also of Chilean society.

Ana Margarida (chapter 11) demonstrates the importance of solidarities and friendship in building the groundwork for the emergence and sustainable reproduction of nonalienated economic formations, nonalienated community relationships and emancipated subaltern women. Here it is not only in the public space of the workshop or the meeting that the pedagogical plays a role. Rather, it is in the social space in which friendships, connections, histories, and relationships are forged that affective noninstrumental pedagogical processes are enacted. These blur the boundaries between the political (public) and social (private) and between educator and educatee creating the conditions of possibility for the overcoming of internalized forms of oppression. It also creates fertile terrain for the public spaces of the movement to overcome informal raced, classed, and gendered hierarchies; create horizontal relationships; and individual and collective voice. However, the forming of affective relationships and deep friendships can also be exclusionary and reinforce classed and raced hierarchies. As she demonstrates, the "inner circle" of the movement tended to become de facto leaders despite aiming to transgress such hierarchies.

These pedagogies intertwine the processes that enable the emergence (and sustainability) of new, popular political actors and institutions with the development of movements' strategy and understanding. They suggest that affective pedagogical processes, and reoccupations and re-creations of space, which overcome the dualism between the public and private and between friendship and politics, are key in creating the conditions for the emergence and sustainability of new forms of popular politics in the region. They also illustrate the uncertain, creative and fragile nature of these popular political processes of transformation.

Decolonizing Pedagogies of Everyday Life

Just as our contributors highlight that the pedagogical processes of movements do not separate the ends from the means for social and political transformation so do movements expand the practice of social transformation and the pedagogical means that enable such transformation. The praxis of popular politics moves away from a monological closure toward a dialogical opening to multiple forms of knowledge, multiple ways of creating knowledge for social transformation and multiple subjects of social transformation. Paradigmatic of such pedagogical and emancipatory plurality and creativity is the work of the Escuela Politíca de Mujeres Pazíficas in Cali, Colombia—a feminist autonomous education center that combines nonviolent, feminist philosophies with popular education in their work with women. Norma Bermudez cofounder and participant in the project tells us the story of the school's history and practice through the lens of a journey in four stages: earth (grounding and roots), air (taking flight into the new), water (flowing in calm and turbulent waters of discovery) and fire (individual and collective transformation). The form of her chapter mirrors the ritual pedagogical practices with which the diplomas offered to women from diverse backgrounds and experiences begin.

The politics of knowledge of the school presents an affirmative challenge to the epistemologies of colonial patriarchal capitalism by embracing and nurturing a dialogue of knowledges—from the women's everyday lives, activist practice, feminist philosophers, to legal experts that weaves a rich tapestry of understanding and agency. The emancipatory practices of the School are also therefore multiple: conceptualizing the workings of power as through the construction of docile gendered bodies, subjectivities and social relationships, which invisibilize the knowledges and wisdom of the subaltern, and particularly of excluded women, the subaltern of the subaltern. Social and political transformation therefore involves the reoccupation and remaking of the space of public politics but also of our everyday lives and brutalized bodies.

The pedagogical practices of the School are also therefore multiple. In seeking to overcome the separations between mind and body and emotions that characterize the militarized patriarchal capitalism of Colombia and more globally, the body becomes both a site of transformation but also the font of embodied pedagogies. Pedagogies that include ritual, dance, theater, sacred touch and embrace enable the unlocking of the embodied traumas experienced by subaltern women. This opens the door to a deepened consciousness of their possibilities and agency. They bring a connection to that deep erotic knowing of which Audrey Lorde (2000) speaks, which once felt cannot be re-imprisoned and creates women who no longer consent to be silenced, oppressed, and marginalized. These pedagogical practices create the possibilities of individual and collective voice and joy, which as Norma Bermudez writes "re-enchants the world and awakens the powers of the periphery" (chapter 13, in this volume).

Pathways to Twenty-First-Century Socialism?

Our contributors paint a portrait of the educational and pedagogical practices of Left governments and popular social movements in the region, which foreground the multiplicity, creativity and radicality of these political and social processes. They demonstrate the central role of the politics of knowledge—who controls the production of knowledge, what is considered knowledge, how that knowledge is produced and who that knowledge is for—in the creation of alternatives to colonial, patriarchal capitalism (whether that be explicitly named 21 cs or not).

Educational struggles in Left governments occur at multiple spatial scales and encounter multiple contradictions in the relationship among state, government and movements. They involve attempts to occupy and transform national educational institutions, curriculum and teacher training, and also attempts to develop popular decentralized and democratized educational institutions that transgress the logics of the capitalist state. When movements are articulated and combine with a consolidated national government, they are able to create radical openings toward mass intellectuality and the creation of new subjectivities and a new society. When movements are fragmented and governments embedded within a hostile state, counterhegemonic educational struggles often remain marginalized and at risk of criminalization or co-optation.

The pedagogies of movements across the region expand the practice of emancipation to include the subjective, embodied and affective; they develop decolonizing pedagogies of everyday life in which popular education is combined with feminist and postcolonial traditions and they transform not only the content but also the process through which we create the conditions for the emergence of new emancipatory subjects and sustainable alternatives. These experiences suggest that the pedagogical is at the heart of creating the conditions of emergence and the conditions of sustainability of popular politics that reimagines the nature, content and objectives of revolutionary struggle in the twenty-first century.

Both those struggling within Left governments for counterhegemonic and decolonizing educational alternatives and those constructing such practices in the everyday struggles of social movements and community struggles are enacting a theoretical and political revolution in which those silenced, criminalized and invisibilized by colonial patriarchal capitalism are raising their voices. It is wise for those of us engaged and committed to a world beyond capitalism that we learn to listen to these voices and begin to dialogue across borders so that we might sustain each other's struggles and strengthen each other's voices.

References

Cole, M. and Motta, S. C. (2011), "Opinion: The Giant School's Emancipatory Lessons," *Times Higher Education*, January 14, 2011.

Dussel, E. (2008), *Twenty Theses on Politics*, Duke University Press.

Lorde, Audre (2000), *The Uses of the Erotic: The Erotic as Power.* Tuscan: Kore Press.

Mignolo, W. D. (2002), "The Zapatistas's Theoretical Revolution: Its Historical, Ethical, and Political Consequences," Review (Fernand Braudel Center) 25(3): pp. 245–275.

——— (2009), "Epistemic Disobedience, Independent Thought and De-Colonial Freedom," *Theory, Culture & Society* 26(7–8): pp. 1–23.

Motta, S. C. (2014a) "Epistemological Counter-Hegemonies from Below: Radical Educators in/and the MST and Solidarity Economy Movements," in S. C. Motta and Mike Cole *Constructing Twenty-first Century Socialism in Latin America: The Role of Radical Education*, New York and London: Palgrave Macmillan.

——— (2014b) "Decolonisation in Praxis: Critical Educators, Student Movements and Feminist Pedagogies in Colombia," in S. C. Motta and M. Cole *Constructing Twenty-first Century Socialism in Latin America: The Role of Radical Education*, New York and London: Palgrave Macmillan.

——— (2014c) "Constructing Twenty-First Century Socialism: The Role of Radical Education," in S. C. Motta and M. Cole *Constructing Twenty-first Century Socialism in Latin America: The Role of Radical Education*, New York and London: Palgrave Macmillan.

Part I

On the Philosophies, Theories and Histories of Emancipatory Education in Latin America

Chapter 1

Naming the World: Situating Freirean Pedagogics in the Philosophical Problematic of *Nuestra América*

Jon L. Mansell

Since the first publication of his *Pedagogy of the Oppressed* in Brazil in 1968, the work of Paulo Freire has come to be a source of inspiration to political militants, socially engaged educators and critical scholars throughout the world. In particular many theorists and practitioners working across both the global north and south have seen in Freire's work rich resources for a renovation of the praxis of emancipatory politics. An important contribution in this volume to this renovation is offered by Sara Motta, developed in dialogue with theorists of Open Marxism, to challenge the monological representative politics of twentieth-century socialism. Instead, according to Motta, the Freirian approach to pedagogy is suggestive of a form of politics that is lived through "the transformation of subjectivity into non-alienated social flows of being, doing, living and loving" (chapter 3, in this volume). Here politics becomes a process of everyday life, of the construction of self that inherently contests the separation between politics and life implied within twentieth-century social democratic and socialist theories of the state.

Also in this volume, Liam Kane has assessed the resonances between Freirean pedagogy and the broad Marxist tradition, considering ten particular points of contact. In particular it is suggested that popular education diverges from Marxism in certain points, notably in the conceptualization of agency, focusing on the "oppressed" or the people, rather than the more narrowly defined proletariat of Marxian political economy. In addition, popular education offers a more open approach to knowledge, based upon the recognition that people develop "knowledge acquired from their own particular lived experiences" (chapter 2, in this volume) rather than the more limited, abstract productivist conception of knowledge found in orthodox historical materialism. Finally, Kane suggests the importance of an ethical concept of "humanization" influenced by Christian thought that distinguishes Freire from the secular rationality of Marxism, which has been dominant in Europe for much of the twentieth century. These dialogues and engagements suggest that the relationship between Freirean pedagogy and emancipatory thought developed in Europe is then highly productive, but also complex and often composed of both resonances and divergences.

In seeking to contextualize some of these productive dialogues, in this chapter I will offer a reading of Freirean pedagogy that situates his unique contribution as a particular moment in the development of Latin America thought. I suggest this approach is useful as questions of literacy, grammar and education have always been central to philosophical thought in Latin America, in the development of a sense of identity, geography and history. I therefore discuss three historical periods: (1) the role of literacy in the development of scholastic humanism during the sixteenth-century colonial period, (2) nineteenth-century post-Independence positivism and (3) concluding in what I suggest as a distinctive philosophy of *Nuestra América* in the latter half of the twentieth century of which Freirean pedagogy is a part.

These discussions draw heavily on the Latin American modernity/coloniality school, in particular Walter Mignolo and Enrique Dussel whose work is paradigmatic of the critical renovation of a distinctively Latin American philosophy in the twentieth century. I conclude by suggesting what I see as three of the fundamental theoretical implications of reading Freire through this tradition: (1) the primacy of the ethical to the rational, (2) an epistemological privileging of the margins and (3) a commitment to the body against abstract, disembodied knowledge.

Naming and Philosophizing América

The Colonial Naming of América

At the center of Freire's understanding of critical pedagogy and adult literacy is the idea that the power of the word is the power to name the world (1996, p. 69); to name however does not imply capturing the exteriority of the world (rendering the world static as a fixed word) but instead expresses only a certain partial fixing of meaning within a totality of knowledge (language, discourse, representation). It is in this sense that language constitutes something of a (para-) reality that is inherent to the American experience, from the moment that Christopher Columbus set foot on the island of *Guanahani* and renamed that island through the vocabularies of Latin Christendom as San Salvador. Moreover, drawing on the flawed cartographic assumptions of Latin Christendom Columbus subsequently names the natives of this island as *Indios*, an initial misrecognition that continues to denote the indigenous inhabitants of the continent until the present day. Two decades after Columbus *discovered India*, the Portuguese navigator Amerigo Vespucci re-cognizes these territories as different from the previous assumptions. This difference is thus named as a derivation of his own name: America. For Eduardo O'Gorman (1961, p. 42) this process of de-naming and re-naming suggests that the *American* was not *discovered* by Europeans, but instead from the very first moment of encounter, *invented* through European words and discourses. In this view the original encounter between European and Amerindian is fundamentally non-dialogical, it is literally monological, that is, purely articulated through the logic of the conqueror's performance of speech. As such Enrique Dussel has suggested Columbus' *discovery* actually amounts to an original act of *covering over* of America, as knowable: "As a result the Other, The American Indian disappeared, The Indian was not discovered (*des-cubierto*) as Other, but subsumed under categories of the Same...denied as Other, covered over (*en-cubierto*)" (1995, p. 32). It is this process of naming and the loss that it involves which it might be argued constitutes the original *American* philosophical problematic.

It is striking that the complicity between the word and territorial power is already explicitly understood by the Spaniards at the onset of the colonial period. As Walter Mignolo has discussed (1995, pp. 37–58), the year of conquest was also the year of the conquest of language, the publication of the first systematic Castilian grammar by Antonio de Nebrija. In presenting this document to Queen Isabella, Nebrija affirms the profound implications of his achievement with reference to the role of Latin in the expansion of the Roman Empire, thus drawing a timely parallel: Nebrija asserts, "always language was the companion of empire...together they begin, grow and flower and together they fall" (2007). Within this rhetorical construction, Castile is presented as the new bearer of Christian civilization and while force of arms may secure conquest, it is only through the closely related disciplines of law and language that civilization may establish itself upon solid ground. For Mignolo, this original connection between grammar and statecraft is of real importance, imposing discipline on the popular impurities inflicted upon the spoken word, characterized by the anarchical impulses of dialect, distortion and innovation "speakers would pronounce in one way and write in another...[Nebija thus perceived the] need for a remedy which will prevent the deterioration and subsequent disintegration of the language (e.g., the control of the voice by means of letters)" (Mignolo, 1992, p. 189). The construction of an approved standardized grammar was thus an effort at the disciplining of language as a fixed, complete system; establishing the rules of both what can and cannot be correctly said, but also firmly connecting this discipline to social hierarchies through epistemological constructions that were essential to the ideological legitimacy of emerging national and colonial projects.

As Mignolo (1995) demonstrates, in parallel to the conquest of language, the conquest of the American territory was explicitly linked to the standardization of literacy. Indeed, according to the scholastic humanism of the sixteenth century (e.g., the Jesuit theologican Jose de Acosta) the Amerindian is considered more or less human to the extent that her knowledge approximates European models of literacy. The power relations of the colonial difference thus takes on an apparently objective, rational form precisely because Greco-Roman reason involves an essential disembodiment of knowledge: "Spaniards stressed reading the word rather than reading the world and thus made the letter the anchor of language and knowledge" (Mignolo, 1995, p. 105). There is then a divergence between individualized European knowledge codified through alphabetic systems and the collectively constructed oral narratives and pictoideographic representational systems of the Amerindians. This Amerindian heritage could not exist in a meaningfully different way, but must be situated in a subordinate position to European literacy, translated, and thus transformed into the totality of European knowledge. The disciplinality of grammar in the context of colonial conquest thus necessitated that knowledge become detached from place, hierarchically organized and legitimized, universalistic, quasi-autonomous from its referents and as such in the American context became complicit with conquest. In the words of Boaventura de Sousa Santos—epistemocidal (2007). The Amerindian in relation to this totalizing form of knowledge could be legitimately disavowed of the right to speak knowledge as Other— oral tradition, Nahuatl grammar, Mayan myth, Guarani body art, etc. were denied to be forms of knowledge, and deemed irrational, idolatrous, satanic. As such "the traditions embedded in Amerindian languages were overruled by alphabetic writing (the letter) which ended up by controlling the territory...colonising the imaginary" (Mignolo, 1992, p. 199).

The idea of literacy in the sixteenth century is then deeply monological, tied to an imperial project of authoritatively naming and writing over Others' knowledge. The authority of written knowledge could thus be deployed, with an appearance of intellectual neutrality, as a tool of naming and knowing the world in order to dominate the world, producing a para-real system of documentations and discourses, which as Annibal Quijano has suggested ensures that

> the conquered and dominated peoples were situated in a natural position of inferiority and, as a result, their phenotypic traits as well as their cultural features were considered inferior. In this way race became the fundamental criterion for the distribution of the world population into ranks, places, and roles in the new society's structure of power. (2008, p. 183)

The disembodiment and de-placement of early modern European universalistic knowledge represents then the ideological appearance of what Quijano (2008) has called the coloniality of power, whereby the totality of written knowledge becomes for Guardiola-Rivera "an order, a *form* of sovereignty or rule; a self-legitimated (global) state-form...trade relations only become hegemonic, achieving the form of the state, when they appear as culture" (2002, p. 27). The implications of this complicity between the coloniality of power and the apparent autonomy of literacy embedded in a Eurocentric knowledge world are clearly significant, as America is named, Amerindia is gradually covered over: Nahuatl is translated to Spanish, orality is disciplined by grammar, bodies are subjectivated by bureaucratic record-keeping—the local becomes subjugated to the national/imperial, the lived particular to the written universal. As Guardiola-Rivera affirms, in America "there is a relationship between literacy as a global design (the secular religion of the civilizing mission) and the process of colonial spatial differentiation initiated in the sixteenth century" (2002, p. 16). The scholastic philosophical tradition that dominates the early colonial period thus constructs literacy as a key dimension of the colonial project, the construction of European knowledge as global and universal, but this can only be achieved through the covering over of the knowledge of Europe's Others—these parallel processes are inseparable and co-constitutive.

The Post-Independence Thinking of America

The end of Spanish and Portuguese colonial rule in the Americas signaled the decline of Iberian scholasticism as the dominant mode of thought in the newly independent republics. The independence movements had been shaped ideologically by a powerful sense of the struggle for reason (associated with the French and North American revolutions) against the dogmas of the Catholic tradition; as such, the new generation of thinkers was keen to proclaim an intellectual renovation that repudiated the Spanish intellectual heritage (Zea, 1963, p. 41). Against the conservatism of Spanish scholasticism the philosophy of the new world was to be a positivistic liberalism associated primarily with French and British thought, a philosophy of liberty and reason, order and progress. The interpretation of Positivism differed from country to country: Brazil and Mexico drew primarily from the French tradition of Comte; Uruguay, Argentina and Chile turning toward the English thinkers Spencer and Mill. What united these diverse national traditions however was the recognition of a specifically American point of departure, a rejection of scholasticism, a passion for science, a suspicion of the clergy and a fascination with the possibilities of education.

The origin of nineteenth-century Latin American thought was then an affirmation of the American as a distinct moment of universal history. In this view the challenge for the thinkers of the "land of the future" was to enter into universal history, by acting as a vanguard in the struggle of European rationalized culture over and against wild American nature. This particular positionality set out by the Venezuelan Andrés Bello affirms that a "philosophy of history, the science of humanity, is the same in every place and in every time...but the general philosophy of history cannot lead to the particular philosophy of history of a people" (Bello, 1997, p. 176). This challenge of constructing a philosophical voice of the American as part of the universal philosophy of history thus constitutes a distinctive process throughout the nineteenth century. A key text in this context is Esteban Echeverría's seminal novella *El Matadero* (1993), which according to Roberto Echevarría serves to inaugurate "a new Latin American master-story mediated by the most authoritative European discourse produced by the West since the sixteenth century: modern science" (1995, p. 221). Within this meta-narrative we find the construction of a powerful new Creole imaginary, whose subject is able to come into existence through a radical break with the past (the decadent Catholicism of the colonial period) and through the struggle for the future against the barbarism of American nature. The importance of this text according to Echevarría is that it establishes a new self-consciousness in Latin American thought, that of the rational, detached observer, surrounded everywhere by the savagery of nature—"From now on the Latin American narrative will deal obsessively with that 'other within' who may be the source of all, that is the violent origin of the difference which makes Latin America distinct and consequentially original" (Echevarría, 1995, p. 223).

An important theorist of this new imaginary in the nineteenth century was another Argentine dissident Domingo Faustino Sarmiento (1811–1888) forced into exile by the dictatorship of Juan Manuel de Rosas (1829–1852). Sarmiento's autobiography of the provincial Caudillo Juan Facundo Quiroga captures the spirit of the age: the struggle between "civilisation and barbarism." This binary opposition is for Sarmiento the basis of the Argentine tragedy, by which the capital Buenos Aires "the only city in the vast Argentine territory which is in contact with European nations" (Sarmiento, 1998, p. 12) is surrounded on all sides by barbarian menace "on the north and the south are savages ever on the watch...to fall like packs of hyenas...upon the defenceless settlements" (p. 10). The ascendency of the Caudillo Facundo (who is a substitute for Rosas himself) marks for Sarmiento the apogee of this tragedy, the domination of the barbarian Gaucho over the educated gentleman, the domination of the wild Pampas over the cultivated City of Letters. The racial undertones of this analysis are quite explicit, the Gaucho being the product of several centuries of mixing among Spaniard, Indian and Negro, by which "a homogenous whole has resulted from the fusion...it is characterised by love of idleness and incapacity for industry...to a great extent this unfortunate result is due to the incorporation of the native tribes" (p. 17). As Echevarría suggests, with Sarmiento "the authoritative language of knowledge" (1995, p. 230) is deployed where once religion had been, yet the essential relations are re-produced, the new subject-position of the rational, detached observer remains situated in imitation of the European, while also as before the target of knowledge is the Other, as nature, as wild savagery opposed to civilization. Positivism, as scholasticism before it, thus constructs "an Other that it depicts, classifies and as it creates a discourse of power [it creates] an object that it has molded for itself" (p. 238).

Rather than a pure philosophy of Latin America, nineteenth-century Positivism is better understood as imitation (though not without often significant and creative innovation) of dominant European models, applied to the American context. It is in this sense that Sarmiento's contemporary (and critic) Juan Bautista Alberdi (1810–1884) observes: "Everything in the civilisation of our land is European...we who call ourselves Americans are but Europeans born in America" (quoted in Zea, 1963, p. 47). The political expression of this philosophy can be seen when Sarmiento came to complete his journey from exiled dissident to president (1868–1874 in two closely associated policies of civilization). On the one hand Sarmiento's presidency involved an unprecedented effort to encourage mass immigration from Europe (particularly Italy and Germany) designed to replenish the nation's racial stock. On the other hand, the government pursued an unprecedented extension throughout the national territory of a system of public education aimed at civilizing the Argentine citizenry "to separate himself from the world of manual labour, and to become a part of the society of cultivated souls" (Altamirano and Sarlo, 1995, p. 157). The public school system envisioned by Sarmiento was heavily influenced by his travels in the United States, a good education was perceived as providing a solid ethic of discipline and industriousness premised upon a commitment to the authority of the written word (law, constitution etc): "to accustom the spirit to the idea of regular, continuous duty, providing him with regular habits in his actions: to add another authority to the paternal one...to mold the spirit to the idea of an authority outside the family circle" (quoted in Katra, 1995, p. 82). In this context, the public school was understood quite explicitly as an institution of nation-building, the civilization of barbarian tendencies, and above all social disciplinality: "The best and cheapest police system that could be adopted" (quoted in Katra, 1995, p. 83). The Positivist goal of social order was thus a primary task of public education, set in the service of the achievement of a humanistic project of progress, as set out by the father of the Chilean system of public education Andres Bello: "Education, which enriches his spirit with ideas and adorns his heart with virtues is an effective means of promoting his progress...(through education) man, the only being on the face of the globe capable of making progress, shall fulfil his destiny completely" (Bello, 1997)

For Sarmiento then, public education sat comfortably alongside European immigration and the colonial genocide of the Amerindians as part of the great project of the rationalization and disciplining of wild nature in the Americas, the means by which the fully civilized and Europeanized cities might eventually complete the total conquest and domination of the Pampas, the jungles, the deserts, the expulsion of all remaining Otherness from the American continent. As Leopoldo Zea (1963) has analyzed, while there are important distinctions in the way Positivist thinkers understood the role of education, there is a basic homology, the rationalization of the Latin American mind—"It was thought that through a Positivistic education a new type of man could eventually be created, freed from all defects he had inherited from the colony, a man with a great practical mind such as had made the United States and England the great leaders of modern civilisation" (Zea, 1963, p. 30). Positivism in Latin America was undeniably a philosophy of Latin American independence, albeit imitative, rather than genuinely original, yet it retains an understanding of knowledge as totality, a monological system of European origin, to be deployed through education and literacy in the struggle of civilization against barbarism. As such the construction of knowledge remains closely connected to the Europeanization of the American, the project of rationalization, the annihilation and submission of Otherness from the American continent, as such even in embracing the era of independence, Latin American philosophy remained in a relationship of dependence on European thought.

Toward a Philosophy of *Nuestra América*

The Peripheral as a Perspective

During the nineteenth century, Positivism was nowhere more institutionally embedded than Mexico, particularly during the long liberal dictatorship of Porfirio Díaz (1876–1911). In Mexico, as with other countries in the region, Positivism in this period became the ideological expression of an emergent urban elite, scientifically minded and committed to economic liberalism and "modernization" against an entrenched rural oligarchy grounded in relations of patronage and traditional Catholicism. What makes Mexico unique is that these tensions culminated in a long, bloody and traumatic revolution (1910–1920), which involved not only conflict between rival elite national projects, but a significant challenge from below, from guerrilla armies led by Pancho Villa in the north and Emiliano Zapata in the south. These represented expressions of a new popular imaginary, which signaled a move beyond the nineteenth century throughout the region.

Mexican thinkers of the post-Revolutionary era were thus confronted with a new challenge, to develop a national consciousness: *Mexicanidad* beyond traditional Catholicism, but also post-Independence Positivism. The key philosophical influences in this project came from Spain (which was experiencing conflicts and tensions very similar to those of Mexico during the 1920s), most notably José Gaos, who relocated to Mexico in 1939 to escape Franco's fascist takeover of his homeland, and José Ortega y Gasset, whose concept of "historical perspectivism" would become a major influence on twentieth-century Latin American thought. For Ortega y Gasset, any understanding of the world is necessarily situated, truth cannot be abstracted from perspective; on the contrary, perspective is constitutive of truth. This argument was particularly attractive for a revolutionary generation in Mexico struggling to assert a new sense of national self-identity that involved a break from the past yet also remained distinct and independent from North American and European traditions.

One of the most significant figures in the post-Revolutionary generation was Leopoldo Zea, who sought to analyze Latin American thought as a situated response, but within a universal context. This is developed by Zea in his study of *The Latin American Mind* (1963), which opens with a reflection upon Hegel's famous declaration that in order to become the land of the future "America must sever its ties with the land where, up to the present time universal history has developed" (quoted in Zea, 1963, p. 3). Zea asks if Hegel's dialectical logic of negation and synthesis can be said to have matured in Latin American thought, to the point where "something is assimilated completely, it is not felt as something belonging to another, a hindrance, an obstacle but something which is one's very own, natural" (p. 4). Zea concludes that in Positivism this process has not yet occurred, Latin American history "is not yet a history of denials," on the contrary "our past has still not become a real past; it is still a present which does not choose to become history" (p. 6). The task of the historian of ideas is then to draw out the ambiguities, in order to understand the interpretation and assimilation of the universal subject of philosophy into the Latin American context, as "a philosophy of history, on a universal level, from the point of view of what…I myself am, namely, a Latin American." As such Zea affirms "that a unique Latin American philosophy does exist. Ours is a philosophical interpretation of a reality that is being lived" (in Maciel, 1985, p. 13).

Zea's position can be situated in the context of the ideological currents emanating from the Mexican Revolution. Yet in his study of the Latin American mind, Zea clearly believes his analysis speaks beyond Mexico for Latin America as a whole. It is therefore noteworthy that thinkers, particularly from South America, have often offered different interpretations to Zea. These differences have been analyzed by J. M. Garrido, who points out that the great Peruvian Marxist theorist José Carlos Mariátegui explicitly questioned the existence of a distinctively "Latin American thought." Even more strongly critical of Zea, Augusto Salazar Bondy suggests that Zea achieves only an elitist analysis, which merely traces "the history of European philosophy *in* Latin America rather than the history of an *authentic* philosophy of Latin America" (quoted in Garrido, 2007, p. 23). For Salazar Bondy and other theorists of liberation, an authentic philosophy of *Nuestra América* cannot be imposed, imitated or even neatly translated from outside, Latin American thought in order to understand itself must come to express itself through its own categories, developed through its own experience and particularly from below, from those whose knowledge has been devalued and marginalized. In this context, Enrique Dussel has argued that Latin American thought comes to know itself not through its articulation of universal history but through a radical affirmation of its exclusion, its unique historical trajectory as

> the "outside of history" ("*el fuera de la historia*")...now interpreted as an "outside," as an "exclusion," as an "exteriority" of the "community of philosophical communication itself." It is a position of exclusion that is imitated by the colonial "universalist" philosophers. And it is with respect to this supposedly universal "philosophy" (to be precise: European and North American) that we are excluded. (Dussel, 1994, pp. 35–36)

This sense of being inserted into history only through being "outside of history" is conceptualized by Dussel as exteriority. This is a recurring theme in twentieth-century Latin American literature, repeatedly expressed as a sense of being lost, out of place, on the margins, in the condition of "solitude." The meaning of solitude here as "outside of history" is deeply rooted in the incommensurability between the para-reality of written knowledge and the experienced reality of lived, embodied traditions developed among the popular social sectors. This heritage, suggests García Márquez, "offers us writers very serious problems, that of the insufficiency of words." Moreover the insufficiency of the word makes the understanding of self all the more complex as "the interpretation of our reality through patterns not our own serves only to make us ever more unknown, ever less free, ever more solitary" (1992). In his famous Nobel Prize acceptance speech on *The Solitude of Latin America*, García Márquez captures one of the definitive philosophical problematics of Latin America's reality in the twentieth century:

> Swedish academy of letters...(Ours is) A reality not of paper, but one that lives within us and determines every instant of our countless daily

deaths...We have had to ask but little of imagination for our crucial problem has been a lack of conventional means to render our lives believable. This my friends is the crux of our solitude. (1992)

This point is recognized as foundational by Enrique Dussel for whom to embark upon an authentically Latin American philosophy is to embrace not simply a world of words but a much more complex and difficult world of the experiences of living, being, and embodied reality, which has often been marginalized and excluded by the written accounts and knowledge construction of the American. Dussel thus offers his own reflections on García Márquez's problematic of the insufficiency of words, through a sustained and thorough re-imagination of ethical epistemology, described by Michael Barber:

> The method of knowing how to believe the word of the Other and interpret it. Committed to the Other, the philosopher gains access to a new world and sets about destroying the obstacles that impede the revelation of the Other. In Latin America, philosophy becomes a cry, a clamour, an exhortation of those who have taught the philosopher...a new and analogical moment in the history of philosophy. (1996, p. 56)

Here then, philosophy does not begin from an accepted totality, the universal history of human reason, the collected reflections of previous generations, but instead begins from humility, an ethical openness to the revelation of those who have been marginalized by universal history, silenced by the reflections of previous generations, in this sense it is a genuinely new moment in philosophy, one that is not simply translation but the emergence of new voices—original and Latin American.

Freirean Critical Pedagogy and Liberation

As with colonial scholasticism and post-Independence Positivism, the development of a distinctive philosophy of *Nuestra América* in the twentieth century continues to place questions of knowledge and literacy education at the center of its project. This new philosophy is indeed perhaps most original when it reflects upon questions of pedagogy, as with the pedagogy for liberation suggested by Salazar Bondy, and more systematically in the various theorizations of critical pedagogy developed by Paulo Freire. In these thinkers there is inevitably a dialogue with what has gone before. Indeed it is impossible not to note the divergence from previous monological approaches to literacy, when Freire affirms: "Dialogue cannot occur between those who want to name the world and those who do not wish this naming—between those who deny others the right to speak their word" (1996, p. 69). For Freire knowledge does not exist as a fixed totality of words and facts (a bank) from which individuals might make withdrawals in order to learn to act rationally in accordance with the norms of civilization. Rather knowledge is constructed through the dialogical process of engagement between the Self and the Other, mediated by the world (Freire, 2001, p. 25). The understanding of knowledge as an abstract totality that constructs its subjects, as Mignolo said of the Spaniards of the sixteenth century who "stressed reading the word rather than reading the world," is rejected as stagnant, degenerate knowledge by which "words are emptied of their concreteness and become a hollow, alienated verbosity" (1996, p. 52). In such circumstances, knowledge becomes the master of people, people become mere vassals (pp. 40–41) to be filled with knowledge. Knowledge is in this context totalitarian: distant, remote, imperial grammar, to be recited without innovation, without questioning; in this context knowledge disembodies people, turns them into mere repeaters and imitators rather than allowing them to develop their radical personhood as unique creators of meaning. This is a power relation that clearly recalls the colonial processes described by De Sousa Santos as "epistemocide" by which Other(s) knowledge(s) are annihilated, denied as knowledge, covered over. Freire can then be read as contributing to a critique of a dominating model of modern rationality existent since the original monological naming of San Salvador. In this dominant totalizing rationality, the object of knowledge became a fixed object within a world of abstract knowledge. The reality of the person as Other became invisibilized in a para-real system of power relations—the lived body a nodal point in an alienated system of signs and most profoundly her ability to speak her knowledge was denied. For Freire and the thinkers of liberation such as Dussel, Salazar-Bondy etc., knowledge built into such structures of inequality and domination as colonialism, capitalism, or patriarchy cannot be rational, precisely because it is not ethical, it denies the revelation of the Other. On the contrary, the critique of knowledge developed from the marginality of *Nuestra América* is an expression of the ethical commitment to find ways through which to understand other forms of knowledge, to allow revelation from the margins, without reducing their difference to an echo of the dominant paradigm.

   In this context, Freire's critique of the nexus between knowledge and power could not maintain the modernistic separation of mind from body. On the contrary, there is an explicit connection: in order that the oppressed speaks her knowledge, she must also live, her development must be fostered. There is an ethical obligation in the rational pursuit of knowledge. Here Freire's thinking is clearly influenced by a strong Semitic tradition and, particularly in the context of Latin America in the 1960s, the currents of Liberation Theology. This influence is most striking where Freire deploys the Christian concept of love as an ethical commitment to the oppressed, as such "love is an act of courage...love is commitment to others. No matter where the oppressed are found the act of love is commitment to their cause—the cause of liberation" (1996, p. 70). Here the preferential option for the poor clearly parallels and enriches the preferential option for the epistemological margins. On this basis, Freire affirms that an education for liberation must begin from an ethical commitment to the oppressed, and that in order "to reclaim their right to live humanly, the marginalized must confront in praxis those institutions, processes and ideologies which prevent them from naming their world" (Lankshear, 1994, p. 42). Freire's approach is thus based on both the ethical and rational recognition of the oppressed, as historically and socially excluded from knowledge. Yet this ethico-rationality is premised upon a "universal human ethic," an understanding of the human as "a being born in the womb of history...(whom) bears in itself some fundamental archetype without which it would be impossible to recognise our human presence in the world as something singular and original" (Freire, 1998, p. 25).

Freirian pedagogy then begins not from the preexisting totality of knowledge but from a commitment to the exteriority (the excludedness from knowledge) of the oppressed, as living, breathing, embodied creators of knowledge. As such, Freire is clearly keen to avoid suggesting that the oppressed are only excluded from knowledge; this exclusion is inherently linked to their conditions as exploited, socially excluded, physically vulnerable etc.

> The life which is denied its fullness...Living corpses...victimised by an endless invisible war in which their remnants of life are devoured by tuberculosis, schistosomiasis, infant diarhhea...by the myriad diseases of poverty. (1996, pp. 152–153)

What Freire achieves, through the pedagogical model he develops, is to offer a way of developing an ethically (and of course politically) informed model of the production of knowledge, which is deeply connected to the projects of exploitation and de-humanization more commonly associated with relations of material production. This concern for the socialized margins of knowledge clearly parallels and enriches the Latin American concern for the geographical margins of thought, by extending this to the universal marginality of those bodies excluded from the production of knowledge, those who have been understood historically as only bodies outside or on the margins of the world of words. The body here, its project of living with dignity, thus becomes for Freire the point zero of humanization; as such while "life affirming humanisation does not lie simply in having more to eat…it does involve having more to eat and cannot fail to include this aspect" (1996, p. 50). The ethical preference for the body marginalized by dominant knowledge paradigms challenges the history of thought, but also offers that tradition new directions, new voices, from which it may develop in a radically altered form.

Conclusion

In this chapter I have sought to situate the emergence of Paulo Freire's pedagogy in the historico-intellectual context of Latin American thought, particularly relating to thinking about theories of knowledge, literacy, and the role of education. I have suggested that previous dominant philosophies of Scholastic Humanism and Positivism conceived knowledge and literacy as systems of rational totality embedded in a European paradigm of rationalization and universal history through which everything that is outside European knowledge is subsumed or destroyed, by the world of letters and its disciplining of the mind. Yet I have also attempted to demonstrate that in Latin America this philosophy has never entirely captured the lived reality of the American. In contrast, the search for an authentic philosophy has achieved a unique and distinctive form by drawing on the experience of marginality to European knowledge as an "outside of history," a "reality not of paper," beyond grammar, even beyond words. It is the effort of recognition of this reality beyond fixed knowledges, marginalized by dominant paradigms of knowledge, which I would suggest signals the foundational moment in Freirean pedagogies, the ethical effort to build dialogue with those whose voices have been silenced. In developing this position Freire's pedagogies reflect a primary commitment to the socially and politically oppressed, yet this oppression is not understood simply as exploitation, but is inherently epistemological, a response to the social, political, and historical silencing of knowledges. The concept of oppressed is thus distinct from the Marxian concept of proletariat—the proletariat refers to those exploited by capital, the oppressed is a concept that demands more of us, a broader recognition of our own complicity in processes of silencing, and an ethical commitment to challenge ourselves in the ways in which we may marginalize knowledge, a process of self-transformation and epistemological transformation. Freirean pedagogies, in its American context, is thus not a methodology but an ethics, concerned with the problematics of transformative dialogue, not to empty ourselves of meaning nor to negate truth, but to recognize the difficult processes by which we might speak with others in historical contexts of oppression.

Acknowledgments

This chapter has benefited from the contributions from participants in the Education and Social Change in Latin America Workshop, as well as the editorial support of Sara Motta.

References

Altamirano, M. and Sarlo, B. (1995), "The Auto Dictat and the Learning Machine," in Donghi, T. H., Jaksic, I., Kirpatrick, G., and Masiello, F. (eds.), *Sarmiento: Author of a Nation*, Berkeley: University of California Press.

Barber, M. (1996), *Ethical Hermeneutics: Rationality in Enrique Dussel's Philosophy of Liberation*, New York: Fordham University Press.

Bello, A. (1997), *Selected Writings of Andrés Bello*, López-Morilla, F. M. (trans), Jaksić, I. (ed.), Oxford: Oxford University Press.

De Sousa Santos, B. (2007), "Beyond Abyssal Thinking: From Global Lines to Ecologies of Knowledge," *Revista Crítica de Ciências Sociais* 78: pp. 3–46.

Dussel, E. (1994), "Leopoldo Zea's Project for a Latin American Philosophy of History," in Chanady, A. (ed.), *Latin American Identity and Constructions of Difference*, Vol. 10, Minneapolis: University of Minnessota Press, pp. 26–42.

——— (1995), *The Invention of the Americas: The Eclipse of the "Other" and the Myth of Modernity*, Barber, M. D. (trans.), New York: Continuum.

Echevarría, R. G. (1995), "A Lost World Rediscovered," in Donghi, T. H., Jaksic, I., Kirpatrick, G., and Masiello, F. (eds.), *Sarmiento: Author of a Nation*, Berkeley: University of California Press.

Echeverría, E. (1993), *El Matadero*, Madrid: Catedra.

Freire, P. (1996), *Pedagogy of the Oppressed*, London: Penguin.

——— (2001), *Pedagogy of Freedom: Ethics, Democracy and Civic Courage*, London: Rowman and Littlefield.

García-Márquez, G. (1992), *The Solitude of Latin America*, Nobel Prize for Literature Acceptance Speech, http://www.nobelprize.org/nobel _prizes/literature/laureates/1982/marquez-lecture.html.

Garrido, J. M. (2007), "The Desire to Think: A Note on Latin American Philosophy," *CR: The New Centennial Review* 7(3): pp. 21–30.

Guardiola-Rivera, O. (2002), "State of Grace: Ideology, Capitalism and the Geopolitics of Knowledge," *Nepantla: Views from the South* 3(1): pp. 15–38.

Katra, W. H. (1995), "Re-reading Viajes: Race, Identity and National Destiny," in Jaksic, I., Kirpatrick, G, and Masiello, F. (eds.), *Sarmiento: Author of a Nation*, Berkeley: University of California Press.

Lankshear, C. (1994), *Critical Literacy: Politics, Praxis and the Postmodern*, New York: SUNY Press.

Maciel, D. (1985), "An Interview with Leopoldo Zea," *Hispanic-American Historical Review* 65(1): pp. 1–20.

Mignolo, W. D. (1992), "Nebrija in the New World: The Question of the Letter, the colonisation of American Languages and the Discontinuity of Classical Tradition," *L'Homme* 32: pp. 185–207.

—— (1995), *The Darker Side of the Renaissance: Literacy, Territoriality and Colonialization*, Ann Arbor: University of Michigan Press.

—— (2000), *Local Histories/Global Designs: Coloniality, Subaltern Knowledges and Border Thinking*, Princeton: Princeton University Press.

Nebrija, A. (2007), "La Gramática de la lengua castellana," http://www .antoniodenebrija.org/indice.html.

O'Gorman, E. (1961), *The Invention of America: An Inquiry into the Historical Nature of the New World and the Meaning of Its History*, Bloomington: Indiana University Press.

Quijano, A. (2008), "Coloniality of Power, Eurocentrism and Social Classification," in Dussel, E., Morena, M., and Juaregui, C. A. (eds.), *Coloniaity at Large: Latin America and the Postcolonial Debate*, London: Duke University Press.

Sarmiento, D. F. (1998), *Facundo or Civilisation and Barbarism*, Mary Mann (trans.), New York: Penguin.

Zea, L. (1963), *The Latin American Mind*, Abbot, J. H. and Dunham, L. (trans.), Norman: University of Oklahoma Press.

Chapter 2

Marxism and Popular Education in Latin America

Liam Kane

At first glance there seems much in common between Marxism and popular education in Latin America. Both are theoretical constructs for analyzing and changing the world; both are concerned with the welfare of the oppressed; both relate to organizations or movements of people, as well as to sociopolitical theory. But drawing too close an association between the two is problematic. Marxists often criticize popular educators and vice-versa, and the different currents, tendencies, interpretations, and expressions of both Marxism and popular education inhibit simple comparisons.

This chapter highlights aspects of Marxism against which popular education might be measured, examines basic principles of popular education, assessing their compatibility with Marxism, and considers how the popular education movement might be viewed through a Marxist lens. Summarizing the similarities and differences between both, the chapter concludes with suggestions as to how and where Marxism and popular education might learn from each other.

Marxism

Briefly highlighting characteristics of Marxism against which popular education might be compared (Eagleton, 2011 and Gonzalez, 2006 provide comprehensive introductions to Marxism), first, the foundational writings of Marx and Engels are based on a "materialist" as opposed to "idealist" conception of history. This means that real-life conditions—particularly our economic situation, whether we are rich or poor, worker, slave or capitalist—conditions both social relationships and the way we think: "the ultimately determining element in history is the production and reproduction of real life" (Engels, 1895). Second, different modes of production give rise to different social classes, each pursuing different interests, with the "class struggle as the immediate driving force of history" (Marx and Engels, 1879). Marx and Engels considered that "all historical struggles, religious, philosophical or some other ideological domain, are in fact only the more or less clear expression of struggles of social classes" (Engels, 1885). Third, in Capital, Marx analyzed and attacked capitalism as a mode of production, explaining how it systematically exploited the working class (proletariat) (Marx, [1867]1887). Fourth, the only way to resolve class conflict was for the proletariat to destroy capitalism and establish a new society under socialist or communist principles (Marx and Engels, 1848). Fifth, since "the ideas of the ruling class are in every epoch the ruling ideas" (Marx, 1845), the working class often acts as a class "in" but not "for itself." Sixth, revolution was possible because (a) capitalism contained within it the seeds of its own destruction, (b) the lived experience of the proletariat caused them to challenge the ruling ideas, (c) though human beings were conditioned by their material environment, they still had scope and agency to enact social change: "Men make their own history, but...they do not make it under self-selected circumstances" (Marx, 1852). Seventh, taking the previous points together, and adapting the ideas of Hegel to a "materialist" philosophy, Marx developed a "dialectical method" for understanding history and contemporary society. Among other things this involved searching for the class interests and conflicts underpinning political, social, and economic change and showing how all change was interconnected. Finally, the point of Marx's work was to link theory with practice to "contribute...to the liberation of the modern proletariat" (Engels, [1883]1978, p. 682).

Subsequent followers of Marx and Engels debated how these ideas should be interpreted, developed, adapted, and put into practice in their own evolving historical contexts. Contradictions, variations of emphasis, and incomplete analyses in the original writings fuelled the debate. Particular areas of dispute were the degree to which economic realities were seen to determine history versus the potential of the working class to shape its own destiny; whether reform was possible instead of revolution; whether the state and other institutions had "relative autonomy" or simply reflected the economic "base" of society; whether the death of capitalism was inevitable, left to its own devices, or whether it had to be defeated in struggle; under what circumstances revolution was more or less likely to take place; whether the formation of social classes was more complex than simply bourgeoisie versus proletariat, capitalist versus working class.

Lenin (1902) championed the leadership role of a revolutionary "vanguard" political party in taking over the state; Luxemburg (1918) argued that revolution "must be the work of the *class* and not of a little leading minority in the name of the class" (para. 5); Trotsky (1931) argued for permanent and international revolution from below to prevent any elite from taking power. Gramsci (1935) criticized over-deterministic interpretations of Marxism and argued that capitalists also ruled through "hegemony," cultural domination. While not ignoring economic considerations, he placed new emphasis on the importance of politics, culture, ideology and civil society, claiming that the agency of the working class, aided by its own intellectuals—"organic" to the class—was crucial to the struggle for counter-hegemony and thus revolution.

Throughout the globe, individuals and new political parties adapted the ideas of Marxism to their own contexts, though their record on promoting progressive change varied. In Latin America, Mariátegui (1928) applied a Marxist analysis to the realities facing indigenous peoples in Peru. From the Cuban Revolution, Guevara (1965) commented on the role of consciousness, education, and the relationship between party and masses in promoting socialism. The Revolution prompted interest in Marxism throughout the region and, fusing Marxist social analysis with Christianity, the progressive wing of the Catholic Church developed a theology of liberation (Boff and Boff, 1987); in the 1979 Nicaraguan Revolution the first Sandinista government contained six liberation theology priests. With Marxism commonly, if disputedly, associated with the Soviet Block, many saw the fall of the Berlin wall in 1989 as its death knell, with the electoral defeat of the Sandinistas in 1990 reinforcing the idea that large-scale social change had become an unrealistic utopia (Castañeda, 1994).

There followed a period of political disorientation in Latin America—a "crisis of paradigms" (Núñez, 2001)—"grand-narratives" like Marxism were discredited and neoliberalism seemed to emerge triumphant. This brought its own contradictions, however, provoked massive opposition, and, by 2000, with a so-called turn to the Left in formal politics, Marxism started to make a comeback. While currently most obviously associated with Venezuela's attempt to promote twenty-first-century socialism (21 cs)—ostensibly an attempt to combine the egalitarian aspirations of socialism with a less hierarchical, more bottom-up, and participatory form of government—it has also impacted on some of the major social movements whose "dance" with Latin American states has been one of the key pressures driving social change (Dangl, 2010). At the same time, Marxism continues to develop in different directions, adding qualifiers on the way. Open Marxism emphasizes the unpredictability of class struggle, that history is open to being shaped (Motta, introduction); "autonomous Marxism" highlights the importance of everyday forms of resistance to capitalism outside organized political parties, with a broader definition of what constitutes the working class (Hardt and Negri, 2000); some Marxists bring a feminist analysis to the role of labor in capitalism (Motta and Mansell, introduction and chapter 1 in this book). In short, there are multiple, developing and sometimes mutually hostile interpretations of Marxism, making a comparison of Marxism and popular education far from straightforward.

A Marxist Look at Popular Education

As with Marxism, popular education too covers a broad range of theory and practice. Definitions of the term vary (Núñez, 2001; Schugurensky, 2010), none definitive or absolute; differences are often subtle, simply emphasizing some characteristics over others, and occasionally serious, usually reflecting attempts to co-opt popular education for conservative ends (Gibson, 1994). In Spanish and Portuguese the adjective "popular" often has connotations different from its English equivalent. It suggests belonging to "the people," the vast majority of citizens who, in the context of Latin America, are normally poor. Though imprecise, the term carries clear connotations of social class and could often translate simply as poor or working class. Educación/educação popular, then, means an education that serves and belongs to the people rather than the elite. More recently, with people organizing around issues such as gender, ethnicity or human rights, the meaning of popular has stretched to include these initiatives too. But, since their protagonists mainly come from lower economic sectors anyway, class-based nuances generally still apply.

Strongly influenced by the work of Paulo Freire ([1972]1985; 1993), popular education refers to a generic educational practice covering a wide variety of social actors—from peasants to factory workers, women to indigenous people, and so on. Most definitions share a number of common characteristics, summarized elsewhere in ten main principles (Kane, 2012), and this section considers how each principle relates to Marxism.

(1) *Popular education has a political commitment in favor of the oppressed, poor, marginalised or excluded.* All education is considered political, either working to support or change the prevailing unjust social order: "washing one's hands of the conflict between the powerful and the powerless means to side with the powerful, not to be neutral" (Freire, 1985, p. 122). The value of education is measured by its contribution to promoting social justice. Clearly, this resonates strongly with all currents of Marxism. Though Marx and Engels seldom discussed education explicitly, education for change was integral to their project. Where there are differences with popular education, these relate to what is understood by the oppressed and the particular vision of the future that education appears to promote. Marxism attempts to understand how class dynamics operate at any particular conjuncture and has a vision of revolutionary change, overcoming capitalism and leading toward socialism or communism, albeit these labels are imprecise and sometimes problematic. The working class, a product of the capitalist mode of production, is central to this. Building from Freire's *Pedagogy of the Oppressed*, the categories used in popular education are more general and vague, albeit the oppressed at least implies some sort of class awareness. While some currents within popular education talk the language of class and openly criticize capitalism, for others, though clearly committed to increased equity and social justice, any critique of capitalism, as a system of oppression, is either implicit or subdued: a "fairer deal for the poor" may be the extent of its vision for the future.

(2) Epistemologically, *popular education recognizes that all people have important knowledge acquired from their own particular lived experiences: useful knowledge is not the preserve of academics, technicians or experts.* Popular education "starts from where people are at" and while showing an (albeit critical) respect for popular knowledge, many popular education activities concentrate on mapping out a group's view of the world before introducing new knowledge (Kane, 2001, pp. 74–76). This is a significant difference from orthodox Marxist thinking, if education is seen simply as enlightened revolutionaries rescuing people from a brainwashing by ruling ideology. While Marxism need not be patronizing—it can explain why brainwashing happens—it says little about valuing popular knowledge; its starting point would be to spread a Marxist understanding of the world, not consider that a priori people had important contributions to make toward that understanding themselves.

(3) *Education should consist of dialogue between different "knowledges," not simply the depositing of someone's expertise into the mind of*

those perceived to be ignorant, what Freire ([1972]1985) calls "banking education." Instead of education being a one-way transaction, then, everyone becomes both teacher and learner in a process of collective enquiry: "no one teaches another, nor is anyone self-taught. People teach each other, mediated by the world" (53). Again, this differs from orthodox Marxist conceptions of education where the aim is to engage in banking education from a left- rather than a right-wing perspective. Where Marxist education sets out to persuade and pass over a theory of how to understand and change the world, it departs from the concept of popular education. Marxism has often gained that reputation and it is one of the critiques against it made by popular educators (Gutiérrez and Castillo, 1994). On the other hand, this (and the previous) characteristic of popular education do have connections with Marxism in that dialectical thinking, promoted by Marx, underpins Freire's theory of knowledge, both at an idealist level, in that dialogue involves exchanges of (sometimes contradictory) theses, and at a materialist level, as the world is the mediator of these ideas.

(4) *Popular education should develop critical thinking among learners, so that people can recognize and understand the mechanisms that keep them oppressed; increasingly, it encourages creative thinking and the ability to make concrete proposals for change.* This principle, promoting what Freire referred to as "conscientization," clearly chimes with Marxism. There seem to be two differences, however. First, Marxism explains which mechanisms keep people oppressed, whereas popular education is vague. Second, for Marxism, critical thinking might just be considered Marxist thinking, to be passed from teacher to learner. Conscientization, by contrast, refers to a process in which, having been challenged by educators to question aspects of dominant ideology and critically research their own social reality, people arrive at their own conclusions about how they are oppressed. The difference could be understood as promoting passive learning in the former, active learning in the latter.

The metaphor has limitations, however. Popular education is based on dialogue between sets of knowledge and it is perfectly legitimate for the ideas of Marxism to be introduced to the dialogue and processed by learners (as opposed to being handed over for passive consumption). Indeed one critique of popular education is that the notion of banking education overestimates the power of the educator, since people do not learn passively at all, they must engage their active minds; conversely, in learner-centered educational processes the transfer of new knowledge is still important and sometimes key in stimulating learning. As Coben points out, commenting on how landless workers appear to listen to agronomists' lectures but are actually engaged in a game of counter manipulation, "the elaborate game being played out leaves Freire's distinction between banking and problem-posing education, with its assumed transparency of motivation, far behind" (Coben, 1998, p. 211).

(5) *The aim is not to manipulate thoughts or create dependency on charismatic leaders but to enable people to become authentic agents, protagonists or "subjects" of change themselves.* This is key to popular education and, I believe, remains a revolutionary concept in educational theory. It links to the notion of participatory democracy—that people should have the maximum amount of involvement possible in the decisions impacting on their lives (Held, 2006)—and helps progressive educators avoid engaging in mere propaganda and persuasion. Whether it relates to Marxism or not depends on who or what is being referenced. It seems at odds with the notion of populist revolutionary leaders and vanguardist political parties calling on the working class to follow their path to liberation. Popular education acknowledges the importance of leadership, and specialist knowledge, but if the relationship is top-down and "verticalist"—not based on dialogue between leaders and supporters—then it subverts this key principle of popular education. Again, many Marxist practices stand accused of verticalism, bolstered by a banking approach to education, not least the examples of state-driven "real socialism" and "orthodox Marxism." The last chapter of Freire's *Pedagogy of the Oppressed*, in fact, is directed at revolutionary leaders, acknowledging their importance but arguing for a dialogical rather than vertical approach to their political work. On the other hand, Guevara makes observations similar to those of Freire (McLaren, 2000); Marx and Engels (1864) declare that "the emancipation of the working classes must be conquered by the working classes themselves" (para. 1); Luxemburg's last recorded words were: "The leadership failed...The masses are the crucial factor" (Luxemburg, 1919, para. 19); Trotskyism critiques blind faith in leadership and Gramsci's concept of "organic intellectuals," as well as "open" and "autonomous" Marxism, all chime with the notion of the oppressed as authentic agents of change. From a popular education perspective, then, on this issue Marxism has both positive and negative aspects, though overall popular education is more explicit than Marxism on the importance of the oppressed themselves becoming collective subjects of change.

(6) *The methodology of popular education should promote a dialogue of knowledges and encourage people to think and act for themselves.* Popular education in Latin America has developed an impressive

range of "participative techniques" and educational approaches for which it has rightly received world renown (Boal, 1992; Bustillos and Vargas, 1993). Here it is difficult to make direct comparisons with Marxism. Popular education methodology relates to what educators do in a practical sense, when they are planning and conducting explicitly educational sessions with groups of learners. The Marxist "method" (Marx, 1858) refers to a materialist and dialectical approach to understanding society, not how to organize learning. Some argue that Marxist education should emphasize "*activity, collaboration* and *critique*, rather than passive absorption of knowledge" (Marxists Internet Archive, 2011, para. 3) and that learning is achieved through struggle; in general, though, while a renewal in Marxist educational theory pays more attention to this area (Rikowski, 2007), there is little in the way of a specific Marxist educational methodology to discuss. Popular education has made great advances here while Marxism has not. However, the Central American popular education network ALFORJA labeled its educational practice-cum-theory the "Concept of a Dialectical Methodology," bringing together dialectical thinking with a participatory educational methodology, with clear reference to a Marxist method of understanding society. The methodology starts "from where people are at" and people are encouraged to see how all aspects of the social world interrelate, dialectically. The methodology encourages people to go backward and forward between theory and practice—another "dialectical" relationship—in thinking through potential action for change. The education materials produced by ALFORJA, clearly influenced by Marxism, have made a huge impact throughout Latin America (Bustillos and Vargas, 1993).

(7) *The concern is to help enable people progress collectively, not single out individuals for special treatment, albeit individual needs are not ignored.* This characteristic differentiates popular education from conventional education, where individuals pursue qualifications as a means of personal advancement. Popular education aims to help small groups, local communities and large movements of oppressed people benefit from educational processes. For a while, popular education was criticized for having too strong a focus on the collective, ignoring the fact that learning takes place in different ways to different individuals. Now it does pay more attention to the individual aspect of learning but the aim remains for the collective to benefit, a principle clearly linked with the Marxist vision of fairness and justice for all.

(8) Promoting critical consciousness is about helping people bring about change. *Popular education is linked to* action *for change*, then, another departure from conventional education. This clearly echoes

Marx's dictum that "the philosophers have only *interpreted* the world...the point is to *change* it' (Marx, 1938, thesis 11). However, with a preplanned analysis and program for action, the traditional vehicle of Marxist struggle is the organized political party, linked to trade union and workplace activism, focusing on the economic role of the working class in capitalism; not seeking recruits for a particular program, the popular education school tends to be social movements, wherever people have attempted to self-organize in response to social or political injustice. Popular education can enter the fray at any point, however: starting with purely educational work, in a community development project, for example, it can encourage people to think about how they might become organized and take action. Alternatively, where people have already initiated action, it can then help with educational support: movements such as the Brazilian Rural Landless Workers and the Zapatistas in Mexico have even developed their own systematic approach to popular education (EZLN, 2008). Polarizing the difference for clarity, then, Marxist political parties will typically have a developed program of action to recommend; popular education will challenge people themselves to consider what action they might take.

(9) *Some argue that the raison d'être of popular education is "an ethical commitment in favour of humanisation"* (Zarco, 2001, p. 30). This emanates from Freire's critique of banking education as "de-humanizing," resonating, in Latin America, with the emphasis placed on ethics by Christian teaching (see Mansell, chapter 1 in this book). At one level, the principle is entirely compatible with Marxism: the destruction of capitalism and advent of socialism should lead to material conditions that allow people to become fully human. If ethics are presented as an abstract entity, however, with no discussion of how different ethical viewpoints might relate to different material realities, it is at odds with some fundamental philosophical components of Marxism.

(10) Tenth, *the role of the educator is not to provide answers but to ask questions and stimulate dialogue, debate and analysis. But popular educators also contribute to the dialogue and are not merely facilitators: though it should never be manipulative, popular education is undeniably interventionist.* First, we might ask, who are the educators? In Marxism, arguably, it is the political party plus its activists. Traditionally in Latin America "the majority of popular educators have their roots in left-wing politics, the Church or the social sciences" (Rivero, 1993, p. 174), though these tend to be the professionals; another group are the organic intellectuals emerging from different movements, where "the most important popular educator

should be the leader of an organisation" (IMDEC, 1994, p. 64). Some differences between a Marxist and popular educator are implicit in the earlier discussions of methodology and the dialogue of knowledges. Based on the definition of the popular educator expressed here, another difference, exaggerating for effect, is that while popular educators are busy asking questions, and trying to help others do likewise, Marxist educators provide answers! However, despite its problem-posing approach, popular education remains undeniably interventionist and popular educators, variably influenced (or not) by Marxism, also contribute to the dialogue. This theme reemerges in the discussion of what Marxism and popular education might learn from each other.

A final consideration is the extent to which Paulo Freire, the father figure of popular education, might himself have been considered a Marxist. When asked directly he was evasive (Gadotti, 1996, p. 609). But he was influenced by many, sometimes contradictory intellectual traditions and there is "no shared-upon agreement among commentators about the relative impact of the different influences on Freire's theoretical framework" (Schugurensky, 2011, p. 77). Concisely, Elias described Freire as a "Christian-existentialist-Marxist educator" (1994, p. 44). Freire and commentators both recognized that Marxism was an important influence on his thought, however, and that he became more Marxist as he grew older (Youngman, 1986). Schugurensky's (2011) review of critique and counter-critique of Freire, from all political perspectives, suggests that almost any statement made on the extent of Freire's Marxism could be instantly contested by Marxists and non-Marxists alike. In the end, while Freire was a consistent critic of mechanical applications of determinist orthodox Marxism, I think the extent to which he can be considered Marxist is largely in the eye of the beholder.

Marxism and the Popular Education Movement

In its contemporary form I consider the Latin American popular education movement to have had five broad periods of development. The divisions are blurry and debatable but they offer a starting point for understanding the movement today.

Period 1 covers the late 1950s and 1960s, when Freire and others were developing new educational ideas in Brazil. Period 2, the boom period, covers the 1970s to mid-1980s when, against a backdrop of growing authoritarianism and economic hardship, social movements flourished and attempted to bring about change through extra-parliamentary activities. The movements sought out support for their struggles, took hold of the new ideas on education, and radicalized them further in practice; key figures comment on the strong influence of Marxism during this period (Gutiérrez and Castillo, 1994; Núñez, 1992). Popular education centers and networks also started to appear, organizing at the regional level in CEAAL, the Latin American Council for Adult Education, which remains to date the most visible manifestation of the popular education movement. Period 3 covers the mid-1980s to the late 1990s, which saw a crisis in popular education parallel to the "crisis of paradigms" mentioned earlier (Mejía, 1995). From the late 1990s to early 2000s, Period 4 saw a settling down of the various debates and the emergence of a wider range of activities under the banner of popular education, some more overtly radical than others and now with varying degrees of engagement with the state. Finally, in Period 5, from the mid-2000s onward, with a so-called turn-to-the Left in Latin American politics and talk of 21cs, particularly in Venezuela and Bolivia, all accompanied by the rhetoric, if not the delivery, of increasing participatory democracy from below, radical structural change is on the agenda again and this is reflected in popular education too (Kane, 2012).

By nature, popular education is sensitive to the context in which it operates and some developments are/were simply reflections of wider changes in Latin America. Its practice has also varied depending on whether dictatorship, liberated zones, social democracy, or revolution forms the political backdrop. As a general rule, popular education has resonated more with Marxism in times of extreme repression, with the polarization of the oppressor–oppressed duality, or in revolutionary conjunctures when large-scale social change has seemed tangible. The extent to which it might be considered Marxist, then, is not straightforward. Also, in one sense the popular education movement is simply a collective term for all initiatives nominally engaged in popular education throughout the region, of which there is a wide variety. Kane's study of popular education practices and publications (2001, pp. 152–159) found openly Marxist and socialist orientations, predominantly religious concerns, postmodernist and anti-Marxist pronouncements (though these were based on debatable interpretations of Marxism), and initiatives indicating faith in the power of civil society, undifferentiated by class, to bring about social transformation.

In another sense, the popular education movement refers to identifiable national and regional popular education networks, at the apex of which is CEAAL. With its strategic plans, regular "encuentros," popular and scholarly publications, particularly *La Piragua*, CEAAL's explicit allegiances are more open to inspection than initiatives less formally connected. One study of CEAAL concluded that "multiple understandings of popular education have fostered contradictory projects, some with an explicit analysis of the state and social class...and others appearing prone to legalistic and ultimately populist constructions of those same institutions" (Austin, 1999, p. 44). CEAAL remains the dominant barometer of popular education in the region, though it cannot claim to speak for the movement as a whole, and in May 2012 changed its name to become the *Popular* (as opposed to "Adult") Education Council for Latin America and the Caribbean, renewing and strengthening its commitment to popular education and political and social change. Its newer mission statement (CEAAL, 2012) seems a step toward rather than away from Marxism.

Finally, a feature of contemporary popular education is that various social movements have developed in-house popular education programs, tailored to their own needs and aspirations. The Rural Landless Workers Movement in Brazil and the Zapatistas in Mexico are two obvious examples, both acknowledging the influence of Marxism, though neither movement is explicitly Marxist. Other movements vary in the extent to which they have been influenced by Marxism and this is reflected in their popular education programs too.

Popular Education and Twenty-First-Century Socialism

In recent decades there has been discussion about the extent to which an autonomous popular education movement ought to engage with the state (Gadotti and Torres, 1992). In revolutionary Nicaragua, popular education was organized by the state itself, albeit with tensions between trying to promote autonomy, on the one hand, and supporting the government on the other (Barndt, 1991). The same issue arises today where governments claim to pursue 21cs, though the explicit allegiance to socialism offers an additional chance to examine the relationship between Marxism and popular education.

As can be seen elsewhere in this book, however (see Motta, Martinez, Esteves and Hernadez), the concept of 21cs is a work under construction rather than a blueprint for action. Among Marxist commentators, some see it as a significant step forward (Wilpert, 2006) while others suggest it is simplistic, concluding that for advocates of 21cs "in times of crises their operative concepts obscure class divisions through the use of vague non-specific populist categories" (Petras, 2009, "Agrarian Reform," para. 9).

In theory at least, in its claimed pursuit of participative and protagonistic democracy, Venezuela's experiment in 21cs gives high prominence to the educational dimensions of the exercise and has taken popular education to its heart. While an independent popular education movement still exists, the Venezuelan government itself declared education for change one of the five motors of the revolution and, attempting to bring direct and participatory democracy into communities, created social missions to bypass the bureaucracy of the old state and promote popular participation. These include education missions that draw heavily on "Freirian conceptions of popular education...and the importance of debate and dialogue" (Duffy, 2012, p. 157). Studying four different areas of Caracas, Duffy (2012) investigates claims and counterclaims regarding the ability of the education missions to promote critical thinking, independent autonomous action, and participatory democracy. The story is varied but the missions often succeed in their aims, even provoking critiques of the government that promoted them. The same educational values are meant to permeate the work of other social missions too.

Though the terms socialism and Marxism are commonly connected, the relationship among 21cs, Marxism and popular education is not straightforward. With varied interpretations of what each concept should mean, never mind how they translate into practice, attempts to synthesize the three are problematic. But the promotion of good popular education should be essential to any struggle for socialism, prefiguring the values of the society to be forged, though it is not a magic pill for delivering brilliant ideas or preconceived outcomes: it cannot guarantee happy endings. In helping people analyze problems, look for solutions and take appropriate action, however, it has an important contribution to make to any struggle for change.

Synthesizing Marxism and Popular Education

Having considered similarities and differences between popular education and Marxism, I think it is possible to synthesize the best of both worlds.

Starting with popular education, a theoretical weakness, I believe, is that while it proudly parades its political commitment, it says little about the particular ideological baggage educators bring to the table. Inevitably, this must impact on educational processes in two particular areas.

The first is the type of question posed. Good popular educators ask questions for groups to work through. But the questions asked depend on how educators happen to see the world. The question occurring to a Marxist, who sees the hand of capitalism everywhere, will often differ from that of a social democrat, who does not. Asking questions does not tell people what to think, but it channels discussion in particular directions and encourages people what to think *about*.

Second, popular educators do not merely facilitate but also contribute new knowledge to the dialogue, albeit for critical appraisal and not passive consumption, so the different ideological orientations among educators likely result in different experiences for learners. It matters, then, what educators think, though outside of educational processes, popular education does not have a systematic body of knowledge to contribute. Marxism does, however, and it makes a crucial contribution to understanding and acting on social injustice. It is important that it enters the educational mix and good popular educators, if they also happen to be Marxists, enrich the educational process by enabling that to happen.

There is also much for Marxism to learn from popular education. Most obviously, popular education shows how to engage in political education, rather than spreading propaganda, and with honesty and critical respect for others. There is a perceived legacy of verticalism and vanguardism in Marxism, which needs to be overcome, and without ignoring the importance of leadership, popular education supports those interpretations of Marxism promoting the working class and its allies as agents of change, in a spirit of participatory democracy. A Marxism infused with an understanding, methodologically, of how its accumulated systematic body of knowledge might contribute to popular knowledge through dialogue, without engaging in "cultural invasion" (Freire, [1972]1985), will be far better for it. Finally, while Marxism and popular education have been associated predominantly with political parties and social movements respectively, this need not be the case. Just as the most committed activists often belong to both types of organization, political parties can also learn from popular education (e.g., the Workers Party in Brazil) as social movements can and do learn from Marxism (e.g., the MST in Brazil).

Conclusion

This chapter argues that while popular education and Marxism are both understood and expressed in a variety of ways, a comparison of core characteristics shows clear areas of convergence and divergence, albeit some interpretations of popular education lean more toward Marxism than others, and vice-versa. However, each has its weaknesses and they could learn from each other. While popular education rightly asserts the value of grassroots experiential knowledge, it is vague on which systematized bodies of knowledge have most to contribute to its cause. I believe popular educators should ensure dialogical processes are enriched by contributions from Marxist insights and analyses. This may not be easy, if educators are insufficiently familiar with—or have even developed an antipathy toward—Marxism. Equally, open-minded Marxists can learn from popular education about how to promote dialogue effectively, contributing their ideas while recognizing the value of other knowledges and thus overcoming a reputation, deserved or otherwise, for dogmatism and "cultural invasion" (Freire, [1972]1985). Marxist theory is more complex than popular education theory, however, and full-fledged Marxists have an initial advantage over generic popular educators in synthesizing the best of both worlds. But however the two philosophies-cum-practice come together, the interests of progressive social change—including attempts to reinvent socialism for the twenty-first century—will surely be advanced if highly competent Marxist popular educator-activists engage in a variety of practices wherever there are spaces for formal or informal education to take place.

References

Austin, R. (1999), "Popular History and Popular Education: El Consejo de Educación de Adultos de América Latina," *Latin American Perspectives* 26, 4(7): pp. 39–68.

Barndt, D. (1991), *To Change This House: Popular Education under the Sandinistas*, Toronto: Between the Lines.

Boal, A. (1992), *Games for Actors and Non-Actors*, London and New York: Routledge.

Boff, L. and Boff, C. (1987), *Introducing Liberation Theology*, Tunbridge Wells: Burns & Oates.

Bustillos, G. and Vargas, L. (1993), *Técnicas participativas para la educación popular. Tomo 1 & 2*, Guadalajara: IMDEC.

Castañeda, J (1994), *Utopia Unarmed: The Latin American Left after the Cold War*, New York: Vintage.

CEAAL (2012), "Misión y Objetivos," http://www.ceaal.org/v2/cmision .php (accessed October 10, 2012).

Coben, D. (1998), *Radical Heroes: Gramsci, Freire, and the Politics of Adult Education*, New York: Garland Pub.

Dangl, B. (2010), *Dancing with Dynamite: Social Movements and States in Latin America*, Oakland, CA: AK Press.

Duffy, M. (2012), *Venezuela's "Bolivarian Revolution": Power to the People?* PhD thesis submitted to the University of Manchester, February.

Eagleton, T. (2011), *Why Marx Was Right*, Yale: Yale University Press.

Elias, J. (1994), *Paulo Freire: Pedagogue of Liberation*, Malabar: Krieger.

Engels, F. ([1883]1978), "Speech at the Graveside of Karl Marx," in Tucker, R. C. *The Marx-Engels Reader*, New York: Norton, pp. 681–682,

—— (1885), "Preface to the Third German Edition of The Eighteenth Brumaire of Louis Bonaparte," http://www.marxists.org/archive/marx/works/1885/prefaces/18th-brumaire.htm (accessed October 26, 2012), Marxists Internet Archive.

—— (1895), "Engels to J. Bloch In Königsberg," http://www.marxists.org/archive/marx/works/1890/letters/90_09_21.htm (accessed October 26, 2012), Marxists Internet Archive.

EZLN (Ejército Zapatista para la Liberación Nacional) (2008), "Cómo Funcionan Las Escuelas Zapatistas. Boletín especial EZLN," *Referencia No 24, Boletín del Foro Latinoamericano de Políticas Educativa*, http://www.foro-latino.org/flape/boletines/boletin_referencias/boletin_24/referencias24.htm (accessed October 26, 2012).

Freire, P. ([1972]1985), *Pedagogy of the Oppressed*, London: Pelican.

—— (1985), *The Politics of Education: Culture, Power and Liberation*, London: Macmillan.

—— (1993), *Pedagogía de la Esperanza*, Mexico City: Siglo Veintiuno Editores.

Gadotti, M. (1996), *Paulo Freire: Uma Bibliobiografía*, São Paulo: Cortez, Instituto Paulo Freire.

Gadotti, M. and Torres, C. A. (1992), *Estado e Educação Popular na America Latina*, São Paulo: Papirus.

Gibson, A. (1994), "Freirian v Enterprise Education: The Difference Is in the Business," *Convergence* 27(1): pp. 46–57.

Gonzalez, M. (2006), *A Rebel's Guide to Marx*, London: Bookmarks.

Gramsci, A. (1935), *Prison Notebooks*, http://www.marxists.org/archive/gramsci/prison_notebooks/index.htm (accessed October 26, 2012), Marxists Internet Archive.

Guevara, E. (1965), *Socialism and Man in Cuba*, http://www.marxists.org/archive/guevara/1965/03/man-socialism.htm (accessed October 26, 2012), Marxists Internet Archive.

Gutiérrez, F. P. and Castillo, D. P. (1994), *Mediación pedagógica para la educación popular*, San José and Costa Rica: RNTC, Universidad San Carlos de Guatemala, Universidad Rafael Landívar.

Hardt, M. and Negri, A. (2000), *Empire*, Harvard: Harvard University Press.

Held, D. (2006), *Models of Democracy* (3d edition), Stanford: Stanford University Press.

IMDEC (1994), *Ser Dirigente No Es Cosa Fácil: Métodos, Estilos y Valores del Dirigente Popular*, Guadalajara, Mexico: IMDEC.

Kane, L. (2001), *Popular Education and Social Change in Latin America*, London: Latin American Bureau.

———— (2012), "Forty Years of Popular Education in Latin America: Lessons for Social Movements Today," in Hall, B. L., Clover, D. E., Crowther, J. and Scandrett, E. (eds.), *Learning and Education for a Better World: The Role of Social Movements*, Sense: Rotterdam, pp. 69–86.

Lenin, V. I. (1902) *What Is to Be Done? Burning Questions of Our Movement*, http://www.marxists.org/archive/lenin/works/1901/witbd/index.htm (accessed October 26, 2012), Marxists Internet Archive.

Luxemburg, R. (1918), *The Russian Revolution. Chapter 8. Democracy and Dictatorship*, http://www.marxists.org/archive/luxemburg/1918/russian-revolution/ch08.htm (accessed October 26, 2012), Marxists Internet Archive.

———— (1919), "Order Prevails in Berlin," http://www.marxists.org/archive/luxemburg/1919/01/14.htm (accessed October 26, 2012), Marxists Internet Archive.

Mariátegui, J. C. (1928), *Seven Interpretative Essays on Peruvian Reality*, http://www.marxists.org/archive/mariateg/works/1928/index.htm (accessed October 26, 2012), Marxists Internet Archive.

Marx, K. (1845), "The German Ideology. Part I: Feuerbach. Opposition of the Materialist and Idealist Outlook. B. The Illusion of the Epoch. Ruling Class and Ruling Ideas," http://www.marxists.org/archive/marx/works/1845/german-ideology/ch01b.htm#b3 (accessed October 26, 2012), Marxists Internet Archive.

———— (1852), *The Eighteenth Brumaire of Louis Bonaparte*, http://www.marxists.org/archive/marx/works/1852/18th-brumaire/ch01.htm (accessed October 26, 2012), Marxists Internet Archive.

———— (1858), "The Grundrisse. A. Introduction (3) The Method of Political Economy," http://www.marxists.org/archive/marx/works/1857/grundrisse/ch01.htm#3 (accessed October 26, 2012), Marxists Internet Archive.

———— ([1867]1887), "Capital: A Critique of Political Economy. Volume I, Book One: The Process of Production of Capital," http://www.marxists.org/archive/marx/works/1867-c1/ (accessed October 26, 2012), Marxists Internet Archive.

———— (1938), *Theses on Feuerbach*, http://www.marxists.org/archive/marx/works/1845/theses/original.htm (accessed October 26, 2012), Marxists Internet Archive.

Marx, K. and Engels, F. (1848), *Manifesto of the Communist Party*, http://www.marxists.org/archive/marx/works/1848/communist-manifesto/ (accessed October 26, 2012), Marxists Internet Archive.

———— (1864), *The International Workingmen's Association 1864. General Rules*, http://www.marxists.org/archive/marx/iwma/documents/1864/rules.htm (accessed October 26, 2012), Marxists Internet Archive.

———— (1879), *Strategy and Tactics of the Class Struggle*, http://www.marxists.org/archive/marx/works/1879/09/17.htm (accessed October 26, 2012), Marxists Internet Archive.

Marxists Internet Archive (2011), *Marxism and Education*, http://www
.marxists.org/subject/education/index.htm (accessed October 26, 2012).

McLaren, P. (2000), *Che Guevara, Paulo Freire and the Pedagogy of
Revolution*, New York: Rowman and Littlefield.

Mejía, M. R. (1995), *Transformação Social*, São Paulo: Cortez.

Núñez, C. H. (1992), *Educar Para Transformar, Transformar Para Educar*,
Guadalajara, Mexico: Instituto Mexicano para el Desarrollo Comunitario
(IMDEC).

——— (2001), *La revolución ética*, Xátiva: Diálogos.

Petras, J. (2009), "Latin America's 21st Century Socialism in Historical
Perspective," *Global Research*, October 12th, http://www.globalresearch.ca
/latin-america-s-twenty-first-century-socialism-in-historical-perspective/
(accessed October 26, 2012).

Rikowski, G. (2007), "Marxist Educational Theory Unplugged," Fourth
Historical Materialism Annual Conference, http://www.flowideas.co.uk
(accessed October 26, 2012).

Rivero, J. H. (1993), *Educación de Adultos en América Latina: Desafíos de la
Equidad y la Modernización*, Lima: TAREA.

Schugurensky, D. (2010), "Popular Education: A Snapshot," http://legacy
.oise.utoronto.ca/research/edu20/courses/popeddefinitions.html
(accessed October 26, 2012).

——— (2011), *Paulo Freire*, New York: Continuum.

Trotsky, L. (1931), *The Permanent Revolution*, http://www.marxists.org
/archive/trotsky/1931/tpr/pr-index.htm (accessed October 26, 2012),
Marxists Internet Archive.

Wilpert, G. (2006), "The Meaning of 21st Century Socialism for Venezuela,"
venezuelaanalysis.com, July 11th, http://venezuelanalysis.com/analysis
/1834 (accessed October 26, 2012).

Youngman, F. (1986), *Adult Education and Socialist Pedagogy*, Kent:
Routledge.

Zarco, C. (2001), "Review of Chapter 1," in Kane, L. *Popular Education
and Social Change in Latin America*, London: Latin American Bureau,
pp. 29–32.

Chapter 3

On the Pedagogical Turn in Latin American Social Movements

Sara C. Motta

The role of the pedagogical is increasingly important in the construction of new forms of anticapitalist politics in Latin America. This is evidenced by the centrality of popular education and other forms of struggle influenced by radical education philosophy and pedagogy, and by social movements in their construction of new forms of participatory politics and mass intellectuality. It is also evidenced in the creation of formal and informal educational programs, practices and projects that develop varieties of critical pedagogy and popular education with both organized and nonorganized marginalized and excluded communities. Such a multiplicity and plurality of practices challenge many of the taken for granted assumptions about the nature of revolutionary struggle and revolutionary subjects, and the meaning and objectives of such struggle. They suggest the need for self-reflection and renovation within Marxist political categories so that they can maintain their relevance and relationship with the popular struggles and subjects at the heart of the creation of multiple pathways to twenty-first-century socialism (21 cs) in the region.

In this chapter, I address such problematics with a view to mapping popular pedagogical praxis by opening a conversation (of a plethora already occurring) between the Open Marxist tradition and the experiences of popular struggle in social movements in Brazil, Venezuela, Argentina, Colombia and Mexico. I hope in this way to contribute to the renovation of Marxist categories of thought through their engagement with the epistemologies and pedagogies of new popular subjects. I also engage with the contributions of Jonathan Mansell and Liam Kane (chapters 1 and 2, in this volume) and the overall problematic of this edition, which is the nature of 21 cs and the role of the pedagogical and education, broadly defined, in this process.

Building on Jonathan Mansell's chapter, which develops a conceptual and philosophical framing of Freirean popular education within
a distinctly Latin American philosophical tradition, I suggest that the
pedagogical reinvention that is occurring in contemporary social movements is testimony to the embodied praxis and pluridiverse epistemologies of such a tradition. My epistemological commitment to such a
politics of knowledge is also represented in my choice to place Open
Marxism in dialogue with these practices, imaginaries and pedagogies
as this tradition is, arguably, a theory from the margins and under-
side of Marxism of the twentieth century. I hope that through this
dialogue I can contribute to producing Open Marxism as a practice
of border-thinking as opposed to a reified conceptual and theoretical
straitjacket that speaks about and above movements from the outside.

Building on Liam Kane's chapter, which foregrounds both the resonances and dissonances between popular education and Orthodox
Marxism and suggests both can learn from each other, I seek to expand
our conceptual lens and representation of the Marxist tradition. I also
hope to contribute methodologically and epistemologically to opening up the Open Marxist tradition, with which I identify, to self-
reflection and renovation through seeing itself through the eyes of
Latin American movement pedagogies and politics of knowledge.

Thus the dialogue between Open Marxism and social movements
in Latin America is specifically focused on the epistemological and
pedagogical. First I use the conceptual horizons opened by Open
Marxist critique to read and make visible the pedagogical that runs
through the heart of the praxis of many social movements in Latin
America. Second I reread Open Marxism through the eyes of the pedagogical and epistemological practices of movements. I hope that this
will stimulate reflection within the open Marxist tradition about the
contradictions and tensions in the politics and practices of knowledge
construction that they (we) engage with, in which they (we) develop a
systematic critique of representative politics and yet often practise representational epistemologies in their theoretical practice. This reading
of Open Marxism through the practise of Latin American popular
politics fosters open Marxism's rethinking of itself and its complicity
in the epistemological politics of coloniality.

From Twentieth- to Twenty-First-Century Socialism:
On the Post-Representational

The dominant articulation of twentieth-century revolutionary praxis
tended to theorize *the* revolutionary subject as the organized working

class. This tended to imply in reality a privileging of the "white" male manufacturing worker resulting in a strong culture of laborism. This was justified by a theorization of the capital relation in which it was conceptualized as occurring at the point of production, in the relationship of exploitation of laborer by owner and premised on the extraction of surplus value. There were increasing contestations of this conceptualization of revolutionary subjectivity, or theorizations from the margins of Marxist praxis that emerged from the realities of peasant revolutionary politics, indigenous struggle (paradigmatic of this is the work of Mariategui) and Marxist feminist movements across the global south, particularly visible in the South American context of the Nicaraguan revolution of 1979 (see Bonefeld, 2007; Federici, 2004; Holloway, 2005 for more contemporary critiques). These experiences and struggles tended to expand our understanding and conceptualization of the capital relation to: (i) include the realm of social reproduction in our understanding of the extraction of surplus labor; (ii) rethink our conceptualization of the capital relation to an expanded understanding of alienation that viewed the state as a form of the capital relation and capital as a social relation in constant need of reproduction; and therefore (iii) reconceptualize primitive accumulation as not merely a historical moment in the formation of capitalism but as a constant process of reproducing the process of abstract labor, which constitute the subjects of the capital relation. Such practical theoretical expansion also impacted upon the theorization of the strategies and objectives of revolutionary transformation, particularly our conceptualization of the role of the state in social and political transformation.

One example of such conceptual expansion of the capital relation and political categories of revolutionary transformation is developed in the Open Marxist tradition. For Open Marxists, structures of the state and market are perverted human forms; alienated human practices that veil the reality that political power and economic goods are actually the result of our energies used against us. Therefore domination is subjective (collective alienation). As Bonefeld explains:

> What then needs to be explained is not the relation between capital and wage labour in its direct and immediate sense but rather the social constitution upon which this relationship is founded and through which it subsists…The class antagonism between capital and labour rests on and subsists through the separation of human social practice from its means, a separation that appears to invest these means with independent power over the very human social practice from which its springs. Thus capital is a perverted form of social cooperation. (2008b, p. 54)

Capital is thus not a thing but a relation in which our creative capacities are turned backed against us into alienated forms of the party, state, market. It is the way we live and reproduce ourselves and our world (Leeds May Day Group, 2008, pp. 115–126). Resistance therefore, is not about resisting something "out there" but rather changing the way we live. This implies a nondualistic understanding of the relationship between domination and resistance, one in which each is internal to the other. It also implies that transformation is a contradictory and creative open process in which we strive to produce ourselves and our relationships differently. Accordingly any form of representational politics will reproduce alienated human practice and a division of labor with thinkers and doers. Thus as Bonefeld argues: "The society of the free and equal or the mode of production of associated producers cannot be achieved through a politics on behalf of the working class. Theory on behalf of the working class leads to the acceptance of programs and tickets whose common basis is the everyday religion of bourgeois society: commodity fetishism" (2008b, p. 61).

Open Marxists argue that traditional leftism and vanguardism replicates alienated human practice in which the capacity to think and theorize is delegated to a select few. Critique becomes reified in a tome of abstract theorizing and party doctrine in which the mass sacrifice in the name of truth as opposed to creating truth in collective praxis. As Tischler continues:

> Class consciousness appears as a universal attribute of the party or the state; it is not the working class in struggle that forms the content of experience but the party as organisation or the (workers) state as the collective consciousness of the working class. In this sense, the theory of class struggle has undergone a period of stasis, a stasis of a specific historical experience, which was canonised and thus achieved hegemonic position. The institutionalisation of class struggle is precisely this. Institutionalism in the state form or in the party form replaces the self-organisation and self-determination of the working class. In short, canonisation entailed the constitution of a vertical subject. (2008, p. 165)

Open Marxists suggest therefore that transformation into a non-alienated subject or a free collective subject necessitates concrete historical engagement with working-class politics in order to give meaning to concepts as tools of political development, develop theoretically engaged analysis and understand the contradictions of such struggle in order to engage in a strategically useful way. Thus Tischler continues:

If collectivity is not a mere sum of individuals, of groups, of movements, but a kind of illumination (Benjamin's) that gives rise to a new subjectivity and a new subject, then what is the element that gives meaning to it...collectivity is not an abstraction, but a real form of existence that is produced as an instance of negation/overcoming of the logic of separation upon which the rule of capital rests. (2008, p. 166)

This *theorizes* the how of constructing postcapitalist communities suggesting that only concrete engagement between theory and political practice will result in the formation of adequate concepts and understanding to move such post-representational politics forward in our own lives and communities. It also suggests that engaging with the contradictions and politics at the heart of such a construction is politically enabling as it allows the asking of strategic questions by movements. However, much Open Marxist critique remains predominantly at the level of abstract critique.

Tischler's work is perhaps the most embedded in political struggle, which is evident in his suggestion of ways in which we might engage with these practices in a politically enabling way. Thus he argues, "one can argue that revolution is reinvented by the radical social movements of our time. To reinvent revolution under the current circumstances is to change the meaning of words, to create a new language for naming radical change...The rebel subject creates a language that tells us that the desired change will no longer be trapped in the form of a vertically constructed power, but that it will be one of the self-organisation and self-determination of the exploited and dominated" (2008, p. 171). This suggests that the best strategic way forward is dialogue with such movements' practices and theorizations.

Open Marxism therefore opens up lines of analysis and conceptualization along a number of axes: de-alienation, theory as emerging from collective popular struggle, the everyday and subject as key categories of critique, revolutionary subjectivity as process of collective construction, liberation as openness and multiplicity and reflective dialogue with movements practices to forge meaningful theoretical contributions. Along all these axes we find the role of the pedagogical is pivotal. It is to this we now turn.

De-alienation and New Subjectivities

Open Marxism places, the question of the subject and a movement away from the alienation reproduced by the vertical subject of vanguardist traditions of revolutionary praxis dominant in the twentieth century at the heart of contemporary critique. They suggest one of

the ways we might conceptualize this problematic is through negative dialectics (Holloway, 2010; Holloway, Matamoros and Tischler,
2009). Negative dialectics is premised upon a negation of the alienat-
ing social relations and subjectivities through which abstract labor
and the capital relation are produced. This negation does not posit
a positive subject of transformation, but rather is premised upon the
negative critique of capitalism as an opening to a door of recapturing
and building upon that of our dignity, creativity and abilities, which
resist their enclosure as a form of capital. This overflowing of our
being can only be found in the particular and is mediated by collective and individual experiences, histories and beliefs. As suggested by
Mansell's reading (chapter 1, in this volume) of Freire as expressive of
the development of a distinctly Latin American philosophical tradition, the body and the placed become central to the conceptualization of the transformatory subject.

At the heart of critique as de-alienation is openness; openness to
the unknown undergird by a belief in humanity that seeks to break
preformed categories of the subject. The transformation of subjectivity into nonalienated social flows of being, doing, living and loving
that this suggests conceptually resonates with the openness that is
at the heart of collective practices of knowledge construction, which
characterize many of the new forms of popular politics that seek to
create worlds beyond capitalism. As Werner Bonefeld states:

> We have to attain a conception of realism that knows how to dream and
> sing, and dance. Imaginative realism is not just an art-form—it is sub-
> version in practice…This volume is dedicated to the communist indi-
> vidual, her imagination and subversive cunning and reason. It is about
> the beauty of human values—freedom and equality of individual human
> needs, human dignity and respect, solidarity and collectivity, affection
> and warmth, democracy and social autonomy. And it is about subversive
> knowledge, what do we have to know to prevent misery. (2008a, p. 8)

How are such subversive knowledges produced and who are the
subjects of their production Open Marxist leads us to ask? The politics
of knowledge of many social movements in Latin America are creating answers to these questions through the development of collective
processes of knowledge production building on the Latin America
philosophical tradition expressed in the praxis of Paolo Freire.

Collective Processes of Knowledge Construction

Thus we find urban social movements such as autonomous piquetero
groups in Buenos Aires, Universidad de la Tierra, Oaxaca, and the

Comités de Tierra Urbana (CTUs), Caracas, that share with rural movements such as the MST, Brazil, a focus on the importance of participatory democracy and the construction of utopias in the present (MTD Solano and Situaciones Colectivas, 2002; CTUs, 2004; Anon., Universidad de la Tierra, 2009). This emphasizes the practices and processes of constructing social and political change as much as the ends of these processes. At the heart of these understandings is a questioning of the need for intellectual vanguards and an engagement with ideas of mass intellectuality, in which developing their creativity and intellectuality is a central building block of the construction of revolutionary and popular change (Motta, 2009). Thus all these movements use and develop popular education as key to the process of creating intellectual and political autonomy.

Some such as the CTUs seek to develop their theorization and strategization of a CTU project(s) by the development of a methodology of democratic practise, in which it is understood that immanent within the concrete experiences of communities are the global practices of capital and the state. Therefore popular education is used as a tool for challenging common sense by building on the good sense of communities. This enables a collective reading of their experience and struggles through the systematization of themes that emerge from their experiences, recovery and retelling of histories of struggles, identification of community agency and dignity in the face of oppressions and violence and the building of proposals, questions and pathways for further agency out of this systematization (Motta, 2011; see also Martinez, chapter 9, in this volume). Similar to such pedagogical practice is the work of the Escuela Política de Mujeres Pazífica, Cali Colombia (see Norma Bermudez's chapter 13, in this volume) in which a collective and critical reading of the world and women's experiences of oppression, violence and displacement is developed by building on the lived knowledges and experiences of participants. In both works there is focus on the collective wisdom of the group or the community as the basis for self and collective transformation and liberation. Other movements such as the MST have less of an immanent post-representational articulation of popular education. Rather they seek to use popular education to combine different knowledges—those of the academy, popular culture and philosophy and community experience—to build ideological and strategic coherence within particular MST rural communities as the basis for the political development of the movement and realization of its objectives at other spatial and political scales, including the regional, state and global levels (Gadelha de Carvalho and Mendes, 2011).

Despite the differing emphases and assumptions within how different movements articulate popular education they share a commitment to collective knowledge processes that break down the division between thinkers and doers and validate the histories, experiences, cultures and knowledges of subaltern communities. Open Marxism resonates with these practices of movements as both bring to the center of our analytic and conceptual attention the role of the everyday and the placed body in the praxis of social transformation.

Yet as suggested previously, Open Marxism as a heuristic tool of conceptualization of new forms of popular politics neither reduces place-based movements to concrete particularistic struggles in need of outside enlightenment nor assumes romanticized popular subjectivities as pre-given given or outside of capitalism. Rather it suggests that we explore the formation of revolutionary and popular subjectivities as forged through processes of collective construction that engage with the lived contradictions of communities' lives and experiences.

Place and the Particular

As the movements are not formed on the basis of a revolutionary vanguard that externally implants an ideology in particular subaltern communities they therefore stress an organic connection with good sense—those fragments of experience, history, culture and dignity that confront and escape the contradictions of capitalist social relations and their inability to totally enclose and capture the autonomy and desires of such communities. Movements' practice is premised upon the recognition and valuation of the rationality, political agency and dignity of communities' struggles. This results in a different content, sometimes plurality of contents, of revolutionary/popular identity, strategy and objectives. Such processes escape the universal political categories and monological strategies suggested by the vanguardism of much twentieth-century revolutionary theorizations. Some movements such as the MTD Solano, the Universidad de la Tierra and the Escuela Política de Mujeres Pazífica (see Bermudéz, chapter 13, in this volume) embrace building from the particular and a conceptualization of popular struggle and objectives as necessarily plural and open. Others such as the MST and to an extent the CTUs (see Martinez, chapter 9), in this volume, exist in an uneasy relationship with a desire for ideological or strategic coherence at a movement level yet embrace of particularity at a place-based level. In these movements, there is an attempt to move up spatial scales of political articulation through the building on the basis of multiplicity and difference. Nevertheless, the embrace of the concrete and the particular has meant the creation of processes that intertwine everyday forms of religiosity, cultural traditions and moral economies into the praxis of such movements.

Thus many movements have been heavily influenced in their origins and their current praxis by traditions of liberation theology—a Left articulation of Catholicism which stressed that paradise must be created on earth, that true Catholics would choose the option of the poor as a manifestation of their Godliness and that the word of God was open to all and need not be mediated by a caste of priests. Such articulations resulted in place-based politicization in conjuncture with bible study. This produced a moral economy and political culture shaped by practices and imaginaries in which ordinary Catholics (people) were Godly and able to produce and access knowledge for liberation and a belief in the ability and desirability of developing all as agents in the struggle for paradise on earth (see Motta, 2013a, forthcoming). This has colored both the structures of feeling and the ways of organizing in many urban shanty towns and rural peasant movements combining socialist concepts and articulations with biblical language and Christian beliefs.

It has also meant that the spiritual and the cultural become integral elements in the struggle for social and political change. Thus, the MST has developed "mistica" as a means of constructing equal and participatory communities. A mistica is an artistic/cultural event to open and close any MST event, including workshops, meetings, occupations, marches. It can take the form of poetry, a re-action of popular struggle and history, dance, song and often ends with all participants touching each other by either holding hands or a collective embrace. Mistica combines elements of liberation theology with other spiritual beliefs and builds upon them as integral parts of what it means to construct new men and women and a new culture. In the case of Universidad de la Tierra and the Escuela Política de Mujeres Pazífica, spiritual articulation is often intertwined with indigenous heritages recovered and reconstructed to shape the construction of a radically different present from that of the violence of global neoliberal capitalism. Cosmologies and everyday religiosities are considered fonts of knowledge and transformation that are not mere instruments in social transformation but inherent elements of what it means to construct self-governing and autonomous anticapitalist communities. Thus the pedagogical as the means and the ends is constructed through the cultural and spiritual bringing the symbolic and the affective to the heart of the processes of social transformation.

Open Marxism brings into conceptual and political visibility these place-based articulations of popular subjectivities, emotional landscapes, moral economies and everyday religiosities. It enables us to explore the complex dynamics of these processes in a way that confound any simplistic analysis that seeks to invisibilize, infantilize and delegitimize popular beliefs, cultures and practices as representative of backward beliefs and false consciousness. Rather this framework conceptualizes the complexities of subaltern subjectivities, the methodological imperative of learning to listen and the necessity of building conceptual and political categories that engage in solidarity, recognition and with humility with these realities. This also suggests the opening of our conceptual horizons to an expanded practice and theorization of liberation, which includes *politica afectiva* (affective politics) and the embodied.

Integral Liberation: Politica Afectiva and the Body

As we have discussed many popular processes of social and political transformation are premised upon politicization of knowledge in both its form and content. This means that pedagogies of resistance and transformation have become embedded in the complexities of experience and desire of place-based urban and rural communities in struggle. Thus the affective and the embodied have been brought to the heart of the praxis of popular transformation.

There are two main ways in which this occurs: the development of affective and embodied pedagogies and the expansion of the objectives of social and political transformation to include affective and embodied relationships and experiences as a result of these pedagogies. There are of course differing intensities of pedagogical engagement and practice of the affective and embodied.

The CTU's methodology is perhaps the most embedded within the conceptual realm working through and building on reflections upon the everyday practice of struggle and experience of oppression. This aims to enable communities to transform the material conditions of their habitat (housing, health, sanitation, infrastructure, education) at the local scale but also more broadly. However, this often leaves questions, experiences and problematics of the private realm and gendered divisions of labor excluded and depoliticized reproducing contradictions and exclusions in their praxis (see Motta, 2013b, forthcoming).

Movements such as the MTD Solano and Universidad de la Tierra develop an expanded sense of liberation in which the affective and new affective relationships are integral elements in the process and objectives of social transformation. This is perhaps most explicitly discussed in the ideas of some of the autonomous piquetero movements, particularly the MTD Solano and their reflections on how new forms of solidarity and love not premised upon ownership, competition and power over others are formed in their practice and how this constructs in the here and now other subjectivities and social relations. However these are also articulated in the praxis of the Universidad de la Tierra in which the affective and the emotional are central elements to the collective processes of knowledge construction be that the development of urban food production systems that are sustainable or the recapturing and reinventing of cultures of resistance and creation with youth through song, dance, theater. All involve different ways of being and relating to each other and to the earth. They develop and are premised upon another way of seeing and embodying relationships and oneself.

The MST develops affective and embodied pedagogies in a critical reading of the world involving building learning spaces in which the totality of participants' experiences are engaged with. Thus the use of mistica involves pedagogies of the body in which new intimacies and levels of trust are developed between participants in their embodied enactment of their histories of struggle and experiences. Here the wisdom of touch is pedagogical in that it helps form the bonds and openings to intimacies and solidarities beyond competitive individualism.

It is however the pedagogical work of the Escuela Politíca de Mujeres Pazíficas with women in which the most complex pedagogies of crossing between self/other and cosmos are developed. These work through the erotic, which as Audre Lorde (2000) describes "lies in a deeply female and spiritual plane, firmly rooted in the power of our unexpressed or unrecognized feeling." It is a deep knowing or joy that we feel when we authentically express our creativity and desire, which once experienced cannot be forgotten and reburied. As Lorde (2000) continues: "Within the celebration of the erotic in all our endeavors, [our] work becomes a conscious decision—a longed-for bed which [we] enter gratefully and from which [we] rise up empowered." Their development of pedagogies that include ritual, the senses, dreaming, dancing, storytelling, singing, massage, combined with more traditional forms of knowledge produced in textual form builds the conditions for participants reoccupation of the world and ability to challenge and transform conditions of multiple oppression. However, they also open the possibility of a reoccupation of their own bodies.

The internalization of the oppressor's gendered, classed and raced embodied beliefs and practices are subverted and in its place flourish transgressive relationships with the self, others and the world. This cornucopia of pedagogies and methodologies based in popular education do not therefore merely engage with intellectual and theoretical production as if these were disembodied and objective processes. There is a questioning of the alienation of human experience through which capitalist social relations are reproduced and an attempt (sometimes explicit sometimes implicit) to unite and de-alienate our capacities and creativity. Such processes of collective knowledge construction, to differing degrees and in different ways seek to overcome the dualisms between intellect and emotion, mind and body and thought and action that characterize capitalist one-dimensional man.

Re-reading Open Marxism through the Pedagogical and Epistemological Practice of Latin American Movements

We have read social movement practice through the eyes of Open Marxism, which has made visible the complex pedagogical processes and politics of knowledge at the heart of much popular politics in Latin America. However, there are important political questions and reflections raised for Open Marxism by these pedagogical practices and politics of knowledge.

Arguably, Open Marxism's epistemological production remains within capitalist modernity's logic—individuals produce abstraction that enables understanding of concrete political experience. This reinforces a dualism between practice and theory and mind and body in which the construction of theory and the legitimacy of the theorist reproduces the form of politics of coloniality in its construction. While attempting to negate dominant understandings of the world, there is a lack of practical collective negation of the world. This paradoxically reproduces a division of labor between thinker and doer, and between the subject of knowledge production and those about whom knowledge is produced.

If we look to the concrete practices of movements, their practice is the creation of living epistemologies. Through these practices we can open a dialogue on which we can build upon the strengths and possibilities of Open Marxist theoretical production as well as transgress and problematize those elements of alienated human practice that crisscross its production. As we have demonstrated many movements forge post-representational politics in which what we are, what we are becoming and what we want to be are combined. Accordingly, knowledge is not created from the outside in an individualized manner, nor is it seen as being in an external relationship with practice. This involves a negation not only of traditional leftism in its political form but also in its academic form. This suggests the deconstruction of the subjectivity of the radical academic and lines of escape and invention that transgress reified conceptual and theoretical production. It points to possibilities for developing living concepts and abstractions, theory as part of everyday life, an overcoming of the separation between those who think and act and a reuniting with our intellectual and political capabilities that are alienated from us in the form of specialized objects that we cannot reach.

It suggests travesías/crossings of becoming in which as critical scholars we reach to our borders, again and again, embracing the power and creativity of disruption and discomfort. When talking to Andres Antillano, one of the founders of the first CTUs in La Vega, he suggested that as well as learning to listen, we need to desaprender/ unlearn many of the taken for granted of twentieth-century Left political categories and conceptualizations. This is not a call to forget. It is a call to enter into the borderlands, as Gloria Anzaldúa explains, "[to] loosen our borders, not closing off to others. To understand that bridging is the work of opening the gate to the stranger, within and without... To step across the threshold is to be stripped of the illusion of safety because it moves us into unfamiliar territory and does not grant safe passage" (2002, p. 3). Embracing the uncertainty and the discomfort that arises when our taken-for-granted assumptions about the role and subjectivity of the critical theorist are decentered is an act of decolonization of ourselves as critically engaged scholars committed to enacting alternatives to neoliberal capitalism with others and in our everyday lives.

It is therefore imperative not merely to theorize an overcoming of dualisms between thought and practice, life and politics, mind and body as Open Marxism does but practice this overcoming, construct the "how" of these processes moving beyond the limits of capitalist modernity and an epistemological politics of coloniality. It is also imperative not only to theorize the necessity of making subjugated knowledges visible but to think through post-representational ways of making knowledge that de-throne the academic knower from his epistemic privilege. This involves moving beyond abstract negation to concrete negation and the creation of a living epistemology that can be a basis of the construction in the struggle of post-representational politics. It is, I contend, in the praxis of Latin American social movements that a two-way translation can be enacted that creates the grounds for rupturing the form of the epistemological politics of coloniality that crisscross Open Marxism. This reading through Latin American sub-altern eyes of these traditions and orientations in Marxism begins the double-translation on the basis of dialogue and opens the possibility of an intermingling of traditions, ways of knowing and being that are intensely place-based but are in an open process of self-construction that neither reduces one to the other nor the other to the one. Such networked pluridiverse universalism breaks geographical borders, conceptual categories and essentialized subjectivities taking us into the borderlands, into the unknown beauty of worlds beyond capitalism.

Conclusion

While inevitably a simplification of complex and multiple processes of Latin American popular anticapitalist praxis I hope to have contributed to the praxis of such change and its use for practical theorizing by systematizing some of the key tendencies to be found, with different intensities of articulation, that bring popular education and mass intellectuality to the center of our imagining, living and making of worlds beyond capitalism. This attempt at systematization is framed by an understanding of revolutionary and popular praxis as a living project with a multiplicity of manifestations. It has therefore opened a dialogue between a Marxist tradition from the margins, Open Marxism and the epistemological and pedagogical practice of popular social movements. This dialogue demonstrates the pivotal role of the pedagogical in the reinvention of pathways toward 21 cs in the region and how they escape many of the limits and conceptualizations of traditional revolutionary praxis of the twentieth century.

Through this systematization I have also engaged in an expanded dialogue between Marxism and popular education in the region, contributing to the task begun by Liam Kane. I have hoped to bring concreteness to the distinctly Latin American philosophical tradition reflected through Freire suggested by Jon Mansell, demonstrating the link between the pedagogical, the body and the place of the community. In this dialogue I have used Open Marxism as a tool to bring to conceptual and political visibility the pedagogical in movement praxis. I have also suggested the need for self-reflection within the Open Marxist tradition, on its own implications in the reproduction of alienated epistemological practice through reading itself through the pedagogical practices and politics of knowledge of movements.

The pedagogical is taking center stage in the creation of pathways toward 21 cs. Many movements explore and experiment with participatory, collective and post-representational forms of epistemological practice. These create theoretical and strategic knowledge construction immanent to the concrete political experiences of movements. In this knowledge is practiced as a verb or a practice as opposed to a noun, or a thing. Here movements are not only challenging the content of twentieth-century Left political categories but they very form through which we create these popular Left alternatives.

These pedagogical processes develop out of concrete reflection about the lived realities of excluded and oppressed communities. Thus, the spiritual and cultural become important elements articulated as popular practices, imaginaries and emotional landscapes. Oral traditions, dance, theater, song and ritual are considered knowledges that are not mere instruments of social transformation but a central part of creating the rich and multiple textures of ways of life that contest neoliberal capitalism.

The politics of knowledge and the pedagogies that result do not merely engage with intellectual and theoretical production as if these were disembodied processes. Rather movements seek to overcome the separations between intellect and emotion, mind and body and thought and action that characterize many articulations of twentieth-century Left alternatives, and to create, as Boff and Boff describe, "integral liberation." Thus affective and embodied pedagogies foreground different ways of being and relating to each other and the earth. They enable marginalized and oppressed communities to appear in the world as embodied political subjects. This suggests that the pedagogical (in all its complexity) is at the heart of the reinvention of pathways toward 21 cs in contemporary Latin America.

References

Anon. (2009), *Universidad de la Tierra en Oaxaca, A.C.*, Col. Reforma, Oaxaca: Ediciones !Basta!.

Anzaldúa, Gloria and Ana Louise Keating (2002), *The Bridge We Call Home: Radical Visions for Transformation*, London: Routledge.

Bonefeld, W. (2007), "History and Social Constitution: Primitive Accumulation Is not Primitive," in Bonefeld, Werner (ed.), *Subverting the Present, Imagining the Future: Insurrection, Movement, Commons*, New York: Autonomedia, pp. 77–86.

———— (2008a), "Subverting the Present, Imagining the Future: Insurrection, Movement and Commons," in Bonefeld, Werner (ed.), *Subverting the Present, Imagining the Future: Insurrection, Movement and Commons*, New York: Autonomedia, pp. 7–9.

——— (2008b), "The Permanence of Primitive Accumulation: Commodity Fetishism and Social Constitution," in Bonefeld, W. (ed.), *Subverting the Present, Imagining the Future: Insurrection, Movement and Commons*, New York: Autonomedia, pp. 51–66.

Comité de Tierras Urbanas (CTUs) (2004), "Democratización de la Ciudad y Transformación Urbana," Caracas: Cooperación Solidaria Instituto Municipal de Pubicaciones.

Federici, Silvia (2004), *Caliban and the Witch: Women, the Body, and Primitive Accumulation*, New York: Autonomedia.

Gadelha de Carvalho, S. and Mendes, E. (2011), "The University and the Landless Movement in Brazil: The Experience of Collective Knowledge Construction through Educational Projects in Rural Areas,'" in Motta, S. C. and Nilsen, A. G. (eds.), *Social Movements in the Global South: Dispossession, Development and Resistance*, London: Palgrave Macmillan Press, pp. 131–150.

Holloway, John (2005), *Change the World without Taking Power*, London: Pluto.

——— (2010), *Crack Capitalism*, London: Pluto.

Holloway, John, Matamoros, Fernando and Tishler, Sergio (eds.) (2009), *Negativity and Revolution: Adorno and Political Activism*, Michigan: Michigan University Press.

Lorde, Audre (2000), *The Uses of the Erotic: The Erotic as Power*. Tuscan: Kore Press.

Motta, Sara C. (2009), "Old Tools and New Movements in Latin America: Political Science as Gatekeeper or Intellectual Illuminator?" *Latin American Politics and Society* 51(1): pp. 31–56.

——— (2011), "Notes towards Prefigurative Epistemologies," in Motta, Sara and Alf, Nilsen (eds.), *Social Movements in the Global South: Dispossession, Development and Resistance*, London: Palgrave Macmillan Press.

——— (2013a), "Introduction: Reinventing the Lefts from Below," *Latin American Perspectives*, Special Edition: Reinventing the Lefts from Below, forthcoming.

——— (2013b), "'WeAre the Ones We Have Been Waiting for': The Feminisation of Resistance in Venezuela," *Latin American Perspectives*, Special Edition: Reinventing the Lefts from Below, forthcoming.

MTD of Solano and Colectivo Situaciones (2002), *La Hipótesis 891: Más Allá de los Piquetes*, Buenos Aires: De Mano en Mano.

The Leeds May Day Group (2008), "Anti-Capitalist Movements," in Bonefeld, W. (ed.), *Subverting the Present, Imagining the Future: Insurrection, Movement and Commons*, New York: Autonomedia, pp. 115–126.

Tischler, S. (2008), "The Crisis of the Classical Canon of the *Class Form* and Social Movements in Latin America," in Bonefeld, W. (ed.), *Subverting the Present, Imagining the Future: Insurrection, Movement and Commons*, New York: Autonomedia, pp. 161–178.

Part II

Education Struggles and/in Left Governments

Chapter 4

Nicaragua: Deprivatizing Education, the Citizen Power Development Model and the Construction of Socialism in the Twenty-First Century

Thomas Muhr

"Indeed, we may be witnessing not the terminal decay of Socialism," remarked Joel Samoff in response to the general greeting of the decline of socialism in the late twentieth century, "but the struggles of its rebirth" (Samoff, 1991, p. 1). While Samoff pointed to the Polish workers at the time to potentially take on a lead role in this effort, history has once more put Latin America and the Caribbean—in José Martí's decolonialist terms, Our America—into the spotlight of resistance to capitalism. These transformations are advanced and promoted through the Bolivarian Alliance for the Peoples of Our America—Peoples' Trade Agreement (Alianza Bolivariana para los Pueblos de Nuestra América—Tratado de Comercio de los Pueblos, ALBA-TCP), which I have theorized as a pluriscalar counter-hegemonic war of position that seeks the construction of socialism: a set of processes in which the local and national become dialectically interrelated with the regional and global, and with the notion of "revolutionary democracy" at the core.[1]

Nicaragua joined the ALBA-TCP in 2007 as a full member under the Government of Reconciliation and National Unity (GRUN), led by the Sandinista National Liberation Front (Frente Sandinista de Liberación Nacional, FSLN) as the strongest force in the multiparty United Nicaragua Will Triumph Alliance. Once again, Nicaragua's political economy has become subject to fundamental reorientation: after toppling the Somoza dictatorship in 1979, which was one of the longest-lasting US-supported dictatorships in Latin America and the Caribbean, the FSLN-led Sandinista People's Revolution under President Daniel Ortega sought to transform the dependent capitalist agro-economy toward a democratic socialism. The FSLN's defeat in the February 1990 elections, however, ushered in 16 years of neoliberalization, whereby the implementation of Washington Consensus policies meant the reversal of the revolutionary gains in social justice—land redistribution, relative basic food security, free basic health care and a significant reduction in illiteracy. In a climate of pervasive hopelessness, Managua's streetscape started changing noticeably in the late 1990s: laboring and begging street children proliferated while the urban geography became restructured according to the needs of the automobile elites.

With the FSLN's return to national government in January 2007 and its reelection in November 2011, GRUN has initiated a process of structural transformation from neoliberalism to socialism within the ALBA-TCP ideational and institutional framework. While still an impoverished nation, the envisioned "reconstruction of Nicaragua" (GRUN, 2009a, p. 5) has involved the restoration of free health care and basic education and the integration of over 23,500 children in risk situations, including street and laboring children, in the education system between 2007 and 2010 (GRUN, 2011). According to a survey by the International Foundation for Global Economic Challenge (FIDEG, 2010), between 2005 and 2010, consumption-based poverty was reduced from 48.3 to 44.7 percent, extreme poverty from 17.2 to 9.7 percent and extreme rural poverty from 30.5 to 18.2 percent. Most significantly, perhaps, the nation was declared illiteracy-free in July 2009 (UNESCO et al., 2009). Unseen in a decade: children playing and reclaiming their childhood.

The following exploration of the Participative Education Revolution (Revolución Participativa de la Educación) and the construction of socialism continues my previous discussions of the construction of the ALBA-TCP in Nicaragua (Muhr, 2008a; 2010a) and the production of an ALBA-TCP regional education space (Muhr, 2010b). Although, during the parliamentary term 2007–2012, GRUN did not have a mandate for outright revolutionary transformation (the Alliance had 38 seats out of 92 in the National Assembly), the Citizen Power development model contains the transformative socialist agenda. Therein, "universal and integral education" (GRUN, 2009a, p. 84) seeks to reconcile education for personal and moral growth with the exigencies of national political and economic development. I concentrate on two aspects of the Participative Education Revolution central to the construction of socialism/revolutionary democracy: the National

Literacy Campaign "From Martí to Fidel," and the 2007/2008 Great National Consultation for the Reform of the Basic and Medium Education Curriculum.

Nicaragua and the Construction of the ALBA-TCP

In accordance with the constitutional mandates (RN, 2010, Article 9), Nicaragua joined the ALBA-TCP as its fourth member on January 11, 2007, the day following Ortega's presidential inauguration.[2] At the time, the country had dropped in the United Nations Development Programme (UNDP) Human Development Index (HDI) from position 71 in 1990 to 120 (UNDP, 1990; 2008); poverty, as measured by the minimum basket of food and nonfood requirements, had reached 46–48 percent, and extreme poverty (food poverty line) 15–17 percent (World Bank, 2008); 21 percent of the population were undernourished (FAO, 2009, p. 48), and 20 percent of the 15–65 year olds illiterate (INIDE in MINED, Unesco et al., 2009).[3] With about 34 percent of the school age population excluded from education (MINED in FEDH-IPN et al., 2007, p. 4),[4] the neoliberal "decentralisation" policies ("autonomous schools" and "municipalisation") implemented from 1993 on had resulted in the violation of the constitutional right to free state-provided basic education. While the failure of World Bank inspired privatization is explored in greater detail elsewhere (Muhr, 2008a), some consequences the current Participative Education Revolution responds to are noteworthy: average schooling had diminished from 8.3 years in 1990 to 4.6 years, whereby the extremely poor could expect 1.9 years (UNESCO/MECD in Muhr, 2008a, p. 152); schools came to be run as largely independent units under the control of Directive School Councils that saved funding directly allocated from the ministry by employing unqualified personnel rather than graduate teachers (33–36 percent of Nicaraguan teachers were untrained when GRUN entered office in 2007);[5] and, with salaries of approximately USD 110 per month, which covered less than the basic food basket, as compared to USD 375 as the Central American average, Nicaraguan teachers were the lowest-paid in Central America in the mid-2000s (Federación Luterana Mundial, 2006, p. 45). Within a climate of "ungovernability," the education crisis provided the grounds for the construction of the ALBA-TCP in Nicaragua from 2004 on, in two key dimensions that characterize the multidimensional development and integration project: energy, and the social-humanitarian in the form of health care and literacy (Muhr, 2008a).

As regards the energy dimension, a mixed enterprise called ALBA Nicaragua S.A. (ALBANISA) has been created between the Nicaraguan state oil company Petronic and Petróleos de Venezuela Sociedad Anónima (PDVSA). Through ALBANISA, Venezuela supplies Nicaragua with petroleum and derivatives under a low-interest, long-term financing scheme, which involves the diversion of 50 percent of the invoice from the Venezuelan coffers to regional and bilateral development funds. Half of these funds are administered in Nicaragua by the cooperative, not-for-profit National Rural Bank (Caja Rural Nacional, CARUNA), the other half by the jointly administered ALBA Fund. Simultaneously, between 2004 and 2006, the ALBA-TCP was territorialized through the Cuban-Venezuelan ¡Yo Sí Puedo! (I Can Do It!) literacy campaign and the Misión Milagro (Mission Miracle) ophthalmology program. In the two years prior to Nicaragua's formal membership, the ALBA-TCP was being constructed jointly by Venezuelan and Cuban state organs and the FSLN, municipal governments, individuals (voluntary university students and private doctors) and civil and organized society actors, such as the peasant umbrella organization Nicarao Farming Cooperative Enterprise (NICARAOCOOP, R.L.), the Carlos Fonseca Amador Popular Education Association (Asociación de Educación Popular Carlos Fonseca Amador) and Médicos del Mundo. Therefore, as my analysis has shown, transnational as well as regional and bi-/multistate integration strategies are deployed by state actors and social forces in the construction of the ALBA-TCP space.

Guided by the principles of solidarity, cooperation and complementarity, the ALBA-TCP explicitly recognizes international power asymmetries and replaces the orthodox comparative (locational) advantage by the "cooperative advantage." Ideologically drawing on Simón Bolívar's vision of the Grand Homeland (Patria Grande), the construction of a production-based, value-adding economy in strategic sectors has involved the creation of bi-/multistate grandnational enterprises (GNEs) (regional production, distribution and commercialization chains and networks), grandnational projects (GNPs) (social action programs) and grandnational institutes (GNIs) (research centers). The emergent regional production and trade chains stand for a democratization of the organization of production with socialist orientation and may, as in 1980s Sandinista Nicaragua, also integrate private actors, especially cooperatives and micro, small- and medium-sized enterprises (micro, pequeña y mediana empresas, MIPYMES) that are created with state support (credits, land titles, guaranteed market/prices) in a process of deproletarianization of the peasantry. The relevance attributed to these forms of social organization is reflected in the creation in 2012 of a Ministry for Family, Communitarian, Cooperative and Associative Economy (Ministerio de Economía Familiar, Comunitaria, Cooperativa y Asociativa). International trade figures show that within the context of global financial, economic and 'aid' crisis, the Venezuela/ ALBA-TCP development cooperation has prevented the Nicaraguan economy from collapsing (Muhr, 2011a, pp. 180–181).

As I argue in detail elsewhere, the definitional foundation of twenty-first-century socialism is the notion of revolutionary democracy in which pluralist representative democracy coexists with Marxist direct democracy and C. B. Macpherson's participatory democracy (Muhr, 2008b; 2011a; 2012). With popular power as the core constitutive element, revolutionary democracy has been used synonymously with 1980s Sandinista democratic socialism (e.g., Hoyt, 1997). As did this unorthodox, pluralist Latin American and Caribbean socialism, the contemporary construction of socialism extends the struggle over democracy to all spheres of social existence without prioritizing a pre-constituted site of struggle (e.g., the point of production) (Slater, 1986, p. 162). Subsequently, direct democracy means social and popular control of the means of production and political organization in a pyramidal council structure (Marx, 1942[1871]). The process of reconfiguring and rescaling state power by social forces within the state apparatus as well as from outside is ongoing in ALBA-TCP members, especially in Venezuela, and in Nicaragua takes the form of the Citizen Power development model. Within the ALBA-TCP, direct democracy is becoming institutionalized as the Council of Social Movements, through which the ALBA-TCP societies become organized in a pyramidal, counter-hegemonic governance structure. The Council of Social Movements is in direct dialogue with the Council of Presidents, which is the highest decision-making body in the ALBA-TCP.[6]

The exercise of direct (as well as representative) democracy, however, is contingent upon political, economic, social and cultural conditions related to "the equal right to self-development," which is the essence of Macpherson's participatory democracy: a process of conscientization (from an individualist consumer identity to personal development and a sense of community), and a substantial reduction of social and economic inequalities for the full development of people's capabilities (Macpherson, 1977). Change of the conditions for participation is promoted through the ALBA-TCP in a number of ways, including: First, the ¡Yo Sí Puedo! literacy method, which has been adapted to 14 linguistic and cultural contexts in 28 countries worldwide, has been inter- and transnationalized as Misión Robinson International, to the benefit of 3.8 million hitherto illiterate people in over 20 Latin America and Caribbean countries by 2009; and the Cuban-Venezuelan Misión Milagro has provided ophthalmological treatment free of charge to 1.9 million people in 33 Latin American and Caribbean countries between 2005 and early 2011 (Muhr, 2011a, pp. 184–185). The missions and other social programs, which in contrast to conventional assistentialist or compensatory welfare schemes (social democracy) combine short-term poverty alleviation with long-term structural transformation (Muhr and Verger, 2006), may be localized under different names in different territories: for example, an ALBA-TCP program for people with disabilities is called Misión Todos Con Vos (All With a Voice) in Nicaragua; Atención al Discapacitado (Attention to the Disabled) in Cuba and St. Vincent and the Grenadines; and Misión Manuela Espejo in Ecuador. Second, the ALBA Caribe Fund, which is one of the aforementioned regional development funds, had by 2010 allocated USD 179 million to 85 social and socio-productive projects in 12 Central American and Caribbean countries (Muhr, 2011a, pp. 198–199). Third, important for the purposes of this chapter, among the GNPs and GNEs that operate in human security areas (especially food, health and education), the GNP ALBA-Education and the GNP Literacy and Post-Literacy operate within Venezuela's "higher education for all" rationale (Muhr and Verger, 2006; Muhr, 2010b). In the next section, I argue that Nicaragua's Citizen Power contains the elements of revolutionary democracy, on which grounds the role of the Participative Education Revolution in the construction of socialism can be illustrated.

Citizen Power: Constructing Socialism in Twenty-First-Century Nicaragua

The draft version of the National Human Development Plan 2008–2012 (GRUN, 2008a) and its 2009–2011 Update in response to the global financial, economic and aid crisis (GRUN, 2009a) identify poverty as a structural problem, the elimination of which requires long-term transformation in which the organized communities become (re)instituted as the new "social subject and political actor" (pp. 5, 11, 17). The government, however, recognizes the structural constraints imposed by Nicaragua's dependent-capitalist position in the global economy. Accordingly, the World Bank, on the one hand, perceives continuity with respect to macroeconomic stability and public debt sustainability for poverty reduction in accordance with the Millennium Development Goals, diversification of exports within the logic of international free trade and attempts to attract foreign direct productive investment. On the other hand, the Bank also observes "important strategic changes," including a refocus from the previous "cluster development strategy" that worked in favor of agents of "big" capital, as well as the abandonment of privatization and assistentialist policies, instead aiming for rights-based universality for human development (World Bank, 2008).

Consequently, Citizen Power is embedded in a critique of global capitalism and grounded in the values of solidarity, community, complementarity, redistribution, inclusion and equality (GRUN, 2008a, pp. 4–7, 14–15). These, essentially, are the ALBA-TCP principles. Citizen Power evolves from this base as a coherent, integral development model that seeks to reconfigure the power structure through the liberation of the human development capacity of the majorities. Grounded in Nicaragua's constitution (RN, 2010, Article 2) and the Law of Citizen Participation (RN, 2003), Citizen Power is composed of ten "fundamental axes" that can be read as containing the elements of revolutionary democracy (direct democracy/participatory democracy), without explicitly stating so in these terms (GRUN, 2008a, pp. 15–30; 2009a, pp. 10, 16–27). Direct democracy through Councils of Citizen Power (Consejos del Poder Ciudadano) and Cabinets of Citizen Power (Gabinetes del Poder Ciudadano) aims to balance out the perceived power asymmetries in public policy-making between state institutions and the predominantly elitist nongovernment organizations (NGOs) on the one hand, and the popular sectors on the other (Stuart Almendárez, 2009, p. 25). Three pyramidal pillars of direct democratic instances have been established: the territorial, that is, organization at different scales of governance; the sectoral, comprising a minimum of 16 defined areas, including health, security, environment and education; and the civil societal, which is made up of sectoral organizations (women, indigenous, etc.), private business organizations, parties, trade unions, and the National Cabinet of Citizen Power, organized in the Council of Economic and Social Planning (Consejo de Planificación Económica y Social, CONPES). The three pillars are interrelated at the national scale (GRUN, 2008a, pp. 208–209; RN, 2007a, b). Responsibilities of Councils of Citizen Power and Cabinets of Citizen Power involve the management, monitoring, follow-up and evaluation of national and local programs and projects jointly by the organized community, the private sector and the national and subnational governments (GRUN, 2009a, pp. 21). In the southern department of Río San Juan, in July 2009, the councils prioritized areas such as production, road building, electricity, water supply and housing.

GRUN's strategy to change the conditions for participation, mobilization and protagonism in Macpherson's sense—the reduction of inequality for the full development of people's capabilities (1977, p. 114)—is manifest in a wide range of ALBA-TCP financed policies and programs.[7] These include the reinstitution of free health care and state-provided primary and secondary education, including the aforementioned ¡Yo, Sí Puedo! literacy campaign, subsidized cooking gas supply and school meal schemes; Casas para el Pueblo (Houses for the People); Calles para el Pueblo (Streets for the People); Plan Techo (Plan Roof, zinc roofs); Programa Amor (Program Love, targeting children in risk situations), supported by the United Nations Children's Fund (UNICEF); and Hambre Cero (Zero Hunger, subsidized food), which is part of the government's food sovereignty and security policies that have been commended by the United Nations Special Rapporteur on the Right to Food (UN, 2010). Many of these program are run jointly by government bodies and the direct democratic Citizen Power structure, thus promoting local-scale popular organization.

The Citizen Power development model epitomizes the continuation of the FSLN's historical trajectory of direct consultation: the 1987 Constitution was drafted through a consultative process of almost two years (Rosset and Vandermeer, 1986, pp. 357–364); the Great National Literacy Crusade of 1980/1981 that reduced illiteracy from over 50 percent to around 13 percent of the population of ten years and older, involved over 225,000 literate adult volunteers (brigadistas) (Arnove, 1986, p. 137; Barndt, 1985, p. 328; MED, 1982); the National Education Consultation of 1981 for the transformation of the educational system drew on the participation of over 50,000 people (Arnove, 1986, p. 97; Barndt, 1985). Three decades later, the National Human Development Plan 2008–2012, presented after 15 months in government, had been subject to national consultation that started with the Programme of Government during the electoral campaign of 2006. The consultation processes involved CONPES and other state bodies; productive sectors, including private businesses; trade unions, federations and confederations; citizen associations, NGOs and movements; political parties; churches; universities and research centers; the international community; and individuals, including from the diaspora in the United States and Costa Rica (GRUN, 2008a, pp. 9, 227–230; 2009a, pp. 34–35; Ortega, 2008). Against this backdrop, the following section explores the Participative Education Revolution and its significance for the construction of socialism, that is, revolutionary democracy.

Nicaragua's Participative Education Revolution

The National Human Development Plan approaches education from three directions: as a human right for personal development; as technical and scientific knowledge fundamental to national development; and for social transformation. While one of the first acts of the incoming administration was to abolish neoliberal decentralization, the proclaimed "absolute de-privatisation" (GRUN, 2008b, p. 10), however, refers to the restoration of free-of-charge primary and secondary education, rather than to the per se outlawing of private education institutions.[8] Education spending has been increased from 3.8 percent of gross domestic product in 2000 to 5.4 percent in 2010 (UNDP, 2011, p. 31).

Identifying children, adolescents (age group 13–17) and "the young" (age group 18–30), who together constitute almost two-third of Nicaraguans, as well as women, as the key actors in the productive, economic, social, political and cultural development of the nation (GRUN, 2009a, pp. 19–20), the education policies consist of five components that combine quantity with quality and participation with diversity:

- *More education*: Elimination of all sorts of charges in the state sector; universal literacy and increase of preschool, primary, secondary, special and technical education coverage through a formal and non-formal subsystem of basic and medium education (age group 5–17).
- *Better education*: Transforming the curriculum and reverse the de-professionalization produced by (the aforementioned neoliberal) fiscal and administrative deconcentration.
- *A different education*: Overcoming the neoliberal "anti-values" of education privatization and commoditization (MINED, 2009, p. 25) through a new set of values regarding the environment, family, economy, health, solidarity, tolerance, cooperation, *compañerismo*, identity, patriotism and self-determination.
- *Participative and decentralized education management*: Education policy formulation and management jointly by national actors and international organizations, centered around the Citizen Power structure. The Great National Consultation for the Reform of the Basic and Medium Education Curriculum outlined further down exemplifies this idea.
- *All educations*: Integral and holistic articulation of the different levels and types of education (rural/urban, public/private, formal/nonformal, university, persons with different capacities, which is

GRUN's term for people with disabilities, the Regional Autonomous Education Subsystem of the Caribbean Coast), to create synergies and permit continued education throughout life. (GRUN, 2008a, b; 2009a)

Strategies for the realization of these objectives include: the National Literacy Campaign "From Martí to Fidel" and the follow-up post-literacy programs ¡Ya Puedo Leer! (I Can Already Read!), ¡Yo, Sí Puedo Seguir! (I Can Continue!), El Maestro en Casa (The Teacher in the Home) and Basic Education by Level (Educacion Básica por Nivel), to universalize basic education up to 6th grade (MINED, 2009, p. 27); the extension of infrastructure (4,200 new schools) and 6,000 new teachers, as well as the creation of 1,200 school gardens through which nutrition education is sought to be contextualized with production (La Lucha Sigue, 2011); environmental education schemes such as the National Reforestation Campaign (Campaña Nacional de Reforestación) that mobilized 265,000 students in the reforestation of 65,343 hectares between 2007 and 2010 (UNDP, 2011, pp. 33, 36); the creation of centers for technical education (e.g., agricultural production, industry, tourism) to strengthen MIPYMES and the productive sector; the Integral School Nourishment and Food Programme; the National System of Education and Training of Nicaraguan Teachers, accompanied by a 30 percent increase of teacher salaries between 2006 and 2008 (GRUN, 2009b, p. 11). Increasing teacher salaries seeks to support the (re)professionalization of education workers as, in 2009, informants identified teacher education (and the lack thereof) as the weakest element in the ambitious education transformation.

Attempting to ensure equality and quality throughout the territory, the neoliberal Directive School Councils were abolished and finance, maintenance and recruitment re-centralized.[9] From 2008 on, the monthly school-based Educational Evaluation, Programming and Training Workshops (Talleres de Evaluación, Programación y Capacitación Educativa, TEPCEs), which already existed in the 1980s (with questionable success, see Arnove, 1986, pp. 90–91), were reintroduced to organize and locally contextualize the new curriculum and materials. In monthly meetings, TEPCEs also serve to integrate delegates from the Citizen Power councils and cabinets as well as the Ministry of Education (MINED) departmental and municipal delegates. Out of resource scarcity and to promote cooperation restructuring has further involved the creation of a satellite system of 1,460 Education Nuclei, which are networks composed of a "Base School" (Escuela Base) where educational resources are concentrated (experienced staff, laboratories, libraries, audiovisual and digital materials), and so-called "Neighbour Schools" (Escuelas Vecinas). Again, this is not entirely new: in the 1980s, the rural education nuclei were an agency for integrating the school with community and national life for problem resolution (Arnove, 1986, p. 96). The following cases of the National Literacy Campaign "From Martí to Fidel" and the Great National Consultation for the Reform of the Basic and Medium Education Curriculum illustrate the protagonistic potential of the Participative Education Revolution.

The National Literacy Campaign "From Martí to Fidel"

The National Literacy Campaign,[10] launched on June 23, 2007, originated in the transnational ALBA-TCP cooperation from 2005 on: that year, the Carlos Fonseca Amador Popular Education Association, which was created by FSLN members in the aftermath of the Sandinista loss of government power in 1990 for the purpose of continuing the struggle for literacy, called on the international community to support the alleviation of the national education crisis. As the only one to respond, the Cuban government provided the innovative alphanumeric ¡Yo, Sí Puedo! literacy method together with material support for 5,000 literacy points (TV sets; video players; sets of videos, primers and facilitator guides). In contrast to traditional literacy methods that require one year or longer to acquire basic literacy, this innovative method facilitates literacy acquisition within 65 days. Between 2005 and 2007, the Fonseca Association was logistically supported by six Cuban consultants, as illiteracy among the 15–65 age group was reduced from 20.1 to 12.7 percent.[11] From 2008 on, after ¡Yo, Sí Puedo! had become national policy, 86 Cuban advisors and 61 Venezuelan *brigadistas* supported the literacy and post-literacy campaigns,[12] and the Association adapted the literacy method to the linguistic and cultural realities of the nation (Creole English; the indigenous languages Miskito, Mayangna and Creole; Castilian Braille). In June 2009, based on a survey that confirmed a remaining illiteracy rate of 4.73 percent, a multi-institutional commission led by the United Nations Educational, Scientific and Cultural Organization (UNESCO) declared the nation illiteracy-free (UNESCO et al., 2009). The following year, the government announced a further reduction of illiteracy to 3.33 percent (GRUN, 2010a, p. 6).

For the purposes here, the most remarkable aspect of the campaign is the popular mobilization that facilitated its success (Muhr, 2008a, p. 157): 57,631 voluntary literacy workers participated (50,531 under 35 years of age, 66 percent women and 77 percent in rural zones); 76.61 percent of the literacy classes were held in private homes, 18.02 percent in schools, the rest in churches, communal centers, prisons and other government and nongovernment localities (MINED, 2009, p. 19). During the campaign's different phases—national census (July–October 2008), sensitization of the population, methodological training for the facilitators, the literacy classes themselves—volunteers from all walks of life joined. These included: individual teachers; civilian and religious community leaders, especially from the Citizen Power councils; students from state and private universities; youth organizations, such as the Federation of Secondary Students (Federación de Estudiantes de Secundaria) and Sandinista Youth 19 July (Juventud Sandinista 19 de Julio); teacher unions; the FSLN base structure; municipal governments; state institutions (ministries, the army, the police); and private enterprises. The ministry's Final Report highlights that the literacy campaign is the only government program that has not been discredited by adversary political parties and the corporate media (MINED, 2009, p. 15).

Great National Consultation for the Reform of the Basic and Medium Education Curriculum

For much of the neoliberal era, Nicaragua's curriculum had been criticized for being irrelevant, decontextualized and nonresponsive to social reality, promoting rote learning with little practical application of knowledge (Arnove, 1994; FEDH-IPN et al., 2007, pp. 4–5; PREAL, 2004). From 2005 on, under the predecessor government, a new curriculum had been devised by the education ministry, which, however, was not implemented due to the government change in 2007. With the objective of creating a truly national curriculum based on consensus, GRUN subjected the previously drafted curriculum to national consultation. The outcome is a curricular framework that provides basic norms with respect to: educational competencies (knowledges/abilities/attitudes and their application); basic contents that consider relevance (conceptual, procedural, attitudinal); and indicators of achievement. About 30 percent of the contents are flexible, to balance national norms with decentralized local input generated through Citizen Power (FEDH-IPN et al., 2007, p. 7).

In 2007, 17,081 individuals from within and without the education system participated in the Great National Consultation in the entire territory: 6,943 teachers (preschool, primary, secondary); 657 primary and secondary head teachers from state, private and state-subsidized private schools; parents and students; 153 civil society organizations; teacher unions, community leaders, as well as the territorial and sectoral instances of Citizen Power. Data gathering methods included: first, 38 discussion forums with parents and teachers, structured around presentations, in all 19 departments/autonomous regions (approximately 300 participants each). Second, workshops were organized with participants from the educational community to elaborate on specific issues. Third, classroom visits to study needs in concrete educational contexts. Fourth, curricular councils, that is, popular assemblies supported by the Citizen Power structure in locations such as *barrios*, markets, free trade zones, shopping centers and universities, for discussion of proposals by participants not directly related to schooling. Fifth, the Education Web-Portal as a deliberative mechanism for teachers, parents/guardians and school students. Sixth, representatives of interest groups (community, union, business, NGO leaders), which underscores the effort of creating a multiclass alliance in the national interest with respect to education and development (see MINED, 2008, pp. 25–54, for methodological details). Parallel to the consultation, a group of NGOs developed a curricular framework (based on the existing draft curriculum) that was subjected to consultation by organizations and institutions associated with the promotion of the right to education (see FEDH-IPN et al., 2007; MINED, 2008, pp. 45–48, for methodological details).

To increase the credibility of the consultation, GRUN had the data systematized by consultants from the National Autonomous University of Nicaragua (UNAN). Nevertheless, the extent to which an enquiry of this kind really shapes the final product can always be doubted. Less questionable, and perhaps of principal relevance, however, is the evident political and socio-pedagogical function of such processes (Arnove, 1986, p. 98). The procedures suggest that GRUN's discourse of participation and national reconciliation is not just rhetoric. The foundation for such protagonism has been laid by the literacy campaign: as has been stated (e.g., Arnove, 1986; Barndt, 1985) and reiterated by a Fonseca Association facilitator in 2009, literacy within a popular or revolutionary education rationale is not merely a skill, but serves conscientization and empowerment—altering self-perceptions of historically excluded groups for participation and transformation, to "seek alternatives" and become actors in their individual and collective development.[13] GRUN makes this explicit: "the future of the country needs their incorporation in the productive, economic, social and political activities [...] generating the analysis and reflection for knowledge and the transformation of reality" (MINED, 2009, pp. 2, 14).

Conclusion

Although, during its first term in office, GRUN did not formally position itself with respect to socialism, in this chapter I have argued that the construction of socialism is under way in Nicaragua through the Citizen Power development model and the nation's ALBA-TCP membership. In summary, Citizen Power can be understood as the government and state-driven mobilization, organization and empowerment of the popular classes. While the prevailing historical structure (global capitalism) is not directly challenged, and in part reproduced through, for instance, foreign investment incentives for the export processing sector, it is simultaneously resisted as an alternative configuration of forces—a rival structure—emerges (cf. Cox, 1981). The construction of socialism, however, does not occur in a unilinear fashion (as for instance assumed by the mainstream "top-down"/"bottom-up" ontology), but through dialectical, pluriscalar processes driven by politically likeminded governments and social forces (see also Mieke Lopes Cardozo, chapter 5, in this volume). This means, for example, that curricular norms generated by the Great National Consultation for the Reform of the Basic and Medium Education Curriculum, such as the notion of integral education for local socio-productive development, also appear in the 2009 ALBA Managua Declaration background documentation, which is a milestone document in the construction of the ALBA-TCP education space. In return, concepts such as Madre Tierra (Mother Earth) and vivir bien/buen vivir (to live well), which originate in the cosmovision of indigenous knowledge and communitarian solidarity economics in Bolivia and Ecuador, as well as the grandnational per se, have been accommodated in GRUN's policy and strategy papers in the production of an ALBA-TCP discourse (see GRUN, 2008a, pp. 5, 16, 44; 2010b).

Understanding the transformation of society and of education as a dialectical process in which "education is both an agent of change and in turn is changed by society" (Fägerlind and Saha, 1989, pp. 225–228), a key issue in Nicaragua's education revolution certainly will be whether the democratization of state and society—as embodied by the National Literacy Campaign and the Great National Consultation—can be extended into the formal school system: Can the democratic practices be institutionalized in the schools through the TEPCEs—the school-based Workshops for Education Evaluation, Programming and Capacitation—that demonstrated, as stated, limited success in the 1980s Revolution? Can the socially reproductive character of schools be broken? As Samoff emphasizes, "socialists' failure to revolutionize their education systems significantly" and to develop fully "an alternative, counterhegemonic, ideology of education [. . .] may well have undermined efforts to transform their societies [...] and to support those initiatives when they came under attack" (Samoff, 1991, pp. 2, 10, 17). With a level of popular support of 60–80 percent, unseen since the mid-1980s, and through Nicaragua's ALBA-TCP membership, the FSLN-led United Nicaragua Will Triumph Alliance appears to be in a strong position to take on this challenge.

Notes

1. For the empirical, theoretical and methodological underpinnings of this argument, see Muhr (2008a, b; 2011a; 2013).
2. In early 2013, formal members of the ALBA-TCP are Antigua and Barbuda; Republic of Bolivia; Republic of Cuba; Commonwealth of Dominica; Republic of Ecuador; Republic of Nicaragua; Saint Vincent and the Grenadines; Bolivarian Republic of Venezuela.
3. Alternative sources, however, suggest illiteracy rates of 32–34% in the early to mid-2000s (UNDP, CEPAL, in GRUN, 2008b, p. 53).
4. Net primary enrolment was at 82.6% in 2004; 36.1% of primary and 66.4% of secondary students did not complete their schooling that year (MECD, 2005, p. 9).
5. Author's interview with MINED policy makers, July 17, 2009.
6. Subordinate to the Council of Presidents are three ministerial councils (political, social, economic) that elaborate policy proposals and projects, a Political Commission for political, social and economic coordination, and a number of Committees and Working Groups. For details and an ALBA-TCP organigram see Muhr (2011b; 2012).
7. Some of which are cofunded by other international organizations, such as the Inter-American Development Bank (IADB) (see UN, 2010).
8. Between 2005 and 2009, the share of private education institutes increased from 18.0% to 22.9%, while participation in state-subsidized private institutes rose from 5.9% to 9.4%, in non-subsidized private centers from 12.1% to 12.8% (FIDEG, 2010).
9. In the most extreme cases, young males from non-deprived urban households enjoy 10.9 years of schooling, young females from severely deprived rural households only 2.7 years (UNDP, 2011, Table 5.1).
10. The Campaña Nacional de Alfabetización 'De Martí a Fidel' honors José Martí (1853–1895), who died in action for Cuban liberation against the Spanish colonizers, and Cuban ex-president Fidel Castro Ruz. Reference to Castro is an expression of gratitude to the (then Castro-presided) Cuban government's support to the campaign from 2004 onward.
11. The Fonseca Association's literacy efforts were paralleled by a ministry of education (then Ministerio de Educación, Cultura y Deportes, MECD) Social Programme of Alphabetisation. In 2005/2006, MECD alphabetized 64,883 persons, the Fonseca Association 73,754 persons (MINED, 2009, Annex. 6)

12. Bi- and multilateral support further included the Spanish Agency for International Cooperation and Development and UNESCO, amongst others (MINED, 2009, pp. 10 and 11).
13. Guillermo Fuentes in interview with author, August 3, 2009.

References

Arnove, R. F. (1986), *Education and Revolution in Nicaragua*, New York: Praeger.
——— (1994), *Education as Contested Terrain in Nicaragua*, Boulder: Westview Press.
Barndt, D. (1985), "Popular Education," in Walker, T. W. (ed.), *Nicaragua: The First Five Years*, New York: Praeger, pp. 317–345.
Cox, R. W. (1981), "Social Forces, States and World Order: Beyond International Relations Theory," *Millennium: Journal of International Studies* 10(2): pp. 126–155.
Fägerlind, I. and Saha, L. J. (1989), *Education and National Development* (2d edition), Oxford: Butterworth.
FAO (2009), *The State of Food Insecurity in the World*, Rome: FAO.
Federación Luterana Mundial (2006), *Centroamérica 2004–2005. Desde una Perspectiva de Derechos Humanos*, Managua: FLM.
FEDH-IPN (Foro de Educación y Desarrollo Humano de la Iniciativa Por Nicaragua), IPADE (Instituto para el Desarrollo y la Democracia)/CEAAL Nicaragua (Consejo de Educación de Adultos de América Latina), Plan Nicaragua (2007), *Consulta del Nuevo Curriculum de Educación Básica y Media. Aspectos Fundamentales de Consulta*, Managua: FEDH-IPN/IPADE/CEAAL/Plan Nicaragua.
FIDEG (Fundación Internacional para el Desafío Económico Global) (2010), *Encuesta de Hogares para la Medición de la Pobreza en Nicaragua*, http://www.fideg.org/files/doc/1283290135_Resultados%20FIDEG%202009web.pdf (accessed November 9, 2010).
GRUN (Gobierno de Reconciliación y Unidad Nacional) (2008a), *Plan Nacional de Desarrollo Humano 2008–2012. Documento Borrador 0 – Para Discusión*, Managua: GRUN.
——— (2008b), *Informe de País*, CONFINTEA VI 2008, Managua: MINED.
——— (2009a), *Plan Nacional de Desarrollo Humano Actualizado 2009–2011*, Managua: GRUN.
——— (2009b), *Plan de Acción del Poder Ciudadano. Hacia la Restitución de Derechos del Pueblo*, Managua: GRUN.
——— (2010a), *Informe Anual del Presidente de la República 2009*, Managua: GRUN.
——— (2010b), *Estrategia Nacional Ambiental y del Cambio Climático. Plan de Acción 2010–2015*, Managua: GRUN.
——— (2011), *Nicaragua Triunfa*, 44, September 21, 2011, http://www.nicaraguatriunfa.com/DOCUMENTOS%202011/SEPTIEMBRE%202011/210911/NICARAGUA%20TRIUNFA%20NO.44.doc.

Hoyt, K. (1997), *The Many Faces of Sandinista Democracy*, Athens: Ohio University Press.

La Lucha Sigue (2011), *Avances Sandinistas II Etapa de la Revolución 2007–2010*, December 11, 2010, http://www.laluchasigue.org/index.php?option=com_content.

Macpherson, C. B. (1977), *The Life and Times of Liberal Democracy*, Oxford: Oxford University Press.

Marx, K. (1942[1871]), "The Civil War in France," in Marx, K., *Selected Works*, Vol. 2, London: Lawrence and Wishart, pp. 446–527.

MED (Ministerio de Educación) (1982), *La Educación en Tres Años de Revolución*, Managua: MED.

MECD (Ministerio de Educación, Cultura y Deportes) (2005), *Plan Operativo Anual 2005*, Managua: MECD.

MINED (Ministerio de Educación) (2008), *La Revolución Participativa de la Educación Nicaragüense: El Caso de la Gran Consulta del Currículo para la Educación General Básica y Media (2007–2008)*, Managua: MINED.

——— (2009), *Informe Final. Campaña Nacional de Alfabetización "De Martí a Fidel,"* Managua: MINED.

Muhr, T. (2008a), "Nicaragua Re-Visited: From Neoliberal 'Ungovernability' to the Bolivarian Alternative for the Peoples of Our America (ALBA)," *Globalisation, Societies and Education* 6(2): pp. 147–161.

——— (2008b), "Venezuela: Global Counter-Hegemony, Geographies of Regional Development, and Higher Education for All," PhD thesis, University of Bristol, http://www.bristol.ac.uk/education/people/person.html?personKey=6uBLaYkxRNHTb9WC7RIalGLHf01j2Q.

——— (2010a), "Nicaragua: Constructing the Bolivarian Alliance for the Peoples of Our America (ALBA)," in Schuerkens, U. (ed.), *Globalization and Social Inequality*, New York: Routledge, pp. 115–134.

——— (2010b), "Counter-Hegemonic Regionalism and Higher Education for All: Venezuela and the ALBA," *Globalisation, Societies and Education* 8(1): pp. 39–57.

——— (2011a), *Venezuela and the ALBA: Counter-Hegemony, Geographies of Integration and Development, and Higher Education for All*, Saarbrücken: VDM.

——— (2011b), "Conceptualising the ALBA-TCP: Third Generation Regionalism and Political Economy," *International Journal of Cuban Studies* 3(2/3): pp. 98–115.

——— (2012), "(Re)constructing Popular Power in Our America: Venezuela and the Regionalisation of 'Revolutionary Democracy' in the ALBA-TCP Space," *Third World Quarterly* 33(3): pp. 225–241.

——— (2013), "The Enigma of Socialism," in Muhr, T. (ed.), *Counter-Globalization and Socialism in the 21st Century: The Bolivarian Alliance for the Peoples of Our America*, London: Routledge, pp. 1–29.

Muhr, T. and Verger, A. (2006), "Venezuela: Higher Education for All," *The Journal for Critical Education Policy Studies* 4(1), http://www.jceps.com/index.php?pageID=article&"&articleID=63.

Ortega, D. (2008), "Daniel Instala el CONPES. Intervención de Daniel en Reunión con el Consejo Nacional de Planificación Económica y Social, CONPES, presentando el Plan Nacional de Desarrollo Humano," October 15, 2008, http://www.lavozdelsandinismo.com/nicaragua/2008-10-15/daniel-instala-el-conpes/.

PREAL (Programa de Promoción de la Reforma Educativa en América Latina y el Caribe) (2004), *Informe de Progreso Educativo en Nicaragua*, Managua: PREAL.

RN (República de Nicaragua) (2003), "Ley de Participación Ciudadana," *La Gaceta*, 241, December 19, 2003.

—— (2007a), "Decreto 113–2007," *La Gaceta*, 230, November 29, 2007.

—— (2007b), "Decreto 114–2007," *La Gaceta*, 236, December 7, 2007.

—— (2010), "Constitución Política," *La Gaceta*, 176, September 16, 2010.

Rosset, P. and Vandermeer, J. (eds.) (1986), *Nicaragua: Unfinished Revolution. The New Nicaragua Reader*, New York: Grove Press.

Samoff, J. (1991), "Socialist Education?" *Comparative Education Review* 35(1): pp. 1–22.

Slater, D. (1986), "Socialism, Democracy and the Territorial Imperative: Elements for a Comparison of the Cuban and Nicaraguan Experiences," *Antipode* 18(2): pp. 155–185.

Stuart Almendárez, R. (2009), *Consejos del Poder Ciudadano y Gestión Pública en Nicaragua*, Managua: CEAP.

UN (2010), *Report of the Special Rapporteur on the Right to Food*, Olivier De Schutter, Addendum, Mission to Nicaragua, Human Rights Council, thirteenth session, Agenda item 3, http://daccess-ods.un.org/TMP/2016671.448946.html.

UNDP (1990), *Human Development Report 1990*, New York: UNDP.

—— (2008), *Human Development Indices: A Statistical Update*, http://hdr.undp.org/en/statistics/data/hdi2008/ (accessed April 26, 2008).

—— (2011), *Informe Nacional sobre Desarrollo Humano 2011. Las Juventudes Construyendo Nicaragua*, Managua: PNUD Nicaragua.

UNESCO (United Nations Educational, Scientific and Cultural Organization), OEI (Organización de Estados Iberoamericanos), INIDE (Instituto Nacional de Información de Desarrollo), UNAN-Managua (Universidad Nacional Autónoma de Nicaragua), IDEUCA (Instituto de Educación de la Universidad Centro-Americana) (2009), *Informe. Comisión Nacional de Verificación: Verificación de la Tasa Nacional de Analfabetismo en Nicaragua 16/06/2009*, Managua: UNESCO-Managua/OEI/INIDE/UNAN/IDEUCA.

World Bank (2008), *Nicaragua Poverty Assessment, Vol. 1, Main Report, 39736-NI*, Washington D.C.: World Bank.

Chapter 5

A Critical Theoretical Perspective on Education and Social Change in Bolivia: A Contested Alternative Pedagogy

Mieke T. A. Lopes Cardozo

An Introduction to Bolivia's Envisaged "Politics of Change"

You have to be committed to study, to become the light and hope that Bolivia needs for its development.
President Morales in an address to secondary school students in Santa Cruz (Ministerio de Educacion de Bolivia, 2011)

In Bolivia, education is seen by many as a promising way out of a life in poverty and marginalization. Similarly, hope is often mentioned in relation to processes of social change, as the epigraph reveals. This education-hope-change nexus becomes particularly relevant in highly unequal societies, such as Bolivia, where historically marginalized groups struggle with great anticipation for a better future. With a "politics of change," the new Bolivian government endeavors—in any case discursively—a restructuring of the economy, politics and society, with education being perceived as a mayor vehicle for such transformations.

Bolivia, situated right in the heart of South America, is a country of wide diversity, contrasts and struggles. Since 2006, the first majority-elected and self-identified indigenous president Evo Morales has given Bolivia a new face. Even though Bolivia is experiencing a period of economic growth in a global context of economic decline (World Bank, 2009), it remains one of the most unequal and poorest countries in the Latin American continent. In the apt words of Kohl and Bresnahan (2010, p. 5), the achievements of the Morales government are thus far much like beauty in the eye of the beholder. Huge inequalities, between rich and poor, between lowland and highland Bolivia and between different ethnic-cultural groups continue to lead to social tensions and conflicts (Latinobarómetro, 2007; Lopes Cardozo, 2009).

Social transformation in Bolivia is—at least ideologically—high on the political agenda and education is seen as a core remedy. A Bolivian ministry official explained in an interview how "society will not change if we do not change education." This comment provides a strong argument for the focus of this essay: if we want to understand processes of social transformation in Bolivia, education provides an important entry point.[1] Education policies represent not only the state's vision on how its population can be best "developed," it also defines what type of citizen is envisaged, or how Bolivia aims to deal with its diverse population and social inequalities.

With this new political push for radical structural societal and educational transformation, Bolivia is marking an exceptional route toward development that stands in stark contrast to mainstream (neoliberal inspired) global tendencies and generates an intriguing area for social science research. This essay aims to shed new light on Bolivian processes of social transformation through education from a neo-Gramscian theoretical lens, while also bringing in additional insights from critical pedagogy and Latin American coloniality debates necessary to understand the specifics of this case. The chapter draws on a five-year research engagement with Bolivian education and social transformation, particularly focusing on potentials and obstacles to transformation in an urban and a rural teacher training institute, or Normales. The Normales are defined here as teacher *training* institutes rather than teacher *education* institutes—bearing in mind the difference between reproductive forms of institutional "training" and more reflexive and transformational "education" (see Cole, 2011, p. 1). Data shows that current practices in Bolivia's Normales relate more to the banking and reproductive training approach, while the new Reform discourse envisages a shift toward what could be called "social justice teacher education" (Lopes Cardozo, 2011).[2]

The research that informs this chapter has been inspired by Roger Dale's meta-theoretical research approach that understands education from an interdisciplinary perspective, and as embedded within a multiscalar context, while acknowledging the relevance of alternative knowledges and the importance of historical analysis. From a critical theoretical perspective, we should look for alternatives beyond the status quo, and explain the "social contract" for education: what does society give to education, and what is expected in return? Through what "logic of intervention" does education work? (Dale, 2006; 2010). Particularly the phenomenon of globalization paints the broader picture in which societal and educational changes take place in Bolivia and elsewhere. Refraining from seeing globalization as an "unambiguous and non-negotiable structural constraint" (Hay 2002, p. 164–166), this text positions the case of Bolivia in a wider context of countertendencies to processes of globalization.

In this chapter, I first explore the processes of sociopolitical transformation in the Bolivian context from a neo-Gramscian perspective, highlighting particularly the role of intellectuals and education within those. Second, I turn to discuss how critical pedagogy debates as well as Latin American coloniality discussions help to understand the rationale behind Bolivia's new education reform "Avelino Sinani Elizardo Perez." As a way of conclusion and discussion, the chapter reflects on empirical findings relating to the possibilities and challenges of Bolivia's quest for a decolonized education system in practice.

Applying (Neo-)Gramscian Thinking to Sociopolitical Change in Bolivia

Bolivia's current "decolonizing politics of change" openly contest neoliberal forms of globalization. Studying present day political and educational developments in this context of Bolivian sociopolitical change fits Bieler and Morton's suggestions for further critical scholarship to problematize and clarify tactics and strategies of resistance to neoliberalism (Cox 2002, in Bieler and Morton, 2004, p. 103). So as to understand Bolivia's present processes of social transformation, being part of a wider Latin American turn to the Left (Rodriguez-Garavito et al., 2008), I draw on (neo-) Gramscian thinking on hegemony and counter-hegemony. Present day processes of social transformation in Bolivia are not just about an economic redistribution of wealth and (educational and work) opportunities among different classes, they are also very much about struggles for cultural recognition and political representation of large and varying groups that for long have been excluded and discriminated in Bolivian society. In this essay I will illustrate the usefulness of Gramsci's ideas, as he acknowledged the need for both political and cultural struggles of (counter-)hegemony. Gramsci's work, which was originally written in the first part of the twentieth century and largely during his imprisonment under Italian fascist

rule, helps to address the overemphasis on structures, and consequently a neglect of agents and agency, of traditional Marxist thinking as Wallerstein's World System Theory (Novelli, 2004, p. 26).
Gramsci's work acknowledges the relevance of cultural hegemony,
and the role of civil society and cultural institutions—including the
education arena—in understanding balances of power and processes
of societal change (Bates, 1975, p. 353; Bieler and Morton, 2004,
p. 92; Femia, 1975, p. 30). Educators, in Gramscian thinking, are
consequently seen as important transmitters in gaining political as
well as cultural hegemony, or in other cases as working as an important counter-hegemonic force.

While recognizing the obvious differences in time and geography
between the case of early-twentieth-century Italy under fascist rule,
and twenty-first-century Bolivia under President Morales, Gramscian
ideas are still useful to develop an understanding of contemporary
changes and counter-forces in Bolivian society, through the lens of
education. Gramsci writes how human nature is not fixed, it is rather
the totality of historically determined social relations, and therefore the study of politics and social transformation should be seen
as a "developing organism" (Gramsci, 1971, pp. 133–134). Various
authors (for instance, Morton, 1999, pp. 5–6; Harris, 2007, p. 2) have
suggested how Gramscian ideas on hegemony are particularly help-
ful in understanding the Latin American "strategic sites of political
struggle," where various forms of resistance to hegemonic structures
(but not necessarily states) take place—for instance, in the case of
the Mexican Zapatista movement, or indigenous social movements
in the Andes region. Obviously, there is no single theory that perfectly explains the dynamics, complexities and (lack of) success of
processes of social transformation around the world, and to look for
one assumes a reductionist approach to science (Harris, 2007, p. 23).
There is, however, a need for understanding the "democratic dialectic," which helps us to grasp the dynamic interconnection between
the state, civil society and the market in processes of social change,
particularly in cases such as contemporary Bolivia and Venezuela
(Harris, 2007). Exploring this relationship is also especially important for understanding education, and particularly the work of teachers (Robertson, 2000). The education sector in Bolivia works and
interrelates with all these terrains, and forms part of this democratic
dialectic. I argue for the relevance of applying Gramscian thinking
on hegemony and counter-hegemony to explain the complexities of
the struggle for state power alongside cultural hegemony through the
project of decolonization of education in Bolivia, with a particular

focus on teachers' pre-service education, as one of the main starting points for educational transformations.

In Gramsci's theoretical writings, hegemony can be understood as a form of social control, of an ideological (and often cultural) domination of one social group over "subordinated" others (Martin, 1997, p. 38). "It means political leadership based on the consent of the led, a consent which is secured by the diffusion and popularization of the world view of the ruling class" (Bates, 1975, p. 352). Educational institutions can be perceived as part of this hegemony, since "intellectual and moral leadership" is exercised through the "ensemble of educational, religious and associational" institutions of civil society" (Femia, 1975, p. 30). Hegemonic systems are constantly contested by opposition parties within the government, social movements and intellectuals. Therefore, capitalist states apply varying combinations of consent and coercion to maintain the hegemony (Crehan, 2002, p. 97; Harris, 2007, p. 2; Kohl, 2006, p. 309).

A Gramscian conceptualization of the state does not limit itself to the "government of functionaries" or the "political society" that exercises "direct dominion," through the "public spheres" of governmental institutions, political parties and the military. Gramsci's notion of the state is inclusive of the realm of civil society, including the "private sphere" of education, religion and media, that fashion social and political consciousness (Bates, 1975, p. 353; Bieler and Morton, 2004, p. 92). Anderson (in Martin, 1997, and in Kohl, 2006), one of the main critics of Gramsci's work, stated how Gramsci gave the notion of hegemony various and even contradictory meanings, and that we should perceive hegemony as a multiple concept that incorporates both civil society and state hegemonic strategies. This critique is, for instance, addressed in Jessop's (2005; 2007) Strategic Relational Approach (SRA) which employs a broad perception of "the state."[3]

"The challenge for any revolutionary movement is to move from protest to power" (Harris, 2007, p. 3). According to Gramsci, popular social forces need to build counter-hegemonic institutions that challenge capitalism and occupy autonomous social and political space. This battle over politics, culture and ideology is what he called "a war of position," in which a principal condition for winning power is to exercise leadership within civil society. Following a "politics of protest"[4] or "direct democracy," the popular masses, movements and unions became a strong force within Bolivian politics at the start of the twenty-first century (e.g., see Brienen, 2002; Domingo, 2005; Gamboa Rocabado, 2009). In Bolivia, the so-called Water Wars in

Cochabamba in 2000 through their successful mass mobilization and victory of social movements created counter-consciousness to neoliberal hegemony, giving rise to further battles over the recovery of gas resources and the extension of democracy.[5] This illustrates a crucial aspect of Gramsci's "war of position," since a new level of confidence and self-awareness stimulated people to organize and become agents of change (Harris, 2007, p. 11). Besides this "war of position," Gramsci developed the notion of a "war of manoeuvre," defined as "a frontal or insurrectional attack against the state or a period of intensive and active struggle, such as strikes and mass protest" (p. 3). Before taking democratic power the political party MAS of Evo Morales was employing a war of maneuver, with its massive demonstrations, and a war of position, becoming a leading social movement that eventually won the elections. In Gramscian language, the Water and Gas wars were a war of maneuver with the various represented sectors creating a new historic bloc of actors (Harris, 2007, p. 13). Gramsci saw these notions of position and maneuver as dialectic and fluid, rather than static and unidirectional.

Creating a counter-hegemonic culture, as is attempted by the current Bolivian government, is a long and conflictive process. These events in Bolivia at the beginning of the twenty-first century can be seen as part of a "new historic moment with resonance beyond its borders" in which opportunities have opened for marginalized and especially indigenous groups to take a vital role in the formation of the agenda, which is concerned with a politics of recognition as well as a politics of redistribution (McNeish, 2007, p. 889). Viewed from a neo-Gramscian perspective, the Bolivian state can be perceived as a site of contestation and a "strategic terrain" upon which both Left and Right political actors and wider civil society strive for their causes. A sense of mistrust in the state is deeply rooted in historical struggles between Bolivian governments and popular movements (Brienen, 2002; Dangl, 2007; 2010; Domingo, 2005; Salman, 2006), and remains an important dimension of social and political tensions.

Morales' political and now governing party *Movimiento al Socialismo* (MAS—movement toward socialism) has retained close ties with its social movement base, creating rather blurred boundaries between the party and social movements as they "at times work for, with and against each other" (Dangl, 2010, pp. 16, 19). The relationship between the social movements and the current government is "a two-way street," since social movements goals are largely supported and taken up by this government, while the MAS receives support for passing legislation and policies through (sometimes even

MAS-funded) mass demonstrations (Dangl, 2010, p. 22). Yet, in spite of Morales' background as a social movement leader of the coca growers union before becoming president, he cannot count on absolute support from all social movements. Several trade unions, neighborhood movements (especially in El Alto) and landless movements protested from the beginning against certain appointments within the Morales cabinet.[6] Zibechi warns of the "dangers of seduction by the state," as he emphasizes how the new Bolivian government can be "the bearer and voice of change," yet it should not disempower social movements in their key roles (Zibechi, 2010, p. 7). Based on empirical findings in the Bolivian education sector, the boundaries between "political society" and "civil society" are rather fluid, and the government is also internally struggling to create a cohesive strategy, since social movements leaders have now become officials within governmental institutions and work next to an older generation of policy makers, in some cases leading to internal tensions.

Furthermore, the government is confronted with serious popular resistance to the new "politics of change" and a decolonizing education reform. The large-scale social movement protests in (August-October) 2011 against the creation of a new highway through the Tipnis natural reserve and indigenous territory showed an ongoing power of popular protest, as the Morales government saw itself forced to denounce this project. Several indigenous movements continue to hold the new government accountable, but now to follow the newly created constitution, as in the case of the highway through the Tipnis reserve, the government seemed to undermine its own legal regulations that should protect indigenous territory as well as "la Pacha Mama" (Mother Earth). These events show a continuing dissatisfaction of parts of the Bolivian population with the governments' political actions, including Morales' voters. There is a sense that promises of change and development are not being met. This might be partly explained by the analysis of Webber (2011) in his recent critical review of the first years of administration of the Morales government, where he illustrates how the new political approach of the Morales government shows several continuities with the inherited neoliberal model. Continuing inequalities and poverty levels in the country can be viewed as the effects of a "reconstituted neoliberalism," as Webber calls it. While certainly convincing with regard to an economic and redistributive approach toward social justice (Fraser, 2005), this perspective does not however fully take into account the *discursive* shift of Bolivia's new education reform, which incorporates elements of cultural recognition and political representation.

Bolivia's current political situation, in which the Morales government is struggling to install a counter-hegemonic project after a long history of elite domination, can be connected to Gramsci's notion of an "organic crisis of the state."[7] Gramsci, in his *Prison Notebooks*, described the organic crisis as a moment of an incomplete transition due to unprepared political forces, when "the old is dying and the new cannot be born" (Gramsci 1975, in Martin, 1997, p. 47). In Bolivia, an organic crisis of the state can be interpreted, in my view, in two ways. The neoliberal governments that ruled the country until Morales experienced an organic crisis of their hegemonic regime, when social movements through mass demonstrations enforced an ending of their reign in the first few years of the twenty-first century (Kohl, 2006). Second, the new, and not yet fully prepared, government, since its installation in the beginning of 2006 up to the time of writing, faces another version of an organic crisis, as it struggles to take the as yet "incomplete transition" further on. In addition to the need to build an alternative economic vision and activity, as Harris (2007, pp. 19, 22) suggests, I argue it is similarly important to follow Bolivia's attempts to build a new education system that supports this alternative vision and a counter-hegemonic culture. In order to do so, there is a need to analyze not only the discursive and perhaps revolutionary shift in educational reforms, but also the incomplete and difficult translation to practice.

Education for Emancipation: Latin American Theories on Coloniality and Knowledges

The importance of the cultural and discursive domains of Bolivia's counter-hegemonic project is reflected in Latin American debates on coloniality. When writing about Bolivian politics of education in the context of the new reform for decolonizing education, one cannot avoid academic discussions related to coloniality theory. "Decolonisation is at the centre of political debate in Bolivia and the wider Latin American region," began Felix Patzi, a Bolivian sociologist and the first Minister of Education in Morales' government in 2006, when he opened a seminar on Decolonisation and Education in October 2008. Patzi was responsible for the very first drafts of the new law for decolonizing education called "AvelinoSinaniElizardoPerez" (ASEP), which is clearly inspired by regional debates on coloniality (Ministerio de Educación de Bolivia, 2010). A growing number of academic debates on education in Latin America deal with issues such as coloniality, critical (border) thinking and "other," "alternative," or "indigenous" knowledges (e.g., see Escobar, 2007; Grosfoguel, 2007a, b; Mignolo, 2000; Mignolo, 2007a, 2007b; Quijano, 2007; Walsh, 2007a, b). These debates are connected to the global rise of social (including indigenous) movements, together with wider processes of economic and cultural globalization that opened up alternative ways of looking at political, theoretical and epistemic approaches (Saavedra, 2007).

From this postcolonial perspective, modern educational systems are considered conservative, Eurocentric and exclusionary. Debates on the coloniality of societies and education systems aim to understand and at the same time deconstruct historical structures of injustices, and construct an equitable and socially, politically and economically just future. The interlinked idea of critical border thinking then suggests that an epistemic dialogue between Eurocentric and other approaches to thinking and knowledges is necessary in order to understand and deconstruct injustices (Weiler, 2003). The construction of knowledge, closely linked to educational processes, is central to the coloniality debate. "Knowledge means power" is also an often-used expression when objectives and goals of education are debated. The construction of knowledge relates to the "politics of knowledge," or the control over and access to a diversity of knowledge cultures (Davies, 2006, p. 1035). Walsh (2007a) discusses the "geopolitics of knowledge" in the context of Latin America, and argues how in this continent the production of knowledge has been subject to colonial and imperial design for a long time. In this continent European thought is dominantly seen as scientific truth, while other epistemes, such as indigenous and Afro-descendent, have long been considered subaltern. Walsh (2007b) argues how social movements, and particularly indigenous movements, have worked on building a cosmology and epistemology based on their own knowledge yet in dialogue with other knowledges (in plural).

Bolivia's current education reform is inspired by a progressive tendency in Latin American pedagogical approaches—also known as popular education (or critical pedagogy in the United States)—that particularly draw on Freire's *Pedagogy for Liberation* and broadly strive for progressive social changes and more egalitarian social relations (Gottesman, 2010). These approaches often entail problem-based learning and critical dialogue, the transformation of teacher–student relations and the incorporation of local or indigenous knowledges in teaching processes. Both the Bolivian 1994 Reform for Intercultural and Bilingual Education and the current ASEP reform also build on Latin American social science and educational work over the past three decades on the concept of "interculturalism," while in the new ASEP reform the notion of "intra-culturalism" has been added—an understanding and appreciation of one's own identity in order to engage in dialogue with "others."

Bolivia is engaged in political discussions and initiatives with regard to a decolonized education system based on this epistemic dialogue, and imagining an alternative future through embracing the critiques brought forward in coloniality debates. To some extent designed in cooperation between social movement actors, intellectuals and progressive political leaders, the reform agenda envisions to go against "western," "European" or neoliberal ideas that until present dominate many education systems worldwide. The envisaged result is a transformative restructuring or deconstruction (Fraser, 1995) of the education system, together with the revaluation of "original" or indigenous knowledges (Walsh, 2007a, b) and values through education; an approach that shows similarities to the ideas of Freire when he was involved in decolonizing the education system of Guinea-Bissau (Freire, 1977). Summarily, the main objectives of educational decolonization in Bolivia are the opening up of different knowledges toward cultural/linguistic diversity and the creation of a critical awareness to function as an instrument of liberation of marginalized groups (Gamboa Rocabado, 2009). Departing from these Latin American debates and ideological developments around education as a form of emancipation and social change, I now turn to discuss insights from both Gramsci and *Critical Pedagogy* on how to further understand the complex relationship between social change and education.

Educating for Social Transformation: A Gramscian and Critical Pedagogy Perspective

Part of the educational function and strategy of social transformation was Gramsci's idea that intellectuals should instill a "critical self-consciousness" in the masses, to free them from dominant hegemonic culture, and to develop an alternative order (Bates, 1975, p. 360; Femia, 1975, p. 35).[8] Intellectuals, according to Gramsci, form a crucial group that can stimulate "the passage from organic terrain of economic life to effective political organisation" (Crehan, 2002, p. 95). Baud and Rutten (2004, p. 6) assert how since Gramsci, and even more so since a cultural turn in social movement studies, a broader conception of "intellectuals" replaced the old dichotomy between the (educated) intellectuals and the masses. Education institutions, including schools, universities and teacher education colleges, can function as places of "creative ideological work and as places where activist intellectual networks may be formed" (p. 213). This essay employs their comprehensive conceptualization of "popular intellectuals," being "persons who—educated or not—aim to understand society in order to change it, with the interest of popular classes in mind" (p. 2), and particularly their argument that individual agency—and hence also teachers' agency—is important in processes of social change. Bolivia's attempt to decolonize the education system and teachers' presumed key role in this political project could be perceived as such a strategy.

From a Gramscian perspective, education is part of the hegemonic functions of the state. This provides theoretical justification for posing the question whether and how educational institutions and actors can and are willing to actually change according to the ideologies of a new regime in Bolivia under Evo Morales (Lopes Cardozo, 2011). Following Gramsci, education institutes are sites of conflict and negotiation in which both state and civil society actions come together and are mediated. Schools are, therefore, neither completely resistant nor fully cooperative to adopt policy reforms from the Bolivian state (Talavera Simoni, 2011, p. 19). Teachers, as popular intellectuals, tend to borrow from globalized ideologies and transform meaning to apply to their local contexts (Baud and Rutten, 2004, pp. 208–209), and often adopt similar strategies of adaptation when it comes to implementing state reforms.

In addition to this state-to-school level of reform adaptation, Tabulawa (2003, pp. 11–12), from a "World System" theoretical perspective, discusses the transferring of certain education reform models at the international level. Teaching methods such as child-centered pedagogy and constructivism, according to Tabulawa, have been transferred from core to periphery states. As a result of these global processes of education policy transfers, the Bolivian 1994 Reform also strongly drew from the constructivist philosophy of knowledge production (Delany-Barmann, 2010, p. 183), and is consequently called neoliberal and foreign-imposed reform by some. This critique fits Tabulawa's (2003, p. 12) criticism that the spread of individualistic Western culture through constructivist-based and child-centered pedagogical reforms are "deemed necessary for an individual to survive in a pluralistic, democratic capitalist society." Tabulawa claims this is part of a reproduction process of capitalism in peripheral states, and indirectly adopted by international aid agencies that see education as an instrument for political democratization (p. 18). In response to these global tendencies, Bolivia's current educational reform undertaking is a search for "Bolivian-owned" and alternative way of pedagogy, meaning a pluricultural and context-specific pedagogy that both revalues and incorporates indigenous values and knowledges. Bearing in mind the premature phase of the decolonization project for education in Bolivia, these alternative and indigenous pedagogies are a necessary field of research (Lopes Cardozo, 2011; Lopes Cardozo and Strauss, 2013; Semali, 2001; Tabulawa, 2003).

Concluding Reflections: Continuity and Change in Bolivian Education and Society

Following a multiscalar "politics of education approach" (Dale, 2000; 2005), and with the aim to understand the dialectics between education and social transformation, we need to understand these broader sociopolitical processes that reach beyond the education sector and the national and state levels. In situations of societal transition, education systems—which might have contributed to the root causes of conflict—should not just be rebuilt but transformed (Bush and Saltarelli, 2000, p. 24; Seitz, 2004, p. 56). While transformation forms the main aim of Bolivia's new ASEP education reform discourse—with a crucial role for the Normales—it remains to be seen whether these current training institutes will indeed transform toward a critical and quality pre-service and in-service long-term "teacher education."

The actual world in education institutes provides valuable information on how these policies work in reality. Teacher education institutes are crucial spaces to bring about educational changes, and ideally to work as a jumpstart for societal change, since this is where a new generation of future teachers is prepared. In order to understand the implications of education reforms, as part of wider state policies, we need to understand educators' roles and agency in these processes. This chapter argues for the usefulness of Gramscian and critical pedagogical theoretical insights for starting to understand the ever-changing and complex strategic context of education—and teachers' training and work—as dialectically related to the recent counter-hegemonic "politics of change" of the Bolivian government under Morales.

Change is a buzz word in Bolivian media, politics and even in the streets and markets—however real or ideational change might be for the real lives of Bolivians. While we can observe some real changes taking place since President Morales' installation in 2006, such as a new Constitution as of February 2009, there are also signs of a continuing lack of economic redistribution leading to persisting inequalities and poverty levels, due to the inheriting of a "reconstituted neoliberal" model (Webber, 2011). Building on the work of Sahlins, Postero (2007, pp. 12–13) writes how there are aspects of continuity in all processes of social change. These struggles for social transformation in Bolivia—with indigenous movements as active agents—are about economic, environmental, democratic and social justice, and Morales' "political discourse of change" envisions bringing forward these struggles for justice. However, this is far from a smooth process, as various processes of conflict continue to exist, and various social groups, including some groups of teachers, disagree with Morales' new project (for a discussion of the challenges of the reform implementation and different actors involved, see Lopes Cardozo 2011; 2012a, b, c). In the words of Gray Molina, "the core of Bolivian democratic politics is about conflict and resolving conflict. Room for contestation is a driver for change" (2009). This room for contestation might create a potential to accelerate progressive changes in a context where change is—slowly—beginning to take place, opening up new horizons amid a context of continuing tensions and struggle. Yet, due to the long-term transition phase at present in Bolivia (Harris, 2007, pp. 13–14) and an impasse in the education sector, we cannot (yet?) speak of a new installed hegemony.

Notes

1. With most academic attention paid to the role of non-formal "popular education" in Latin American processes of social change (Bartlet, 2005), this chapter sets out to understand the potential for social change in the formal education field in Bolivia, where the majority of students are enrolled.

2. Data was gathered during various fieldwork visits of around ten months in total. Methods included a wide range of interviews, discussions, observations and document analysis. For an overview of all respondents of the research, see Lopes Cardozo (2011, Appendix 2, p. 266). Available online at http://educationanddevelopment.files. wordpress.com/2008/04/lopes-cardozo-future-teachers-and -social-change-2011.pdf.

3. "The state is a complex phenomenon. The SRA starts from the proposition that the state is a social relation. [...] States do not exist in majestic isolation overseeing the rest of their respective societies but are embedded in a wider political system (or systems), articulated with other institutional orders, and linked to different forms of civil society [...] an adequate theory of the state can only be produced as part of a wider theory of society and that this wider theory must give due recognition to the constitutive role of semiosis in organizing

social order" (Jessop, 2007, pp. 1–9). Semiosis, in this case, means "the intersubjective production of meaning," including narrativity, rhetoric, hermeneutics, identity, reflexivity, historicity and discourse (Jessop, 2005, p. 159).

4. Or "protest politics" as referred to by Domingo (2005). Alternatively, the term "politics of protest" has been used by David Meyer in his book on social movements in the United States (Krinsky, 2007).

5. In the words of Webber (2011, p. 48), Cochabamba's Water War in 2000 meant the return of powerful left-indigenous struggles in Bolivia, when popular social movements fought against a World Bank initiated privatization of water provision for the city of Cochabamba. These events are generally perceived as leading up to the removal of power of two neoliberal presidents (Sanchez de Lozada in 2003, and Mesa in 2005).

6. The (urban) teachers union for instance rejected the appointment of Felix Patzi Paco as the first minister of education under Morales, because he would lack a background in teaching (Petras, 2006).

7. The concept of the "organic crisis" points to a disjuncture between state and society, between coercion and consent, which created a situation or space in which political agents could enact their agency or "possibility for innovation" (Martin, 1997, pp. 39, 53). Although critics wonder about the current applicability of Gramsci's notion of the "organic crisis of the state" (Martin, 1997), it is still useful to analyze the case of Bolivia, notwithstanding this is a very different geographical and temporal context.

8. Gramsci distinguished between "traditional intellectuals"—officially independent but in reality defending the interests of hegemonic groups, as opposed to "organic intellectuals," possessing fundamental ties to and defending the interests of a particular class (particularly non-hegemonic, yet also hegemonic groups (Baud and Rutten, 2004, p. 3).

References

Bates, T. R. (1975), "Gramsci and the Theory of Hegemony," *Journal of the History of Ideas* 36(2): pp. 351–366.

Baud, M. and Rutten, R. (eds.) (2004), "Popular Intellectuals and Social Movements. Framing protests in Asia, Africa and Latin America." *International Review of Social History* suppl. 12.

Bieler, A. and Morton, A. D. (2004), "A Critical Theory Route to Hegemony, World Order and Historical Change: Neo-Gramscian Perspectives in International Relations," *Capital & Class* 28: pp. 85–113.

Brienen, M. (2002), "The Clamor for Schools Rural Education and the Development of State-Community Contact in Highland Bolivia 1930–1952," *Revista de Indias* 62(226): pp. 615–650.

Bush, K. D. and Saltarelli, D. (2000), *The Two Faces of Education in Ethnic Conflict: Towards a Peace-Building Education for Children*, Florence: Innocenti Research Centre, UNICEF.

Cole, M. (2011), "Introduction," in *Racism and Education in the U.K. and the U.S.: Towards a Socialist Alternative*, New York and London: Palgrave Macmillan, pp. 1–6.

Crehan, K. (2002), *Gramsci, Culture and Anthropology*. Berkeley, LA: University of California Press.

Dale, R. (2000), "Globalization and Education: Demonstrating a Common World Education Culture or Locating a 'Globally Structured Educational Agenda.'" *Educational Theory*.

——— (2005), "Globalisation, Knowledge Economy and Comparative Education," *Comparative Education* 41(2): p. 117.

——— (2006), "From Comparison to Translation: Extending the Research Imagination?" *Globalisation, Societies and Education* 4(2): pp. 179–192.

——— (2010), "Retroducting and Reconstructing 'Education and Conflict,'" Lecture at farewell function for Dr Mario Novelli, University of Amsterdam, August 31, 2010.

Dangl, B. (2007), *The Price of Fire: Resource Wars and Social Movements in Bolivia*, Oakland, Edinburgh, Baltimore: AK Press.

——— (2010), *Dancing with Dynamite: Social Movements and States in Latin America*, Oakland, Edinburgh, Baltimore: AK Press.

Davies, L. (2006), "Understanding the Education–War Interface," *Forged Migration Review Supplement: Education and Conflict: Research, Policy and Practice*, Refugees Studies Centre, UNICEF, Oxford University's Department of Educational Studies, Oxford (July 2006): p. 13.

Delany-Barmann, G. (2010), "Teacher Education Reform and Subaltern Voices: From Politica to Practica in Bolivia," *Journal of Language, Identity and Education* 9(3): pp. 180–202.

Domingo, P. (2005). "Democracy and New Social Forces in Bolivia," *Social Forces* 83(4): 1727.

Escobar, A. (2007), "Worlds and Knowledges Otherwise," *Cultural Studies* 21(2): p. 179.

Femia, J. (1975), "Hegemony and Consiousness in the Thought of Antonio Gramsci," *Political Studies* 23(1): pp. 29–48.

Fraser, N. (1995), "From Redistribution to Recognition? Dilemmas of Justice in a "Post-Socialist" Age," *New Left Review I* 212(July/August): pp. 68–93.

——— (2005), "Reframing Justice in a Globalizing World." *New Left Review* (36): pp. 69–88.

Freire, P. (1977), *Pedagogie in ontwikkeling, Brieven aan Guinee-Bissau*, Baarn, Anthos: Uitgeverij de Toren [original title: Cartas a Guine Bissau: Registros de uma experiencia em processo].

Gamboa Rocabado, F. (2009), *De las criticas contra el sistema al ejercicio del poder: Los movimientos sociales indigenas y las politicas de Reforma*

Educativa en Bolivia, Global Monitoring Report on Education, UNESCO.

Gottesman, I. (2010), "Sitting in the Waiting Room: Paulo Freire and the Critical Turn in the Field of Education." *Educational Studies: A Journal of the American Educational Studies Association* 46(4): pp. 376–399.

Gramsci, A. (1971), *Selections from the Prison Notebooks*. London: Lawrence and Wishart.

Grosfoguel, R. (2007a), "La descolonizacion de la economia politica y los estudios postcoloniales: transmodernidad, pensamiento fronterizo y colonialidad global," in Saavedra, J. L. (ed.), *Educación superior, interculturalidad y descolonización*, La Paz: CEUB and Fundacion PIEB, pp. 87–124.

⸻ (2007b), "The Epistemic Decolonial Turn," *Cultural Studies* 21(2): p. 211.

Harris, J. (2007), "Bolivia and Venezuela: The Democratic Dialectic in New Revolutionary Movements," *Race & Class* 49(1): pp. 1–24.

Hay, C. (2002), *Political Analysis*, Basingstoke: Palgrave.

Jessop, B. (2005), "Critical Realism and the Strategic-Relational Approach," *New Formations* 56: pp. 40–53.

⸻ (2007), *State Power: A Strategic-Relational Approach*, Cambridge: Polity.

Kohl, B. (2006), "Challenges to Neoliberal Hegemony in Bolivia," Antipode.

Kohl, B. and Bresnahan, R. (2010), "Bolivia under Morales: Consolidating Power, Initiating Decolonization," *Latin American Perspectives* 37(5): pp. 5–17.

Latinobarómetro (2007), "Informe Latinobarómetro 2007, Banco de datos en línea," www.latinobarometro.org (accessed April 7, 2008).

Lopes Cardozo, M. T. A. (2009), "Teachers in a Bolivian Context of Conflict: Potential Actors for or against Change?" *Globalisation, Societies and Education*, special issue on "New Perspectives: Globalisation, Education and Violent Conflict" 7(4): pp. 409–432.

⸻ (2011), *Future Teachers and Social Change in Bolivia: Between Decolonisation and Demonstration*, Delft, the Netherlands: Eburon.

⸻ (2012a), "Decolonising Bolivian Education: Ideology versus Reality," in Griffiths T. G. and Millei, Z. (eds.), *Logics of Socialist Education: Engaging with Crisis, Insecurity and Uncertainty*, Dordrecht: Springer.

⸻ (2012b), "Turbulence in Bolivia's Normales: Teacher Education as a Socio-Political Battle Field," *Prospects—Quarterly Review of Comparative Education* 43(1).

⸻ (2012c), *Los futuros maestros y el cambio social en Bolivia—Entre la descolonización y las movilizaciones*, PIEB (Programa de Investigación Estratégica en Bolivia) & Universiteit van Amsterdam, La Paz.

Lopes Cardozo, M. T. A. and Strauss, J. (2013), "From the Local to the Regional and Back: Bolivia's Politics of Decolonizing Education in the Context of ALBA," in Muhr, T., *The Bolivarian Revolution. Democracy, Justice, and Counter-Hegemonic Globalisation*, London: Routledge.

Martin, J. (1997), "Hegemony and the Crisis of Legitimacy in Gramsci," *History of the Human Sciences* 10(1): pp. 37–56.

McNeish, J. A. (2007), "REVIEW Now We Are Citizens: Indigenous Politics in Postmulticutural Bolivia, by Nancy Grey Postero," *Journal of Latin American Studies* 39(4): pp. 889–891.

Mignolo, W. D. (2000), "The Many Faces of Cosmo-polis: Border Thinking and Critical Cosmopolitanism," *Public Culture* 12(3): p. 721.

—— (2007a), "Cambiando las eticas y las politicas del conocimiento: logica de la colonialidad y postcolonialidad imperial," in Saavedra, J. L. (ed.), *Educación superior, interculturalidad y descolonización*, La Paz: CEUB and Fundacion PIEB, pp. 55–85.

—— (2007b), "Introduction: Coloniality of Power and De-colonial Thinking," *Cultural Studies* 21(2): pp. 155–167.

Ministerio de Educación de Bolivia (2010), *Ley no. 70 de Educacion ASEP—Revolucion en la Education*, http://www.minedu.gob.bo/Portals/0/leyeducacion.pdf.

—— (2011), Presidente: "Sin educación, es imposible pensar que Bolivia salga adelante," http://www.minedu.gob.bo/Inicio/tabid/40/EntryId/70/Presidente-Sin-educacion-es-imposible-pensar-que-Bolivia-salga-adelante.aspx# (accessed February 2, 2011).

Molina, G. (2009), *The Challenge of Progressive Change in Bolivia: Run-up to the 2009 Elections*, CEDLA lecture 6–11–2009, University of Amsterdam, Amsterdam.

Morton, A. D. (1999), "On Gramsci," *Politics* 19(1): pp. 1–8.

Novelli, M. (2004), "Trade Unions, Strategic Pedagogy and Globalisation: Learning from the Anti-privatisation Struggles of Sintraemcali," Faculty of Social Sciences, Graduate School of Education, Bristol, University of Bristol, PhD thesis.

Postero, N. (2007), "Andean Utopia's in Evo Morales' Bolivia," *Latin American and Caribbean Ethnic Studies* 2(1): pp. 1–28.

Quijano, A. (2007), "Coloniality and Modernity-Rationality," *Cultural Studies* 21(2): p. 168.

Robertson, S. L. (2000), *A Class Act: Changing Teachers' Work, the State, and Globalisation*, New York: Falmer Press.

Rodriguez-Garavito, C., Barrett, P., et al. (2008), "Utopia Reborn? Introduction to the Study of the New Latin American Left," in Barrett, P., Chavez, D. and Rodriguez-Garavito, C., *The New Latin American Left—Utopia Reborn,*. London, Pluto Press, pp. 1–41.

Saavedra, J. L. (ed.) (2007), *Educación superior, interculturalidad y descolonización*, La Paz: CEUB and Fundacion PIEB.

Salman, T. (2006), "The Jammed Democracy: Bolivia's Troubled Political Learning Process," *Bulletin of Latin American Research* 25(2): p. 163.

Seitz, K. (2004), "Education and Conflict: The Role of Education in the Creation, Prevention and Resolution of Societal Crises—Consequences for Development Cooperation, German Technical Cooperation/Deutsche Gessellschaft fur Technische Zusammenarbeit (GTZ—now GIZ).

Semali, L. (2001), "Review of Reagan, T. & Mahwah, N. (2000) Non-Western Educational Traditions: Alternative Approaches to Educational Thought and Practice (New Jersey, Lawrence Erlbaum Associates)," *Comparative Education Review* 45(4): pp. 643–646.

Tabulawa, R. (2003), "International Aid Agencies, Learner-Centred Pedagogy and Political Democratisation: A Critique," *Comparative Education* 39(1): pp. 7–26.

Talavera Simoni, M. L. (2011), "Educacion Publica y Formacion de las Culturas Magistrales en Bolivia 1955–2005 CIDES," La Paz, Universidad Mayor de San Andres, Doctorado Multidisciplinario en Sciencias del Desarollo.

Tapia, L. (2008), "Bolivia. The Left and Social Movements," in Barrett, P., Chavez, D. and Rodriguez-Garavito, C., *The New Latin American Left—Utopia Reborn*, London: Pluto Press, pp. 215–231.

Walsh, C. (2007a), "Shifting the Geopolitics of Critical Knowledge," *Cultural Studies* 21(2): p. 224.

——— (2007b), "Interculturalidad y colonialidad del poder: un pensamiento y posicionamiento otro desde la diferencia colonial," in Saavedra, J. L. (ed.), *Educación superior, interculturalidad y descolonización*, La Paz: CEUB and Fundacion PIEB, pp. 175–213.

Webber, J. R. (2011), *From Rebellion to Reform in Bolivia—Class Struggle, Indigenous Liberation and the Politics of Evo Morales*, Chicago: Haymarket Books.

Weiler, H. N. (2003), "Diversity and the Politics of Knowledge." Remarks prepared for the concluding session of an international Policy Forum on "Planning for Diversity: Education in Multi-Ethnic and Multicultural Societies" at the International Institute for Educational Planning (IIEP), Paris, June 19–20, 2003."

World Bank (2009), "Country data Bolivia," http://data.worldbank.org /country/bolivia (accessed September 11, 2010).

Zibechi, R. (2010), *Dispersing Power, Social Movements as Anti-State Forces*, Oakland, Edinburgh, Baltimore: AK Press.

Chapter 6

Epistemic Independence Struggles: A Comparative Analysis of Two Indigenous Universities in Peru and Ecuador

Lenin Arturo Valencia Arroyo

This chapter[1] attempts to develop some possible answers to the following questions: How can we explain the rise of indigenous universities in Latin America since the 1990s? Why did this happen now and not before? What does it mean in terms of epistemic breaks in relation to the traditional, dominant (Western) patterns of knowledge production? I try to respond to such questions through the analysis of two indigenous universities—UNIA and UINPI—in Peru and Ecuador, two Andean postcolonial countries in which neoliberal policies have been applied since the 1980s (Assies, van deer Haar and Hoekema, 2000). Based on a neo-Gramscian approach, this essay addresses mainly the sociohistorical conditions in which both educational projects have been gestated. The essay is divided into four parts: in the first part I present the cases under analysis; second I present some theoretical reflections; in the third I explain the processes of state formation/reconfiguration of Peru and Ecuador; finally I present some concluding reflections.

Peru and Ecuador: Similar Conditions, Different Outcomes

Peru and Ecuador are two Andean postcolonial countries sharing similar sociohistorical conditions—the most important being the sharing of Kichwa (Ecuador) or Quechua (Peru) as a language that was propagated by the Incas through the region since precolonial times and later as a language used to evangelize. Both countries are also part of the Amazon basin having in their territories the presence of many Amazon communities with different languages and dialects.

Since the mid-1990s both countries have witnessed increased political demands from indigenous associations for the creation of indigenous universities. As a result, indigenous universities have been created in Peru and Ecuador: the National Intercultural University of the Amazon (UNIA) and the Intercultural University of Nationalities and Indigenous People of Ecuador, "Amawtay Wasi" (UINPI), in 1999 and 2004 respectively.

The UNIA—a public university created in December 1999 (Law No. 27250) at the end of Fujimori's regime—is located in Ucayali, a region with a high presence of indigenous communities (Ashaninkas, Aguaruna, Shipibos).

The UNIA commenced its academic activities in 2005, following a six-year process of bargaining with the Peruvian educational authorities, and specifically with the National Council for the Authorization of New Universities (CONAFU) and the Minister of Finance to receive the budget required. Although the UNIA was created in part as a result of the demand from one of the most important indigenous organizations in Peru: AIDESEP (Spanish acronym for Interethnic Association of Development of the Peruvian Amazon), the national authorities excluded AIDESEP from the process of organization and implementation of this educational project, appointing a special committee that failed in its purpose of implementing a university with intercultural criteria.

In the Ecuadorian case, it can be said that UINPI is the direct result of the efforts of Confederation of Indigenous Nationalities of Ecuador (CONAIE) and the Scientific Institute of Indigenous Cultures (ICCI), two indigenous organizations intimately linked to indigenous social movements in Ecuador. The process started in 1996 and the project of creating a university was seen by these actors as part of a broader political project. The organization was led by two indigenous leaders and members of the Ecuadorian parliament, Luis Macas and Leonidas Iza.

The first stage in the process of creation of this university involved consultation and negotiation with the members of CONAIE to resolve the expectations and needs of the sponsor institutions (CONAIE and ICCI) and determine the characteristics of the university. The purpose was not only to give to the indigenous students the possibility of access to higher education, with learning taking place in their own language, but also to fundamentally challenge *the colonial character* of the Ecuadorian HES. Once a level of internal consensus was achieved, the project was presented to the educational authorities following the requisites established by the new Constitution of 1998 and the Higher Education Act of 2000. Almost ten years after, in 2004, this project was finally approved and legally recognized by the Ecuadorian state.

Since its implementation the university has received international and national support, with non-indigenous intellectuals involved in the process, reflecting in some way the level of legitimacy it has gained. At the national level it is worth mentioning the National Council for Development of the Nationalities and People of Ecuador (CODENPE), a governmental institution directly linked to the executive power and created in 1998 to address issues related to the indigenous communities in Ecuador. The CODENPE played a central role as a mediator between indigenous organizations and the government.

Making a general assessment of both projects we find completely different trajectories: while the Ecuadorian indigenous university has been able to challenge the mainstream higher education system, the Peruvian university has not been able to do so. Both universities have also faced formal and informal institutional barriers and constraints, not just external to the organizations but also internally, in their own organizations. In this essay I argue that this can be explained in part by paying attention to the different situations of the indigenous social movements in each country and how they have been articulated in the process of state formation/reconstitution. In the following sections I will present possible explanations for such differences, focusing my attention primarily on the long-term, structural and historical factors that made possible the differentiated articulation of indigenous social movements and their role in the shaping of higher educational policies. First I present some theoretical considerations in relation to the processes of social (educational) change and how these changes are linked to long-term and institutionalized social relations of production.

Some Theoretical Considerations

As this is a chapter that develops an explanation of the role of social movements in bringing institutional change/inertia to the field of higher education, one first factor to take into account is that of collective action and the structural conditions that make possible its development. Following a neo-Gramscian perspective we can say that collective action is linked and shaped by the configuration of *social forces*. These social forces—"ethnic, nationalist, gender, sexual— derive from common material basis linked to relations of exploitation" (Cox 1992, p. 35, cited in Bieler and Morton, 2003).

The ways in which these social forces interact and make possible the development of collective action depends also on historical structures, "a particular combination of thought patterns [ideas], material conditions [material capabilities] and human institutions [Institutions] which has a certain coherence among its elements. These structures do not determine people's actions in any mechanical sense but constitute the context of habits, pressures, expectations and constrains within which action takes place" (Cox, 1981, p. 135).

As education is one of the *leitmotivs* of indigenous social movements in Latin America, it is also important to reflect on the ways in which education has been historically conceived. It can be said that hegemonic ideas (of education) "are real historical facts which must be combated and their nature as instruments of domination exposed…precisely for reasons of political struggle" (Gramsci 1995, p. 395, cited in Bieler and Morton, 2003, p. 480). From a neo-Gramscian perspective education is one of the underpinnings of the political structure in civil society, as long as it "helped to create in people certain modes of behaviour and expectations consistent with the hegemonic social order" (Cox, p. 51 in Gill. 1993).

However, the analysis cannot be restricted to explaining only the ideational side of education but will also discuss its material structure— of which universities are a central piece as they provide the institutional and material support for the production and reproduction of scientific knowledge, considered since the nineteenth century to be "knowledge" par excellence. The ways in which universities have been structured or institutionalized should be understood as the result of power relations, the stabilization and perpetuation of a particular order, or "particular amalgams of ideas and material power which in turn influence the development of ideas and material capabilities" developed through long historical processes (Cox, 1981, p. 136).

Finally, in order to explain changes and continuities in the higher education systems we have to understand these transformations as a result of the interaction between national and international forces from which the state and consequently the educational policies promoted are just one of their materializations. In this perspective the state is considered a "social relation through which capitalism is expressed," an "entire complex of practical and theoretical activities with which the ruling class not only justifies and maintains its dominance, but manages to win the active consent of those over whom it rules" (Gramsci 1971, p. 244, cited in Bieler and Morton, 2003, p. 482).

Adopting a neo-Gramscian perspective I will describe the social relations in which the production of knowledge has been embedded, giving account of the historical structures that made possible the specific configuration of each university and paying attention to three elements: the process of construction of the hegemonic projects in each country, the ideational and material factors that made possible the rather different performance of indigenous movements of Peru and Ecuador and their subsequent role in the creation of indigenous universities.

From the Nation State to the Developmentalist Project

The first thing to take into consideration is critical junctures in the process of state formation. In addition to the national independence processes of Peru and Ecuador during the 1820s, a central point was the *reconstitution* of national elites at the end of the nineteenth century. By then Peru and Ecuador shared many characteristics in their productive structure and the type of social relations between the state and civil society. At the economic level the Peruvian and Ecuadorian elites began to foster stronger links of dependency with the international economy through a series of state policies. The processes of economic transformation of both countries toward an agro-export economy concentrated along the coast required, among other things, the expansion of work force capacity to respond to the international demands for sugar, cocoa and other agro-export products (Cotler, 1978; Prieto, 2003). Additionally ethnic divisions, upheld ideologically by the notion of distinct "races" modeled the type of social relations between the ruling classes and what was considered by then to be the majority of the population: the so-called Indios.

However, despite these similarities the national elites were facing two different moments of economic and political consolidation. The resolution of these different economic and political moments has been fundamental in shaping the different ways in which the social relations between the ruling classes and other social groups have been articulated in both countries.

In the Peruvian case, after the defeat of Peru in the Pacific war (1879–1883), elites started a process of "national reconstruction" that implied not just the reconstruction of the productive apparatus but the creation and articulation of discourses to explain the reasons for their defeat. The Indios and their "backward conditions" were one of the explanations. Living in conditions of oppression, isolated from the "modern world" and "without any patriotism," the Indios were subject to a "civilizing" set of policies that ranged from education policies to miscegenation between indios and other "races" considered superior. The policies applied to the Indios living in the Highlands (Sierra) and Coast and was in accordance with the prevailing view that indigenous inhabitants of the Amazon region were simply savages and the Amazon was a region to be colonized.

Meanwhile, a new Ecuadorian coastal elite was emerging in Guayaquil (the main Ecuadorian seaport) at the expense of the traditional highland elite concentrated in Quito. The first half of the Ecuadorian twentieth century has been dominated by the hegemony of what some authors like Cueva (1988) and Ayala (1988) have labeled the "liberal oligarchic regime": a period that started in 1894 with the Liberal Revolution and the weakening of the landlord structure of economic power located in the Highlands (with Quito as its center) in favor of an emergent bourgeois located mainly in the Ecuadorian coast (Guayaquil). The role played by the Indios in the liberal side was an important element in the liberal victory. Once in power, the liberal regime established a set of measures aimed to protect the Indios thus starting an ideological debate about the type of policies required to protect these citizens.

The different incorporation of the Indios during the constitution or reconstitution of the elite's project in both countries in the late nineteenth century shaped the type of social transformations that took place until the 1960s when the contradictions arising from social exclusion and the unequal distribution of land led to social protests pressing for land reforms. In Peru, the construction of a national project by a delegitimized elite required more explicit means of repression and the construction of a discourse able to gain consent in the majority of the population to accept the terms of the nation state project (Kapsoly, 1984)—a discourse in which the Indios were identified as one of the reasons for the backward conditions of the country.

Despite state repression, the emergence of leftist political parties and social movements in the first 20 years of the twentieth century challenged the "aristocratic republic" and opened the space for a different type of debate in relation to the Indio. Additional to the mainstream idea of transforming and redeeming the Indios through a progressive and controlled program led by the government, leftist forces (with leading figures like Mariategui and Haya) started to question the material and ideological conditions that made possible the exploitation of much of the Peruvian population. For Mariategui the main problem of the Indios rested not in their "cultural backwardness" but in the material conditions in which they were living. The problem with the indios was foremost a problem of land distribution created first by the colonial regime and then continued by the capitalist system. The solution lay in land redistribution achieved after a socialist revolution led by the working class (Mariategui, 1971). Mariategui's perspective and the role assigned to the Indios in the revolutionary process (not as leaders but as support forces) shaped the type of relation that the leftist movements established with indigenous movements and the ways in which the indigenous movements built their political identity in order to enter the political Peruvian scenario: in classist rather than in ethnic terms (Degregory, 1999).

Unlike Peru, where the debate about the Indio ran between two poles (on the one side a Left position led by the new APRA and Communist parties, on the other side an undeclared alliance between liberals and conservatives), in Ecuador the progressive hegemonic consolidation of the liberal regime narrowed the political space to discuss the conditions of the indigenous population stressing the treatment of subaltern groups in legal, educational and cultural terms, situating the problem in ethnic rather than in class terms.

The accelerated process of penetration of the global capitalist order in this country since the postwar period created profound changes in Ecuadorian society. Of particular importance was the rise of indigenous movements that, unlike in any other Andean country (Peru or Bolivia), established organic relations with political parties, specifically with the Communist Party of Ecuador (PCE). In 1944 this party created the Confederation of Ecuadorian Workers (CTE) and inside this the Ecuadorian Federation of Indians (FEI). In the next 30 years FEI and other indigenous organizations participated in the political scenario promoting especially land reform and land redistribution. They did so without renouncing their ethnic identities.

By the 1960s, the conditions of exclusion and oppression of the indigenous population (manifested mainly in the unequal distribution of land), the processes of urbanization and the international context of socialist revolutions (with Cuba as the main reference for many political movements in Latin America) led to new forms of social protest and reform. Peru experienced the rise of the first guerrilla movements in the early 1960s and the implementation of agrarian reforms to "stop the spread of communism" (Kay, 1982). The most important of these was the reform led by general Velasco between

1969 and 1975. For almost 6 years, influenced in part by leftist social scientists, this regime attempted the implementation of a new hegemonic project aimed at transforming the oligarchic characteristics of Peruvian society, appealing to broader elements of society, particularly in relation to class and nation (Kay, 1982).

This strategy was a response to the shaping of new identities in the urban coast cities, where ethnicity played a much less important role (Quijano, 1980). The leftist military government effectively reinforced class and nationalist identities, encouraging ethnic identities to be cast aside in the formation of a new national project. This shift strongly influenced the treatment of "indigenous populations" (Degregori, 1995). On the one hand the rural inhabitants of the highlands and coast were labeled "peasants" and on the other the ancient inhabitants of the Amazon region were labeled "native communities," avoiding the concept of Indio, because it was considered a pejorative term imposed by the Spanish conquistadors. In 1972 the government created a parallel institution to the Peasant Confederation of Peru (CCP), the National Agrarian Confederation (CAN), in order to gain control over rural organizations. In the next two decades both organizations, CAN and CCP, had limited capacity to articulate any social movement or political proposal in relation to the processes of structural reforms carried on since the 1990s.

In the Ecuadorian case, Quito maintained its economic relevance despite the consolidation of Guayaquil as the main region in economic terms (concentrating the financial and agro-export factions of economic power). In this context, two processes of agrarian reform were carried in 1964 and 1970 by two conservative factions of the Ecuadorian military, explicitly supported by USAID. In the Ecuadorian case, the reforms led to fewer tensions related to land redistribution than in Peru. The reforms attempted to make structural changes without affecting the interests of the ruling classes. Unlike the Peruvian case, where reform implied a process of ideological empowerment of social forces formed by rural and urban workers, the Ecuadorian reforms did not mean the economic and (more important) symbolic breakdown of the Ecuadorian oligarchy. In this context the maintenance of an ethnic identity was important for rural movements to resist the continuation of a nuanced oligarchic order.

The discovery of large oil reserves in the Amazon region of Ecuador in 1972 fundamentally shifted the balance of power and allowed the country to enter a faster process of modernization. Until the end of the 1960s the presence of indigenous movements of the Amazon region in both countries was barely distinguishable. However, the form of capitalist development in both countries had a strong impact on the articulation of social forces in each country. Eight years following the discovery of large oil reserves, the Confederation of Indigenous Nationalities of the Ecuadorian Amazon (CONFENIAE) was created in response to the conflicts that oil companies were generating in the Amazon region. The CONFENIAE was an indigenous organization with an explicitly ethnic discourse. Five years later, CONFENIAE combined forces with other non-Amazon indigenous organizations and became one of the main forces in the creation of the largest indigenous organization in Ecuador, CONAIE, preparing the terrain for social resistance in the 1990s.

New State–Society Relations: Neoliberal Reforms, Higher Education and Rise of Indigenous Movements

The implementation of neoliberal reforms since the 1990s resulted in different responses from indigenous social movements. The economic breakdown that affected both countries during the 1980s led to the implementation of the Structural Adjustment Programs (SAPs) in an attempt to implement a new state project (Watson, 2005) toward a market-based society. These attempts had two different effects in Peru and Ecuador: in the former such programs were developed without organic resistance, in the latter these changes led to a massive response from indigenous social movements.

Throughout the period of the SAPs, political parties in Peru lost legitimacy and social organizations were exhausted and disarticulated as a consequence of internal war.[2] By contrast, the Ecuadorian indigenous movements achieved a gradual process of consolidation since the 1980s. Correspondingly, new indigenous social movements in Ecuador became the main channel of protest for rural inhabitants, who had less fear of being repressed through legitimized state means of violence. During the same period, in Peru any social movement that challenged Peruvian state policies would be misrepresented as a terrorist group linked to the Shining Path (SL), which had been repressed under the framework of National Security and Pacification policies.

The process of consolidation of Ecuadorian indigenous movements did not happen just in the framework of national and international ideological changes such as the fall of the Berlin wall, the demise of traditional political parties and the celebration of 500 years of indigenous resistance. Rather, the consolidation formed part of the tensions in the social relations of production of that country. The indigenous uprisings that started in 1990 were mainly a consequence of old relationships between the indigenous movements with the sate and other political actors, and new processes of land accumulation and policies affecting small farmers. The sustainability of the indigenous movements relied in its capacity to appeal to an ethnic discourse that could generate not just internal cohesion among the diverse groups but international sympathy in a context where unions and political parties had lost political influence. Since the protests of 1990, indigenous social movements in Ecuador moved from a corporatist agenda toward a more hegemonic agenda, trying to include in their project not just their own interests but also the interests of the Mestizo and even urban-Criollo populations. Their active participation in a turbulent political scenario meant that they ascended from their station as mere beneficiaries of state policies to becoming an integral part of the policy-making process of the country.

In the Peruvian case, the Fujimori government was able to gain consensus among weakened Peruvian social forces, first through repressive measures and later through legal reforms (in what Gills has labeled as new constitutionalism) and patronage relations with rural and urban social organizations. The political space for social organizations contesting the established order was minimal. The processes of the liberalization of the economy and subsequent extraordinary growth of investment in mining activities (Albó, 2008), however, gave rise to the formation of one of the most important social forces in the last 15 years—CONACAMI. This organization represented indigenous minorities affected by mining activities but was not organized specifically along ethnic lines. The organization has not incorporated the ethnic dimension in its platform since ethnicity—as elucidated in this essay—had gradually lost its capacity to generate cohesion in the formation of counter-hegemonic groups in the Peruvian historical context.

The higher education system was also affected by these structural processes and was at the same time a space for political struggle. By the 1990s, both the Peruvian and Ecuadorian higher education systems began processes of structural change. The international shift in the educational agenda of developing countries led to the non-prioritization of higher education, the retraction of the state financing for the creation of new public universities and the growing participation of the private sector in the provision of this service (World Bank, 2000). However, Ecuadorian universities have better resisted these processes of reform, in part due to their strategic alliance with indigenous social movements to resists budget cuts.

In contrast, Peruvian universities suffered the direct intervention of the state throughout the 1990s as a means of closing the possibilities of resistance to the marketized policies implemented in the sector. In the specific cases of the universities, until 1998 the Fujimori government sent military forces to take control of the main public universities and eliminate the influence of the SL. Additionally student assassinations were perpetrated by paramilitary forces, prolonging an environment of fear and academic censorship initiated by SL in the 1980s. These events happened with the consent of university authorities and the National Association of Rectors (ANR). In the process, a discourse stressing the necessity of "depoliticized education" gained consensus among authorities and students. It entailed among other things the promotion of depoliticized private universities responding to "the needs of the market". It is in this light that the creation of the UNIA followed the same pattern as any other university. Despite their discourse to promote the conservation of indigenous knowledge, the curriculum reflects instead traditional patterns of scientific and technical knowledge.

Some Conclusions

It is through the framework previously described that we can better understand the rise of indigenous universities, paying attention to the ideological configuration that allowed for the emergence of ethnic identities as well as taking into consideration the following two factors: first the historical institutionalization of specific types of social relations between indigenous movements and other social forces; and second, the reconfiguration of state–society relations in the last 30 years, and as part of such reconfiguration the participation of international actors in the processes of global resistance. The analysis of these three aspects offers an important account of the encounter of two *longue durée* processes in the construction of ethnic identities in Perú and Ecuador: the postcolonial heritage and the process of capitalist formation.

The historical factors presented here help us to understand first why indigenous universities have appeared in these specific contexts and second why the UINPI has a more challenging proposal than the UNIA. In the Ecuadorian case the UINPI is the result of a political project started formally in 1985 with the creation of the CONAIE but whose process of institutionalization can be traced back to the incorporation of indigenous actors in the construction and/or contestation of the Ecuadorian nation-state project. The degree of relative autonomy of this project is evident in the innovative character of its curriculum; the limits are evident in the barriers this project has faced to be recognized as a public university, especially given that the students at whom this proposal is aimed, indigenous students, face continued conditions of social and economic exclusion.

In the Peruvian case, the creation of the UNIA was made possible by the intervention of AIDESEP but the academic proposals do not reflect the incorporation of indigenous knowledge or interests in the curriculum. The absence of AIDESEP in the implementation of the project is evidence of the limited political influence of this organization in the HES (represented in CONAFU). Their absence also reflects the consolidation of a mode of knowledge production in the Peruvian higher education system that responds to the hegemonic discourse reinforced since the implementation of the neoliberal agenda since the early 1990s.

What lessons can be learned for future political action? First, the degree of influence of social movements in the political scenario of the Andean countries depends on their capacity to articulate discourses with an integrative character. While in the Ecuadorian case ethnic discourse will foreseeably remain a unifying discourse, in the Peruvian case other elements could foster and promote processes of ideological articulation. The Peruvian organization that has been able to articulate actors of diverse Peruvian regions has been CONACAMI. They have appealed to discourses of environmental protection to gain national and international support. It does not mean that they dismiss the ethnic identities that form their support base, but rather that they are pragmatically conscious of the limits imposed by the particular configuration of nation state project in Peru. Accordingly, ethnic identities or environmental discourses are not artificially created ideological constructions. They are objective realities resulting from specific social relations.

The UINPI is a valuable example of a social movement's potential to transform spaces traditionally closed to the participation of citizens. The university system in Peru and Ecuador has been a site and example of corporatism that has extended to a corporatism based on the dominance of the Criollo/Mestizo culture. The strengthening of the UINPI will depend on the capacity of CONAIE to exert political pressure in the national scenario and to negotiate terms of cooperation with international institutions. In the long term, the UINPI should rely mainly on public funds, otherwise its economic dependence can compromise the independence of its pedagogical proposal.

As long as the postcolonial heritage is a burden for Latin American societies, the generation of knowledge production is a necessary but not sufficient condition to forge alternative collective projects of life.

The issue of epistemic justice is of extreme importance (Mignolo 2000; Sousa 2006) but its achievement is uncertain if we are not able to understand those material and ideational conditions—historically articulated—that impose limits on our actions. Generalizations are not possible, and the generic understanding of our postcolonial condition is not enough to raise concrete actions for change. Rather we need to develop concrete, historically-specific analysis of particular places, states, struggles, which I have attempted to do in the case of the two indigenous universities discussed in this chapter

Acronyms

AEU	Assembly of the Ecuadorian University
AIDESEP	Interethnic Association of Development of the Peruvian Jungle
ANR	National Association of Rectors
APRA	Popular Revolutionary American Alliance
CCP	Peasant Confederation of Peru
CAN	National Agrarian Confederation
CEUPA	Ecuadorian Corporation of Private Universities
CODENPE	National Council for Development of the Nationalities and People of Ecuador
CONACAMI	National Coordinator of Communities Affected by Mining in Peru
CONAFU	National Council for the Authorization of New Universities
CONAIE	Confederation of Indigenous Nationalities of Ecuador
CONAP	Confederation of Amazon Nationalities of Peru
CONAPA	National Commission of Amazon, Andean and Afro-Peruvian Peoples
CONEA	National Council of Evaluation and Accreditation
CONESUP	National Council of Higher Education
CONFENIAE	Confederation of Indigenous Nationalities of the Ecuadorian Amazon
COPPIP	Permanent Conference of indigenous Peoples of Peru
CTE	Confederation of Ecuadorian Workers
CVR	Commission of Truth and Reconciliation
DINEBI	National Office of Intercultural Bilingual Education
DINEIB	National Direction of Intercultural Bilingual Education

DINEIBIR	National Office of Intercultural Bilingual and Rural Education
ECUARUNARI	Confederation of Indigenous Nationalities of the Ecuadorian Amazonia
FENOC	Federation of Peasant Organizations
FEI	Ecuadorian Federation of Indians
FORMABIAP	Training Program of Bilingual Teachers in the Peruvian Amazon
GLE	General Law of Education
ICCI	Scientific Institute of Indigenous Cultures
INDEPA	National Institute of Development of Andean, Amazon and Afro-Peruvian Peoples
MBA	Market-Based Approach
PDPIA	Development of Indigenous People and Afro-Peruvians
PCE	Communist Party of Ecuador
SAPs	Structural Adjustment Programs
SETAI	Technical Secretariat of Indigenous Affairs
SL	Shining Path
UC	Cuenca University
UINPI	Intercultural University of Nationalities and Indigenous People of Ecuador: "Amawtay Wasi"
UNIA	Intercultural National University of the Amazon
UPS	Salesian Polytechnic University

Notes

1. This chapter is based on my MA thesis, "Epistemic Independence Struggles: A Comparative Analysis of Two Indigenous Universities in Peru and Ecuador," at the Institute of Social Studies (Valencia, 2010).
2. According to the Commission of Truth and Reconciliation of Peru, the internal armed conflict in Peru between 1980 and 2000 was the most intense, extensive and prolonged episode of violence in the Republic period (the period that started when Peru got its independence from Spain—1821 onward—and became a Republic), causing an estimated 69,280 casualties (CVR, 2003).

References

Albó, X. (2008), *Movimientos y poder indígena en Bolivia, Ecuador y Perú*, La Paz: CIPCA.

Assies, W., van der Haar, G., and Hoekema, A. (eds.) (2000), "The Challenge of Diversity: Indigenous People and Reform of the State in Latin America," Thela Thesis Latin America Series, Amsterdam.

Ayala, E. (1988), "De la revolución alfarista al régimen oligárquico liberal (1895–1925)," in Ayala, E. (ed.), *Nueva Historia del Ecuador*, Vol. 9, Quito: CEN.

Bieler, A. and Morton, D. (2003), "Globalisation, the State and Class Struggle: A 'Critical Economy' engagement with Open Marxism," *British Journal of Politics and International Relations* 5(4): pp. 467–499.

CVR (Commission of Truth and Reconciliation) (2003), Final Report, Lima: CVR, 9 vols., http://www.cverdad.org.pe/ifinal/index.php.

Cotler, J. (1978), *Clases, Estado y Nación en el Perú*, Lima: IEP.

Cox, R. (1981), "Social Forces, States and World Orders: Beyond International Relations Theory," *Millennium: Journal of International Studies* 10(2).

Cueva, A. (1988), "Literatura y sociedad en el Ecuador: 1920–1960," *Revista Iberoamericana* (144–145): pp. 629–647.

Degregori, C. I. (1995), "El Estudio del otro: cambios en el análisis sobre etnicidad en Perú," in Cotler, J. (ed.), *Perú 1964–1994: Economía, sociedad y política*, Lima: IEP.

—— (1999), "Estados Nacionales e Identidades Etnicas en Peru y Bolivia," in *Construcciones Etnicas y dinámica sociocultural en América Latina*, Quito: Abya Yala.

Gill, S. (ed.) (1993), *Gramsci, Historical Materialism and International Relations*, Cambridge: Cambridge University Press.

Kapsoly, W. (1984), *Ayllus del sol. Anarquismo y utopía andina*, Lima: Tarea.

Kay, C. (1982), "Achievements and Contradictions of the Peruvian Agrarian Reform," *Journal of Development Studies* 18.

Mariategui, J. C. (1971), *Seven Interpretative Essays on Peruvian Reality*, Austin: University of Texas Press.

Mignolo, W. D. (2000), "The Role of the Humanities in the Corporate University," *Publications of the Modern Language Association of America* 115(5): pp. 1238–1245.

Prieto, M. (2003), "The Liberalism of Fear. Imagining Indigenous Subjects in Postcolonial Ecuador, 1895–1950," Unpublished PhD Thesis, University of Florida.

Quijano, A. (1980), *Dominación y cultura: lo cholo y el conflicto cultural en el Perú*, Lima: Mosca Azul.

Santos, B. S. (2006), *La universidad popular del siglo XXI* (1st ed.), Lima: UNMSM.

Valencia, L. (2010), "Epistemic Independence Struggles: A Comparative Analysis of Two Indigenous Universities in Peru and Ecuador," MA Thesis, International Institute of Social Studies, Erasmus University of Rotterdam.

Watson, M. (2005), *Foundations of International Political Economy*, Basingstoke: Palgrave-Macmillan.

World Bank (2000), *Higher Education in Developing Countries. Peril and Promise.* Washington DC: World Bank.

Chapter 7

Education for the Creation of a New Venezuela

Francisco Dominguez
Dedicated to the memory of Hugo Chávez Frías

Introduction—Key Features of the Bolivarian Cultural Revolution

The revolutionary transformation of Venezuela has in 13 years involved a drastic structural change between the state and society as well as between the state and the economy; this has also crucially involved the revolutionizing of the Venezuelan people. No revolutionary transformation could be sustained for such a long period otherwise. In an amazing dialectical process in which the downtrodden, the driving social and political force of the Bolivarian process, not only push for radical transformations through mass activity, they themselves undergo an intellectual transformation by becoming increasingly conscious agents of the change they began spontaneously to push for back on February 27, 1989, when they shook the foundations of the IV Republic by staging the now legendary "Caracazo."

The previous regime, known pejoratively as *puntofijismo* to signify the two-party-led (AD and COPEI) corrupt political system that presided over Venezuela since 1958, had by 1998 left a heavy legacy of external debt, economic dependence, gross socioeconomic inequalities, huge amounts of corruption, underdevelopment, poverty, squalor, illiteracy, and above all, de facto social and political exclusion of millions of ordinary Venezuelans. Worse, the *adecocopeyanos* (supporters of AD and COPEI) left the country in ruins, and burdened with a huge debt. The ancient regime was so discredited that by 1989 it began to disintegrate of its own accord, so much so that it was beyond repair. It had to be fully replaced lock, stock and barrel, hence the christening of its alternative, under Hugo Chávez's leadership, of V Republic, aimed at replacing the old, thoroughly corroded IV Republic.

Since Hugo Chávez's election as president of Venezuela in December 1998, the oil-producing South American nation underwent substantial structural transformations, and though always being subjected to the unrelenting hostility of the world corporate media, there is little doubt that, its heavy dependency on the export of oil revenues notwithstanding, the transformations underway have been highly positive for its economy, politics and society.

There is plenty of bona fide information about the considerable progress made by Venezuela and its people under Chávez not only in official publications, such as the Instituto Nacional de Estadisticas, but also in the research of highly prestigious bodies such as the Economic Commission for Latin America and the Caribbean (ECLAC) and the United Nations Development Programme (UNPD). The former report indicates that Venezuela has the lowest percentage of social inequality in Latin America (0.38 percent—Venezuela's income per capita is USD 10,000), while the latter shows that Venezuela has the lowest gender inequality index (0.56) in the region (0.6) (UNDP Report, 2011); furthermore, the 2011 UNDP Report shows that in terms of the Human Development Index (HDI) Venezuela's is 0.735, above the regional average (it had been 0.646 in 1995).[1]

Despite the overwhelming body of irrefutable evidence to the contrary, sections of the corporate media and of academics associated with Venezuela's opposition make strenuous efforts to demonstrate that under Chávez Venezuela was not only on the verge of economic ruin but that his policies since 1998 did very little to reduce poverty or that they have even increased poverty. See, for example, the Our World BBC Documentary *Venezuela—Oil Politics and Hugo Chávez* (James Robbins, February 18, 2011) where it is asserted that apart from the "extravagant cable cars" that link shanty towns perched in the hills around Caracas as "a showcase for Hugo Chávez's revolution...it seems in some ways to conceal the fact that so little else has gone on the country so little of Venezuela's oil wealth of the country has been spent on similar infrastructure projects...which is desperately needed to bridge the gap between the poorest and the richest in this society"; the documentary interviews one Venezuelan who asserts, "it seems as if the government wants everybody to be equal, but not equal in improving their lives but equal in getting poorer."

The rather extraordinary socioeconomic progress achieved by Venezuela under Chávez's presidency in no way suggests that there are no unresolved social ills or that all the structural distortions that have beset its economic development have disappeared. Despite being massively reduced, poverty remains high, and urban crime, an offshoot of urban poverty, is also very high. Furthermore, the levels of economic informality are still inordinately high; however, the proportions between the informal and formal sectors of the economy have been reversed (53.1 percent was informal in 1999, and 46.9 percent was formal; by 2011 the proportions were 56.5 percent and 43.5 percent respectively), and inflation has come down to 18 percent (though between 1989 and 1998 the average rate of inflation was 48 percent with the average between 1994 and 1998 being 60 percent). Nevertheless, considering the country's exorbitant levels of poverty and social exclusion in 1998, the progress made is indeed impressive.

In an official report made by various Venezuelan officials to the UN Council for Human Rights on October 7, 2011, in which the following was highlighted:[2] Venezuela's social investment has gone from 36 percent of GDP to 62 percent representing a total of about USD 400 billion; investment in education went from 3 percent of GDP in 1999 to 6 percent of GDP in 2011 (almost 12 million people are registered at some level of the Venezuelan education system) and this has involved greater inclusion of disabled persons (over 354,000 people with disabilities have benefited from the José Gregorio Hernández Mission); infant malnutrition has been reduced by 58 percent (from 7.7 percent in 1999 to 3.2 percent in 2010). The number of children and adolescents enrolled in school increased by 24 percent between 1998 and 2010, standing at 7.7 million in the academic year 2009–2010; net enrolment rates increased by 28 percent in nursery education, and in 2020, UNESCO recognized Venezuela as the country with the fifth highest levels of higher education enrolment in the world and the second highest in Latin America and the Caribbean (in 2005 UNESCO recognized Venezuela as a country free of illiteracy). In 2003 Venezuela launched a health plan called "Mision Barrio Adentro," thanks to which 24 million Venezuelans, 80 percent of the population, are now served by 13,510 free public health centers (free care and free drugs are provided to 37,000 HIV-AIDS sufferers, and other expensive treatments, like cancer, are also subsidized by the government). In Venezuela poverty has been halved in 12 years of Bolivarian policies (from 43.9 percent of the households in 1998 to 26.9 percent in 2010; out of which 17.17 percent of the households were living in extreme poverty, which by 2010 had declined to 6.9 percent—poverty has continued to decline further in 2011); 6,000 places have been set up to provide free food to low-income people and about 900,000 are benefiting daily; Venezuela's school program provides free food to more than 4 million children. The number of people who have been given a decent pension has gone from about 300,000 in 1998 to nearly 2 million in 2011 (Venezuela has also reached FAO's aim of 2,700 daily calories per person—it was 2,140 in 1998 and 2,790 in 2011). Venezuela's minimum wage (120 Bs in 1998; 1,548 Bs in 2011—USD 360 or £220 for the last figure) is the highest in Latin America (unemployment is less than 7 percent). In the period 1999–2010 there have been 15 elections in Venezuela where there is well-structured opposition organized in over 60 political parties who control about 40 percent of parliament, several governorships, mayoralties, local authorities, municipalities. The opposition controls most TV stations, and the overwhelming majority of newspapers and radio stations. Thanks to the vigorous efforts of the Venezuelan government, the number of people registered to vote has increased from about 10 million in 1998 to 17 million in 2011. By the 2012 presidential election the number of registered voters had gone up to nearly 20 million (http://www.cne.gov.ve/web/index.php).

Since 1998 against then world's dominant trends the government began a spate of Venezuela's nationalizations, which has so far included electricity generation, steel making, telecommunications, large swathes of the food industry and of the banking industry including Banco Santander, sections of commerce, some manufacturing, cement, the conversion of operating agreements and strategic associations with foreign companies in the oil sector to majority Venezuelan government control (the latest casualty being Exxon), coffee, sugar, flour and milk production facilities, agricultural landed estates, gas, sections of transport, and even the gold industry. Furthermore, about 5 million hectares of arable land have been expropriated by the Bolivarian government, which has benefited hundreds of thousands of peasant families.

The badly neglected infrastructure of Venezuela has benefited from the state's economic intervention under the Chávez administration and this has included over 1,000 km of railway lines, a third bridge over the Orinoco river, two new lines in the Caracas metro, plus two new metros in Maracaibo and Valencia, the Metro-cable, thousands of kilometers of motorways, and much more. To endeavor to administer all of these massive infrastructure undertakings, President Chávez established the National Company for Public Works.

Venezuela's armed forces have also changed substantially under the presidency; they now see themselves as an integral part of the Bolivarian socialist project. Thus in the Venezuelan Army's website we find the link for Radio Ejercito, "The Socialist of the High Command," with the motto "Independencia y Patria Socialista." The bulk of the armed forces went over to the people during the short-lived coup d'etat that overthrew President Chávez on April 11, 2002, and ever since the commitments of all of the armed forces to the Bolivarian project has intensified. Congruent with the assertion of Venezuela's national sovereignty, the Chávez administration removed any US military presence, expelled the DEA (on rather strong spying grounds) and has even expelled the US ambassador. Thus Venezuela has "ceased to be linked to the US regional military structures (US Southern Command); it does not send military officers to be trained in the US School of the Americas (which has trained so many of the military dictators of the continent); it does not participate in joint military exercises with US forces; and it has steered a totally independent foreign policy from that of the US—something unthinkable only a decade ago."

To top it all, the 1999 Bolivarian Constitution of Venezuela is explicitly anti-neoliberal but it grants the people the right to self-organize in order to make the general will prevail, creating the conditions for a polity that has been described as participatory democracy. Furthermore, indigenous people enjoy special rights and, despite their small demographic weight, are entitled to their own parliamentary representation, and their culture is being actively promoted by the state. Similarly, under Chávez Venezuela vigorously celebrated its African roots.

Inclusion and Citizenship in Venezuela

Beyond the basics (food, health, education, etc.) Venezuela's growth in telecommunications has been staggering (see table 7.1).

The government has established Infocentros and made them available to the poor so that everyone has access to modern telecommunications

Table 7.1 Telecommunications expansion and social inclusion

	1998	2010	Percent variation
Landline subscribers	2.517.220	7.054.603	280.25%
Mobile phones	2.009.757	29.152.847	1,450.53%
TV subscriptions	603.200	2.483.847	411.78%
Internet users	322.244	9.956.842	3,089.85%

Source: Venezuela de verdad, http://www.venezueladeverdad.gob.ve/content/independencia-tecnológica.

Table 7.2   Distribution of Infocentros per province/state and inhabitants per Infocentro

State	Infocentro	Population	Inhabitants per Infocentro
Amazonas	14	157,293	11,235
Anzoategui	28	1,574,505	56,232
Apure	24	520,508	21,688
Aragua	27	1,574,505	58.315
Barinas	30	821,635	27,388
Bolivar	51	1,648,110	32,136
Carabobo	46	2,365,665	51,428
Cojedes	26	324,260	12,472
Delta Amacuro	9	166,907	18,545
Distrito Capital	68	2,109,166	31,017
Falcon	51	966,127	18,994
Guarico	22	802,540	36,479
Lara	39	1,909,846	48,790
Merida	34	907,938	26,704
Miranda	73	3,028,965	41,493
Monagas	44	926,478	21,056
Nueva Esparta	24	462,480	19,270
Portuguesa	46	942,555	20,940
Sucre	33	975,814	29,570
Tachira	42	1,263,628	30,086
Trujillo	25	765,946	30,638
Vargas	19	646,598	34,031
Yaracuy	34	342,845	10,084
Zulia	43	3,887,171	90,039
Infomoviles	28		
	852		

technologies. There are 820 Infocentros throughout Venezuela (810 of which have connectivity), 544 of which are connected to the Simon Bolivar Satellite. One can see this distribution in table 7.2.

The total number of visits to use the *Infocentros* in 2011 alone was 12,344,714, whereas in 2001 it had been 1,335,647. There are *Infocentros* in 85.6 percent of the municipalities of Venezuela (see figure 7.1).

It is not very well known but Infocentros played a central role in the eradication of Illiteracy from Venezuelan soil: between 2006 and 2011 the total number of people technologically alphabetized was 1,432,281 (see figure 7.2; the technological literacy program has benefited prisoners as well). Further, in December 2012 the Fundacion Infocentro received the UNESCO Rey Hamad Bin Isa Al Khalifa Prize in recognition of its contribution to the technological alphabetization

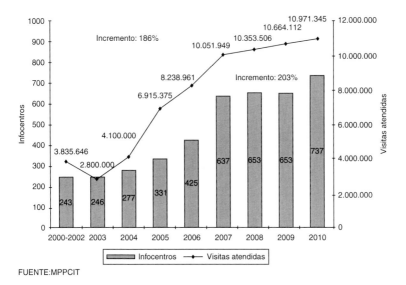

Figure 7.1 Number of people who have used the Infocentros services

Source: Infocentro Foundation, Achievements of the Infocentro Project, 2011, Ministry for Science and Technology, December 14, 2011, p. 146.

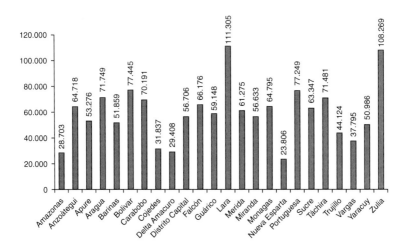

Figure 7.2 Number of people taught to read and write through technology—1,432,281

Source: Infocentro Foundation, Achievements of the Infocentro Project, 2011, Ministry for Science and Technology, December 14, 2011, p. 16.

of adults, with Venezuela being deemed the best (first) among 49 similar programs presented by 37 countries (Fundacion Infocentro, 2011, p. 15).

Apart from making this telecommunication technology available to very large numbers of people and centrally contribute to the eradication of illiteracy (the program includes online literacy courses in Wayuunaki language), Infocentros also significantly contribute to the development of a citizen's consciousness by providing online free-of-charge training courses and practical programs for millions of ordinary Venezuelans. They include text processing, multimedia, use of calculations and data in excel, surfing the internet, social networking, computer-generated presentations, PNAFT program for the visually impaired (available in Infocentros in 22 out of the 24 Venezuelan states), guides to create a communicational product, treatment and classification of sources, how to create a digital phototeca, manipulation of images, how to publish websites on the web, how to edit audio files, use and care of multimedia projector, use and care of a camcorder, how to publish information in twitter, get and circulate information through Google, computer-generated drawing, multimedia resources for video forums, how to look after your computer, how to learn from your own experiences of participation in communal councils, how to generate specialist websites such as for tourism with a regional focus, communal socialist commercial exchange, polls, for Infocentros, for community events, news and information of local communities' activities, digital newspapers, and how to improve your writing, your public speaking and spelling (Fundacion Infocentro, 2011, pp. 18–22). The president of the Fundacion Infocentro is a woman, Nancy Zambrano. The incorporation of the masses to be the actors of politics and culture can be seen in the fact that for the period January–November 2011, ordinary people in their communities throughout the country just by the use of Mobile Infocentros (Infomoviles) staged the following activities: 465 PNAT, 210 conversatorios, 245 open air cine, 102 political debates, 107 sport events, technological "tomas," 240 actions of voluntary work, and 6 activities to humanize prisons (Fundacion Infocentro, 2011, p. 41).

The Infocentros are complemented by the Simon Bolivar satellite for services of broadcasting and reception through 2,055 antennae (aerials) and whose distribution shows the stress on education: 1,475 are for education purposes, 169 for food, 133 for defence, 82 for villages, 44 for health, 42 for economic development, 41 for government, 39 for energy, 18 for CANTV (state telecommunications company), 10 for security and 2 for media. The beneficiaries are educational establishments, schools, libraries, training centers, missions as well as hospitals, *Barrio Adentro* centres, Integral Centres of Diagnose, High Technology Centres, integral Intensive Care Units, and the like.

Additionally, by September 2011, the government had distributed, free of charge, a total of 2,638,506 Canaima computers, entirely assembled in Venezuela, for students to use in their education (the quality control in the Venezuelan company that assembles them—Complejo Tecnologico Simon Rodriguez—is highly rigorous). The allocation of Canaimas in 2011 was as follows: First Grade 298,506; Second Grade 480,000; Third Grade 500,000; Fourth Grade 480,000; Fifth Grade 450,000; and Sixth Grade 430,000 (see figure 7.3). In September 2011, the government began the distribution of 900,000 more Canaima computers. We get an idea of the type of education pupils of the First Grade get since the curriculum includes themes such as Indigenous Resistance, Bicentennial of Independence, Educators and Democracy, Protection of the Environment, Friendship, Solidarity and Love, Equality, Fraternity and the Environment, as well as Holidays, Christmas and Work and the Family. Some of the slogans of the Canaima Project are telling, regarding the nature of the educational curriculum that animates it: "Technology for a liberating

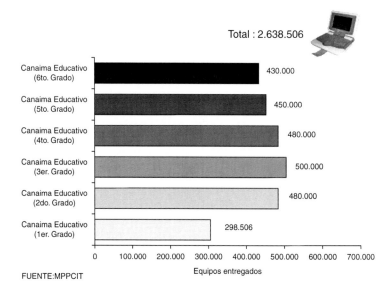

Figure 7.3 Educational Canaima Project, 2009–September 2011

education" and Simon Bolivar's February 15, 1808 dictum "The first duty of a government is to educate the people."[3] Millions of hitherto impoverished and excluded Venezuelans have seen their lives thoroughly transformed for the better through a sustained process of socioeconomic improvement (income, health, education, food) but also have been given the constitutional, legal and political means (enfranchisement, communal council, funding of community projects and the explosion of social and political organizations) so as to become the key subjects of the Bolivarian process in a way that no previous generation of Venezuelan could even dream. They, the masses, have been empowered in a shift of political power that has wrested the state (and state institutions) from the hands of Venezuela's oligarchy and its vast resources are being put to achieve very different objectives. A while ago I formulated it thus:

> Although the process is by no means complete, the Venezuelan state has undergone so many qualitative changes that it has already ceased to be a normal capitalist state apparatus; nor can it be seen as one led temporarily by a socialist government (such as with Allende, for instance). The state now serves totally different interests and tasks from those it set out to fulfill back in 1958, when it was "modernised."[4]

In short, Venezuela has developed a broad education system that seeks to culturally equip citizens so as to bring about their intellectual and political emancipation. That is, the two intimately and dialectically interlinked *sine qua non* conditions for the emancipation of the downtrodden are the constant rise of their cultural and intellectual levels, and their collective involvement in their own emancipation as protagonists.

Broadening Society's Perception of Itself

One of the fundamental principles that informs the Bolivarian government's approach to the transformation of Venezuelan society is the cultural betterment of the masses so as to create a qualitatively new citizenry, akin to the rest of the societal, economic and political transformation underway. Jose Marti's maxim "Ser cultos para ser libres"[5] was fully embraced by the Chávez government. The raising of people's cultural levels is absolutely central to the Bolivarian transformation process and its leaders therefore posit that if it is not cultural it is not a revolution. Consequently a highly developed system of all kinds of literature has been made available, mostly free of charge, involving the publication and distribution of literally tens of millions of books, pamphlets, novels, magazines, documentaries, films, music CDs. A considerable proportion of this massive production, in the same way as the new curricular conception that animates the formal education system in Venezuela under Chávez, aimed at fomenting a culture of human rights and the search for peace, the fostering of a pro-environment consciousness, the development of a patriotic and republican mind based on the fundamental ideas of Simon Rodriguez, Simon Bolivar, and Ezequiel Zamora, among other iconic figures of Venezuela's history, the rescuing of the historic memory and the strengthening of Venezuelan identity, as well as the strengthening of multiculturalism and acceptance of diversity. Bolivarian education stresses the formation of people as social beings seeking to vindicate indigenous and Afro-descendant cultures, thus rejecting the notion of a national identity based on genetic-cultural integration. The Constitution (Art. 100) makes this totally explicit:

> The folk cultures comprising the national identity of Venezuela enjoy special attention, with recognition of and respect for intercultural relations under the principle of equality of cultures. Incentives and inducements shall be provided for by law for persons, institutions and communities that promote, support, develop or finance cultural plans, programs and activities within the country and Venezuelan culture abroad. The State guarantees cultural workers inclusion in the Social security system to provide them with a dignified life, recognizing the idiosyncrasies of cultural work, in accordance with law.

Furthermore, the 1999 Bolivarian Constitution is also very clear on educational matters.

> Education is a human right and a fundamental social duty; it is democratic, free of charge and obligatory [...] the state assumes responsibility for it [...] [It] is a public service [...] [and seeks that citizens engage in] active, conscious, collective participation in the processes of social transformation embodies in the values which are part of the national identity, and with a Latin American and universal vision. (Art. 102)
>   Every person has the right to a full, high-quality, ongoing education under conditions of equality, subject only to such limitations as derive from such persons own aptitudes, vocational aspirations. [State education] is free of charge up to undergraduate university level [...] The law shall guarantee equal treatment to persons with special needs or disabilities, and to those who have been deprived of liberty." (Art. 103)

Environmental education is obligatory in the various levels and modes of the education system [...] Spanish, Venezuelan geography and history and the principles of Bolivarian thought shall be compulsory subjects at public and private [educational] institutions. (Art. 107)

Native peoples have the right to maintain and develop their ethnical and cultural entity, world view, values, spirituality and holy places and places of cult. The State shall promote the appreciation and dissemination of the cultural manifestations of the native peoples, who have the right to their own education, and an education system of an intercultural and bilingual nature, taking into account their special social and cultural characteristics, values and traditions. (Art. 121)

However, it is the Organic Law on Education (OLE) of August 15, 2009, that make these principles even more tangible; Art. 3 of the OLE states that "education is public, social, obligatory, free, of quality, secular, integral, permanent, socially relevant, creative, artistic, innovative, critical, pluricultural, multi-ethnic, intercultural and plurilingual."

In order to fulfill the broad objectives of educating the people for them to become protagonists of their history and emancipation, a *Sistema Masivo de Revistas* (SMR, Massive System of Magazines) has been made available free of charge. The SMR consists of ten magazines: *Asi Somos, A Plena Voz, Arte de Leer, La Roca de Crear, La Revuelta, Poder Vivir, Se Mueve, Memorias de Venezuela*, and the two recent additions *Buen Vivir* and *Ocho Estrellas*. Each has 64 pages and 60,000 copies of each issue are feely distributed; they are also available online free of charge. To this list the magazine *Imagen, Revista Latinoamericana de Cultura*, should be added (a publication of the *Fundacion Editorial El Perro y La Rana*): it contains literary critique, analyses, reviews and indepth articles on Latin American fiction, theater, poetry and popular music (as with the other magazines it is available online, free of charge). There is also the weekly *Todos Adentro* that should be added to the list (it is a 16-page magazine dedicated to popular culture), and the over 300-page *Revista de la Cultura* with scholarly articles and analyses of national cultural developments.

Conclusion

Regardless of standards of measure, the Bolivarian effort to raise the cultural and intellectual levels of the Venezuelan people is the biggest in that country's history and must rank as one of the biggest in Latin

America. A similar attempt to educate the population on a mass base was in Allende's Chile where the state publishing house Quimantu, in only 32 months managed to publish a total of 12 million copies of books, pamphlets and other educational and literary material (more than the total output of Chile's publishing industry in 2002). As stated earlier, the Imprenta de la Cultura has printed 95 million.

As is well known, the dominant culture of a nation is the dominant culture (values, principles, accepted truths, view of national history, received wisdom, ideology, religion, official lingua franca, in a nutshell, a worldview) of its ruling class. This cultural dominance perforce cohabits with the cultures of subordinate groups with which it is in constant competition and, sometimes, conflict. One of the characteristics of Venezuela's dominant culture is its snobbish acceptance of foreign values and formats whose most grotesque manifestations in the Venezuelan case were weekend shopping sprees in Miami, a heavily Hollywoodenized television industry, beauty contests, massive use of plastic surgery, implants and world brand cosmetics, exacerbated obsession with fashion, consumerism, individualism, hedonism, sexism, racism, tackiness, tawdriness, which altogether led to an overrated perception of Hollywood glamor, coupled with contempt for what is viewed as a backward, unsophisticated local culture. Its corollary has made official Venezuela a rather poor imitation of the "American way of life." Caracas epitomizes this neurotic syndrome of the Venezuelan oligarchy.

For decades, Venezuela's oligarchy lived off the oil revenues that it pilfered from the nation through all sort of dubious legal mechanisms and kept the bulk of the nation excluded from any social or economic benefits that came about as a result of its erratic Hollywoodian modernizing impulses. The crucial connection was with the chief consumer of Venezuelan oil, the United States. All the oligarchy's privileges, benefits, prestige, enjoyment of the perks of office, lifestyle and everything else that went with it depended heavily—in fact, totally—on the subordination of Venezuela to US strategic and geopolitical considerations on Venezuela's oil. Thus, there was a material, objective reality on which Venezuelan oligarchy's tacky culture rested.

Thus, it is not just exclusion, ignorance, lack of education, poverty, discrimination, exploitation and so forth that needs to be eradicated; to develop the self-esteem of the Venezuelan people entails a massive task. People's minds must be decolonized through their own education. In the words of literary critic Roberto Fernandez Retamar: "[The colonialist] calls us *mambi*—Black fighters in 19th century wars of liberation—they call us *nigger* to offend us, but we claim as a medal of honour to be the descendants of the *mambi*, descendants of the *negro alzado*, Maroon, independence fighter: and never descendant of the slave-owners."[6] The historic-intellectual roots to build the future are being supplied in abundance in an effort with a content that is a breath of fresh air. An academic, though a bit tongue-in-cheek, accurately described the process thus:

> For many on the left accustomed to seeing socialism in terms largely derived from the Russian Revolution, the recent developments in Latin America are startling, even bewildering. These reflect very different revolutionary conditions, and a very different theory and practice of socialism. For some of those still firmly wedded to old models, and who see only one possible path to socialism, this is simply "not the right way" to carry out the transition to socialism. The victories that brought these revolutionary-popular governments to power were through the ballot box, not armed struggle. The seizure of the state and economy is by no means complete. The role of the revolutionary political instrument (the party) is very different from that of old. Most disturbing of all, perhaps, is the fact that these revolutions seem to be inspired initially not so much by Marxism, as by revolutionary traditions indigenous to Latin America that go back centuries. Chávez has played a leading role in this, defining the Bolivarian Revolution, in relation to Bolívar himself, his teacher and mentor, Simón Rodríguez, and Ezequiel Zamora, the leader of the peasant revolt in the federal wars of the 1850s and '60s.[7]

In the concrete historic circumstances of Venezuela of the twenty-first century, this could be done only by infusing in them large doses of national pride, which in turn could only be achieved through the positive projection, affirmation and promotion of every aspect associated with the culture of the downtrodden and the history of resistance of the underdog. This is what is being carried out in Venezuela under the Bolivarian government.

However, the only source of national resources available for such a massive undertaking was the control over the country's oil revenue, which the Bolivarian government only managed to do after it wrested PDVSA from Venezuela's oligarchy as the outcome of the oil lockout the opposition staged in 2002–2003. Given that the state of the IV Republic was organized around the private appropriation of the oil by a small retinue of bureaucrats and comprador capitalists, no education of the people on the scale carried out by the Bolivarian government would have been possible.

Such an endeavor is also possible because a state that responds to the interests of the majority is being built and is being charged with entirely different social, political and economic aims, with the mass education of millions of ordinary Venezuelan being central to it. The more the population gets educated along the lines being carried out by the Bolivarian government discussed in this essay, the more the people become transformed into conscious agents of the very transformation underway. The new society being constructed necessitates a new type of citizen—this new citizen now counts in the millions.

Notes

1. UNDP report: http://hdr.undp.org/en/reports/global/hdr2011 /download/.
2. Report to the Universal Periodic Review of Venezuela (Bolivarian Republic of), 12th Universal Periodic Review, October 7, 2011, full address by Nicolas Maduro Moros, then Venezuela's minister of foreign affairs, based on 23-page submission to the UPR 2012, http://www .unmultimedia.org/tv/webcast/2011/10/upr-report-of-venezuela -12th-universal-periodic-review.html.
3. From a statement Bolivar wrote as a kind of title to his decree on the creation of an education system in Venezuela issued on December 11, 1825, in the city of Chuquisaca; Simon Bolivar (2010), *Para Nosotros la Patria es America, Ayacucho: Fundacion Biblioteca*, p. 164. Author's translation.
4. Soundings No. 37 (Winter 2007); http://www.lwbooks.co.uk/journals /soundings/issue/37.html.
5. Jose Marti ([1963]1884), *Maestros Ambulantes*, originally published in La América, Nueva York, mayo de. Reproduced in *Obras completas*, Vol 8, La Habana: Editorial Nacional de Cuba, 288–92; http://www .ensayistas.org/antologia/XIXA/marti/marti3.htm.
6. Author's translation. http://www.cubadebate.cu/wp-content/uploads /2009/05/todo-caliban-roberto-fernandez-retamar.pdf.
7. http://monthlyreview.org/2010/07/01/foreword-to-the-summer -issue.

References

Bolivarian Constitution (1999), Constitución de la República Bolivariana de Venezuela, http://www.tsj.gov.ve/legislacion/constitucion1999.htm.
Fundacion Infocentro (2011), Logros del Proyecto Infocentro, Ministerio para Ciencia y Tecnologia, December 14.

Chapter 8

Hugo Chávez, Social Democracy and Twenty-First-Century Socialism in Venezuela: An Alternative to the Neoliberal Model

Mike Cole

In chapter 7 of this volume, Francisco Dominguez describes in great detail the massive social programs initiated since 1998, when President Hugo Chávez won the presidential elections in Venezuela by a landslide. These measures, of course, entail an educational project *for* the Venezuelan people, and other peoples in the region and indeed the world.[1] They represent a major challenge to US neoliberal capitalism and imperial hegemony, and its attendant ideological and repressive apparatuses (Althusser, 1971). However, while the innovations allow the export of socialist ideas and ideals, they are in themselves classic social democracy rather than socialism, somewhat akin to the policies and practice of the post–World War II Labor governments in the United Kingdom. What makes Venezuela unique, however, is that whereas these British Labor governments were posing social democracy as an *alternative* to socialism, and, indeed, attempting to fight off attempts by revolutionary workers to move toward socialism, Chávez was presenting reforms as a *prelude* to socialism.

These reforms were seen by sections of the Chávez government and by large sections of the Venezuelan working class[2] as a step on the road to true socialist revolution. Thus for Chávez, "[t]he hurricane of revolution has begun, and it will never again be calmed" (cited in Contreras Baspineiro, 2003). On another occasion, Chávez asserted: "I am convinced, and I think that this conviction will be for the rest of my life, that the path to a new, better and possible world, is not capitalism, the path is socialism, that is the path: socialism, socialism" (Lee, 2005).

As Maria Paez Victor (2009) argues, one of the biggest achievements of the Bolivarian Revolution is existential:

> A new sense of identity, a new sense of belonging...The great majority of Venezuelans feel they are now in control of their own government and destiny—despite the continuous attacks from the oligarchy and its satellites. Now the Chávistas frame all the political discourse and its name is Socialism of the 21st Century.

Socialism cannot be decreed from above (see the comment on this by Gerardo in the case study toward the end of this chapter). The people discuss Chávez and they support him, but they are aware that they are the motor of the revolution. It is worth quoting Victor (2009) at length:

> For the first time since the fall of the Berlin Wall, a country in the world repudiates the barbaric version of capitalism that has prevailed since Ronald Reagan and Margaret Thatcher, and embraces a new socialism, one that has its roots in the indigenous people's socialism, in Liberation Theology[3] which was born in Latin America, in Humanism, in the inspiration of Cuba, as well as the works of Marx, but not exclusively in European socialism. It is not Stalinism,[4] it is not a copy of what has passed for socialism to date, but Venezuela's own brand infused with the idea that the people are the protagonists of democracy, that the economy should serve people, not the other way around, and that only their active and direct participation in political decision making will free the country from corruption and inequality.[5]

In 2010, Chávez asserted that, as well as a Christian, he was also a Marxist (Chávez, 2010), describing Marxism as "the most advanced proposal toward the world that Christ came to announce more than 2,000 years ago" (Suggett, 2010). Chávez made it clear that he was not arguing for the *reform* of the Venezuelan capitalist state, but its overthrow. As he put it, in perhaps his most clearly articulated intention to destroy the existing state:

> We have to go beyond the local. We have to begin creating...a kind of confederation, local, regional and national, of communal councils. We have to head towards the creation of a communal state. And the old bourgeois state, which is still alive and kicking—this we have to progressively dismantle, at the same time as we build up the communal state, the socialist state, the Bolivarian state, a state that is capable of carrying through a revolution. (Cited in Socialist Outlook Editorial, 2007)

This strategy has been described as the "state for revolution" strategy (e.g., Artz, 2012, p. 2), as part of a strategy of "parallelism"—the creating of parallel institutions—social "missions," which not only provide basic social democratic reforms, but in tandem with the existing capitalist state build a "self-government of workers" (p. 2). The communal councils that discuss and decide on local spending and development plans provide, in the words of Roland Dennis, an historic opportunity to do away with the capitalist state (cited in Piper, 2007). Sara C. Motta (2010, p.11) has described the politics of the establishment of communal councils as revealing the struggle between "old" and "new" politics, the development of new state/society relations and the formation of a new popular democracy. While she notes that it could be argued that the way in which the councils were created—from above, by presidential decree—is in contradiction with the idea of popular self-government and "leaves little room for community experimentation and involvement in the design and development of new institutions" (Andrés Antillano and Nora Machado, interviews, Caracas, July/August 2006), this underestimates "the lived experience of popular political agency and the ideological, organizational, and political realities of the popular classes," who "are neither politically uneducated nor incapable of working to produce forms of democracy and development that transform traditional state/society relationships and transcend the limits of liberal democracy." Experiences such as these, she concludes, suggest that equating the Chávez Government with illiberal populism—which tends to be the dominant form of "Western" analysis of Venezuela—"makes invisible the popular democratic subjects who are at the heart of contemporary Venezuelan politics" (Motta, 2011, pp. 11–12).

If it is the case that Chávez genuinely supported socialist revolution from below, which will eventually overthrow the existing capitalist state of Venezuela, and I believe that he did, then, for Marxists, he must be seen as an ally. Whether he was or not, however, is less important than the fact that he openly advocated and helped to create genuine revolutionary consciousness among the working class.

In discussing the necessity of destroying the bourgeois state, and replacing it with a socialist state, Ana Marin, a militant and key member of the *El Panel 2021 comuna* (multiple communal councils), the Alexis Vive collective, argued as follows:

> We have to remember that following the *Caracazo* in 1989 and the failed 1992 uprising, the Bolivarian revolution has assumed a democratic path through elections, beginning with the election of Chávez

in 1998. We've not seen a revolutionary war like in the Cuban or Russian revolutions. Of course we study the teachings of Mao and Lenin in the necessity of insurrection and the destruction of the capitalist state. However, at this point, in order to destroy capitalism we have to compare the approaches, capitalism produces death, we produce life, in a capitalist bakery, they produce exploitation, we have a bakery where we develop consciousness, where we work as a collective, this is our insurrection, to show that there is another way of life, another system. Currently our form of insurrection depends on developing the consciousness of the Venezuelan people, creating popular power. If you ask me, how do we overthrow the old state? My answer is through the comunas. (McGill, 2012)

Education for Socialism

We can make a distinction between schooling, on the one hand, and education on the other, with the former referring to the processes by which young people are attuned to the requirements of capitalism both in the form and the content of schooling, and the latter, a more liberatory process from birth to death, a process of human emancipation and socialism. While the former sustains and nourishes neoliberal capitalist hegemony and imperialism, the latter poses a counter-hegemonic challenge to capitalism and imperialism. I would like to make a brief but, from a Marxist perspective, important comment about critical pedagogy—the dominant from of radical Left pedagogy in the United States. A number of writers have described it as reformist (in that it aims to reform capitalism rather than to oppose it). Jerrold L. Kachur (2012), for example, has warned of a "liberal virus" in critical pedagogy, where "democracy" is promoted as a kind of "anti-capitalist" challenge to inequality, oppression and exploitation, which in reality assumes that liberal democratic capitalism can be harnessed for a yet-to-be named "something" that never arrives. The concept of a "yet-to-be named 'something' that never arrives" is commonplace in many reformist (non-socialist) movements and schools of thoughts, that is to say movements and schools of thought that do not both challenge capitalism directly *and* pose socialism as an alternative: for example, poststructuralism and postmodernism (see Cole, 2008, for a critique); Critical Race Theory (see Cole, 2009, for a critique); the "Race Traitor" movement (see Cole, 2012, for a critique).

For critical pedagogy to fulfill its radical promise, it is essential that this virus be eradicated. Glenn Rikowski (2012) has suggested that a truly anticapitalist critical pedagogy has the following features:

- It is based on the works of Marx and Marxism first and foremost [and therefore has revolutionary socialism at its core];
- The starting point is the critique of the basic structuring phenomena and processes of capitalist society—which involves a critique of the constitution of capitalist society;
- The second most significant level of critique is the host of social inequalities thrown up by the normal workings of capitalist society—and issues of social justice can be brought in here;
- The third level of critique brings in the rest of capitalist social life—but relates to the first and second levels as frequently as possible;
- Two keys fields of human activity in contemporary society stand in need of fierce critique: capitalist work and capitalist education and training (including the social production of labor power);
- Labor power—as capital's "weakest link"—deserves special attention as it has strategic and political significance.

Education and the Bolivarian Revolution

In many ways, the Bolivarian project of twenty-first-century socialism (21 cs) is *in its very essence* education in the liberatory counter-hegemonic sense of the word. Education, as a liberatory process from birth to death, a process of human emancipation and socialism was articulated in 2010 by Chávez in describing the nature of the Bolivarian Revolution, and the role of knowledge and education as the first of three forms of power in the revolutionary process, the others being political power and economic power:

> When we talk about power, what are we talking about…The first power that we all have is knowledge. So we've made efforts first in education, against illiteracy, for the development of thinking, studying, analysis. In a way, that has never happened before. Today, Venezuela is a giant school, it's all a school.
>
> From children of one year old until old age, all of us are studying and learning. And then political power, the capacity to make decisions, the community councils, communes, the people's power, the popular assemblies. And then there is the economic power. Transferring economic power to the people, the wealth of the people distributed throughout the nation. I believe that is the principal force that precisely guarantees that the Bolivarian revolution continues to be peaceful. (Cited in Sheehan, 2010)

Venezuela as "a giant school" and "education for socialism" is exemplified by the Revolutionary Reading Plan launched by Chávez in

2009 (Pearson, 2009). "A change in spirit hasn't been achieved yet," Chávez suggested, and argued that the plan will be the "base for the injection of consciousness through reading, with which our revolution will be strengthened even more" (cited in Pearson, 2009).

The plan involves the distribution by the government of 2.5 million books to develop communal libraries. Chávez said that part of the plan was a "rescuing of our true history for our youth," explaining that many standard textbooks do not acknowledge the European imperialist genocide of the indigenous peoples and their resistance (Pearson, 2009). Chávez went on to recommend that people do collective reading and exchange knowledge, mainly through the communal councils and the popular libraries. He called on communal councils as well as "factory workers, farmers, and neighbors, to form revolutionary reading squadrons," one of whose tasks is to have discussions in order to "unmask the psychological war...of the oligarchy" (cited in Pearson, 2009).

"Read, read and read, that is the task of every day. Reading to form conscious and minds," Chávez noted, "[e]veryday we must inject the counter revolution a dose of liberation through reading" (cited in MercoPress, 2009). Moreover, the revolutionary reading plan is intended to reaffirm values leading to "the consolidation of the new man and the new woman, as the foundations for the construction of a Socialist motherland, unraveling the capitalist imaginary" (cited in MercoPress, 2009; see Dominguez, chapter 7, in this volume, for further details).

The Bolivarian Government's Educational Project for Schools

As far as more "formal" education is concerned, since the election of Chávez, there was a massive increase in funding for primary, secondary and higher education. With respect to the curriculum, the Venezuelan Ministry of Culture stated on its website that there is a need to help schoolchildren get rid of "capitalist thinking" and better understand the ideals and values "necessary to build a Socialist country and society." Education is increasingly put forward by the state as a social good, and a central factor in shaping the system of production (Griffiths and Williams, 2009, p. 37).

Tom Griffiths and Jo Williams (2009) outline the essential factors in the Bolivarian Revolution's approach to education that make it truly counter-hegemonic. The Venezuelan approach, they argue, draws on concepts of critical and popular education within the framework of a participatory model of endogenous socialist development (p. 41). In representative democracies such as the United Kingdom and the United States, political participation is by and large limited to parliamentary politics—which represent the imperatives of capitalism, rather than the real needs and interests of the people.[6] Participatory democracy, on the other hand, involves direct decision-making by the people. At the forefront, they note, is "the struggle to translate policy into practice in ways that are authentically democratic, that promote critical reflection and participation over formalistic and uncritical learning" (p. 41).

As in the United Kingdom and the United States, formal school education in Venezuela is based on an explicit, politicized conception of education and its role in society (pp. 41–42). However, whereas in the United Kingdom (e.g., Beckman et al., 2009) and the United States (e.g., Au, 2009), the capitalist state increasingly uses formal education merely as a vehicle to promote capitalism, in the Bolivarian Republic of Venezuela, "the political" in education is articulated *against* capitalism and imperialism and *for* socialism. In 2008, a draft national curriculum framework for the Bolivarian Republic was released. It stated that the system is "oriented toward the consolidation of a humanistic, democratic, protagonistic, participatory, multi-ethnic, pluri-cultural, pluri-lingual and intercultural society" (Ministerio del Poder Popular Para la Educación, 2007, p. 11, cited in Griffiths and Williams, 2009, p. 42). It went on to critique the former system for reinforcing "the fundamental values of the capitalist system: individualism, egotism, intolerance, consumerism and ferocious competition...[which also] promoted the privatisation of education" (p. 42).

One central message of the Bolivarian Revolution tells us is that a fundamental counter-hegemonic shift in the political economy toward socialism, including *universal* free access to education, with a high degree of equity in terms of opportunity and outcomes, can be achieved quite quickly (p. 34). As Griffiths and Williams conclude, the Bolivarian system consistently refers these back to the underlying project to promote the formation of new republicans, with creative and transformational autonomy, and with revolutionary ideas, and with a positive attitude toward learning in order to put into practice new and original solutions for the endogenous transformation of the country (pp. 42–43).

The Realities of Educational Practice

It should be stressed at this stage that, in terms of actual practice in the schools and universities, education based on the above revolutionary principles is by no means universal. Indeed, as Griffiths and Williams (2009, p. 44) point out, discussions with education academics and activists during fieldwork in Caracas in 2007, 2008 and 2009, repeatedly raised the challenge of the political and pedagogical conservatism of existing teachers, often in opposition to the government's Bolivarian socialist project (e.g., Griffiths, 2008).

While such a model of education undoubtedly articulates with anticapitalist critical pedagogy, Tamara Pearson (2011) has pointed out that, "so far such a vision for education is limited to a number of 'model' schools and the majority of Venezuelan children continue to be educated [we might say 'schooled'] in the conventional way." She goes on, while education in Venezuela is now accessible to almost everyone, illiteracy has been eradicated the working conditions and wages of teachers are much improved, and education is more linked to the outside world, mainly through community service and the communal councils, "structural changes in terms of teaching methods and democratic organising of schools and education have been very limited" (Pearson, 2011).

She concludes:

> Building a new education system is an important prong to building a new economic and political system, because the education system is where we form many of our values, where we learn how to relate to people, where we learn our identity and history, and how to participate in society. Hence we need an alternative to the conventional education systems that train us to be workers more than anything else, to be competitive, to operate under almost army-like discipline, to focus only on individual results not collective outcomes, and to not really understand our history, or the more emotional aspects of life...The effort to change Venezuela's education system is intricately connected to its larger political project. (Pearson, 2011)

Pearson (2012) has commented on one of the latest government documents. In a generally extremely positive account of Chávez's 39-page proposed plan for the 2013–2019 period of the Bolivarian revolution, she notes that with respect to education, while the plan mentions increasing enrolment, the building of new schools, the introduction or improvement of certain elements of the curriculum content—such as "the people's and indigenous history of Venezuela"—as well as strengthening research into the educative process, there are "no structural or methodology changes." There have hardly been any changes, she argues, in the last 12 years. She concludes:

The achievement of literacy and enrolment of the poorest sectors is important, but the teaching methods are still traditional authoritarian, competitive ones, and while some schools have become more involved in their community life, many are still merely producers of obedient workers and a source of income for the teachers. More radical change than what has been proposed is needed. (Pearson, 2012)

Bearing Pearson's prescriptions in mind, there is much to learn from alternative schools, such as the one in Barrio Pueblo Neuvo, Merida.[7] The creation of a parallel set of popular educational institutions may be viewed as a process of construction—as part of a longer-term process of anticapitalist struggle, which can eventually serve as a model and help to free the official state schools from the stranglehold of the long-standing bureaucracy, created in part before the presidency of Chávez. Revolutionary socialist speeches and other forms of government communication are important, but need to be complemented by practical struggles on the ground.

Revolutionary Education in an Alternative School in Barrio Pueblo Nuevo, Mérida

Creating Space

The school is a small project,[8] started by committed socialist revolutionary residents and activists of Barrio Pueblo Nuevo, perhaps the poorest community in the city of Mérida in western Venezuela. It caters to students aged between eight and fifteen, and since, at the time of the research, it had been operating for only six months, it was very much in its initiatory phase. The teachers want to create an alternative for young people who have been left behind in the public school system and reengage them in participatory pedagogy consistent with socialist and democratic values. The school is currently linked to the Ministry of Education under the title of "alternative school" and receives some state funding.

Reflecting on the overall context of his fieldwork at the school, Edward Ellis (unpublished fieldwork, 2010) points out that the fact that the school is the exception rather than the rule as far as education in the country as a whole is concerned "need not be understood as distressing. It can be seen...as a great opportunity to empower and encourage new forms of change." He underlines the spaces that the Chávez government opened up—in this case for "independent and autonomous...new projects to grow and develop." As Gerardo, a part-time collaborator at the school, a long-time community activist from the barrio and an organic intellectual of the working class par excellence states: "Ten years ago this wouldn't have been possible. This would have been called 'terrorist' and would have to be underground." As he puts it, revolutionary teachers, unlike before, can advance faster, no longer having "to worry about being hunted down."

Gerardo points out that the school has opened many doors for people and that there are "a lot of expectations" from the Ministry of Education, which is hoping that the school might work as "a model for other schools."

Twenty-First-Century Socialist Praxis

Gerardo is committed to socialist praxis, noting that "socialism is done, not decreed." Given that the words "revolution" and "socialism" are omnipresent in Venezuelan society, and can be used "without much thought," Gerardo is working on the *construction* of socialism in the school being "a bit more responsible in this sense." As he explains, "here we practice socialism with concrete elements from everyday life...sharing, working in a collective way, friendship, getting along, the fundamental bases of socialism with praxis." Having seen societies torn apart in a capitalist system based on consumption, and underlining Chávez's stress on participatory democracy, Gerardo notes that the teachers are trying to teach the children to be "critical and proactive"—"not just criticism but how things can be changed," "we are trying to show that the children have a participatory role in society, and that this role can be transformative." Communication tools are crucial in this process—"the radio, the television, the written word...these things can lead to the transformation of society."

Lisbeida, a university student studying criminology and a dance instructor, working at the school and in the community as a volunteer, says of 21 cs, it "is being redefined, something that is flexible. I believe there are new understandings of what socialism is and how it can be implemented":

> But basically, the core concepts are the same: equality, social justice, elimination of class differences, more horizontal processes, all of this inside our school is an intrinsic part of what we are doing. It's our base...So we are trying to transmit these values of equality, solidarity, cooperation, collective work.

James Suggett, a writer for venezuelanalysis.com[9] who is also a community activist and a volunteer at the school, reflects Freireian[10] analysis when he says he is critical of those teachers who view socialism as being authoritarian, those who believe they should be getting students into line. For Suggett, "socialism means creating a democratic space in the classroom," encouraging people "to recognize oppression and overcome it" (see Kane, chapter 2, in this volume, for a discussion of the resonances and dissonances between Latin American traditions of popular education and Orthodox Marxism).

Communal, Cooperative and Democratic Living and Learning

At the alternative school in Barrio Pueblo Nuevo, each day starts with a communal breakfast, after which students are brought together to discuss what will take place that day. Sometimes communal cleaning of the community center where the classes are held ensues; sometimes the day starts with group activities, focused on reading, writing, or mathematics, depending on what students wish to work on, or need to improve.

Addressing the socialist roots of Venezuela's indigenous communities, Gerardo illustrates Freire's process of conscientization (the pedagogical process by which counter-hegemonic awareness is achieved) as he points out that indigenous peoples have a tradition of companionship, solidarity, respect and sharing, and that private property did not exist, and how the teachers are trying to break the paradigms of Western society that value "capital more than people," and that prioritize individualism and competition. The school aims to provide the children with a point of departure so that they can all advance together toward socialism. Gerardo points to the use of a pedagogy that "involves the children in collective work and thinking" and includes cooperative games. When the teachers meet with the children, as Jeaneth (the main teacher of the school, a member of the community whose children are studying at the school) explains, the teachers try to emphasize "that we are a collective and if something happens to the group it affects us all."

Learning at the school is in line with Freire's advocacy of "dialogic education," which entails a democratic learning environment and the *absence* of authoritarianism, of "banking education" (where teachers deposit "facts" into empty minds) and of grades. As Jeaneth puts it:

> We plan activities and then ask the children which they would like to work on. They choose the area. We have some basic parameters that

they need to work in but they choose. Also, when we leave the school for a trip, we propose the idea to them and they take part in the discussion about how to plan the trip.

Tamara Pearson, like Suggett, a writer for venezuelanalysis.com and also a volunteer teacher of reading at the school, points out:

> No one is forced to do anything and there are no punishments. If they don't want to participate in an activity, they can simply go somewhere else, or sit and watch. Hence, the weight is on the teacher to properly motivate the students and draw them in through the activity rather than discipline and threats of lower grades or whatever.

"There is no grading or competition," Pearson explains, "there's simply no sense of them competing with others." "The idea of the school," she believes, "is to teach using more creative and dynamic methods, without the usual competition and grades and failure and passing and who is first etc, with teachers who are very supportive and friendly, while also involving the community in school life, and vice versa."

Socialism and the Community

As Edward Ellis states, "there is a real emphasis on trying to increase students' participation in all activities." He gives the example of how "the students watched a movie and then discussed how to organize a screening of that same film in their community. A group conversation was held to identify what the steps necessary would be to put on this screening." As Ellis explains, "there is a lot of collaboration on the part of the community and different activities are led by different folks...It is quite common for the students to leave the classroom to attend an event in the community." In addition, as Lisbeida points out, the school's "activities [are] open to the entire community so that the community is a protagonist in what happens in the school. In that way, the dance group which is part of the school is also part of the community." Emphasizing how Participatory Action Research (PAR)[11] works in the community and school, Lisbeida explains:

> The idea is that the children have an impact in their community, carrying with them this experience to their homes and to their families so that their families also become integrated in the educational process that the school is trying to carry out. So there's a kind of feedback

that we are trying to accomplish between the community and the school. And school- community means family, workers, etc. There is an important interaction which is very relevant to the educational process in the school.

This is not to glamorize the students' community. As Gerardo explains, some of the students come from homes where there are problems of violence, alcohol, drugs, or unemployment and its attendant problems. However, as Lisbeida believes, this can also be a source of strength for the students:

> As these students come from backgrounds that are very difficult, I think that this gives them the ability to see certain social realities with more clarity: justice, the marked differences between violence and love. I see this as a potential to create criticisms and questions with more meaning. Because they have experienced very difficult things, they are not going to be afraid and they are going to have a very strong base to be critical of things.

Gerardo points out that there is help from some government missions, such as Mission Barrio Adentro (literally "mission inside the barrio"), which provides comprehensive, public-funded health care, and sports training to poor and marginalized communities. Barrio Adentro delivers de facto universal health care from cradle to grave.

In addition, the teachers are trying to improve human relations, not only with cooperative games, from which the teachers are also learning, but also physical spaces "with a community vision," such as a community library and a community radio station. As Lisbeida puts it:

> We've noticed that the children are arriving at their house with new attitudes, and although we don't have a way to scientifically measure it, we can feel a difference in the attitude of the parents as well…how they treat their children. Something very interesting is happening. Things are changing…[the children] learn things based on what they already know and live. In this way, they can also learn that they have the potential to change the reality that surrounds them.

The students at the alternative school in Barrio Pueblo Nuevo are in a process of self-liberation, and already there are signs of progress. As Lisbeida enthuses, "one of the things that we have seen with this process in the school is that the ones who were thought to be completely without potential or capacity to learn are making people turn their heads. They are doing some incredible things." As Gerardo concludes:

> We've only had a short time operating but I have noticed a change in the way the children see things. Before, their world was just the barrio, but now they are looking a little bit beyond this. And I have seen that the children are speaking now, they are conversing…Before everything was resolved through violence. Now there is more talking. There are still some very sharp words, but we are working on it. This has opened many doors for people. There are a lot of expectations…And there are many things that we have learned about ourselves due to the students.

Revolutionary Education in an Alternative School in Barrio Pueblo Nuevo, Mérida: Update, 2012

In mid-2012, Edward Ellis revisited the school, and talked to its cofounder Miguel Cortez. Cortez describes how someone from the Ministry of Education described the school as the concretization of the Bolivarian curriculum, so that in one sense the school is not an *alternative* school. However, in another sense, because no one is actually implementing the Bolivarian curriculum to the same extent elsewhere, it *is* an alternative school. He repeated what has been referred to above, namely the central contradiction between the very progressive ideas in government documents, and the difficulty of translating them into practice in the day-to-day curriculum.

What is happening in the alternative school in Barrio Pueblo Neuvo serves as an example of the radical change that is needed to create educative practices along the lines of the features of a truly anticapitalist pedagogy as outlined by Rikowski (2012), and referred to at the beginning of this chapter. The processes involve a lived critique of capitalist society, both educationally and socially, the forefronting of social justice and socially productive labor with revolutionary socialism at the core. All this is in direct opposition to schooling to produce obedient workers. Cortez states that when the alternative school was started, the staff decided not to be indifferent to the needs of the students, and soon found out that the students wanted to participate, that they needed to be a part of everything happening in the school. He describes how the staff proceeded to give the students more and more responsibility, and how the relationship between them and staff is one of mutual respect. In Venezuela, he argues, there is now a generation who understand what is going on—and who need to be subjects of social transformation. "We are building a community," he stresses, which realizes it has an impact on the barrio.

He gives the example of a money-raising initiative initiated by the students whereby they made pizza to sell from scratch. In doing this, he argues, they were acting as true researchers. Everyone got a chance to be involved, to write, to look after the money and so on. The students provide a model for participatory democracy, and, as Cortez notes, "they are more democratic than us." Everyone has access to the money and the treasurer is currently a five-year-old girl. Crucially, the students take their activities to the central location of the street. Indeed, Cortez talks of "taking the streets," which would otherwise be under the control of gangs and narco-traffickers. In so doing, the students are helping to foster democratic socialism in the community.

In tandem with the 2013–2019 Plan, Cortez concludes by stressing the importance of democratizing history, of the centrality of local history to bridge the gaps between generations. All histories are important, he concludes, because they occur in the context of life in the barrio. For the development of participatory democracy and 21 cs, the barrios need to be organized, and a discourse has to be constructed. The students at the alternative school in Barrio Pueblo Nuevo are actively involved in this construction, thus providing an exemplar for the resolution of the major contradiction between the progressive policies of the government, and schooling as practiced in Venezuelan schools.

Conclusion

The government of the Bolivarian Republic of Venezuela, led by Hugo Chávez, represented, I believe, the best currently existing model in the world for a future socialist society. As Chávez declared to supporters from the People's Balcony of the presidential palace, after his victory was confirmed in October 2012: "Venezuela will never return to neoliberalism and will continue in the transition to socialism of the 21st century." However, as noted here and stressed by Gerardo, the part-time collaborator in the alternative school in Barrio Pueblo Nuevo, and by Chávez himself, the revolution will not be decreed from above. From a Marxist perspective, it is important to stress the Chávez government's dialectic and symbiotic relationship with the Venezuelan working class.

Martinez et al. (2010, p. 2) argue that President Chávez was "the defining political factor" as revealed "by the typical political labels that . . . divide many Venezuelans between *Chavistas* and *anti-Chavistas*." However, it is "precisely in the relationship and tension between the Venezuelan government and the social movements that the process of building a participatory democracy comes alive most vividly." Greg Wilpert (2010, pp. viii–ix) underlines this fact:

> To learn about…the movements that stand behind the Chávez phenomenon is…as important as learning about the Chávez government itself. One cannot truly make sense of one without the other. And making sense of and defending what is happening in Venezuela is perhaps one of the most important tasks for progressives around the world today, since Venezuela is at the forefront in the effort to find a real progressive alternative to capitalism, to representative democracy, and to U.S. imperialism.

Central to the Bolivarian Revolution, as we have seen, is the idea of participatory democracy, as opposed to representative democracy, which was a pillar of Chávez's philosophy since his first election victory in 1998. There seems to be an abundance of hope for the future at the local and societal levels *despite* the forces opposing the revolution (see Cole, 2011, pp. 146–149).

With respect to education, we have witnessed that, viewed as a lifelong liberatory process, education is a key pillar of the revolution. I have noted how this is manifested in Chávez's concept of Venezuela as "a giant school." At the "formal" institutional level of education, the principles of the revolution have not been fully put into practice. Moreover, given the aforementioned conservatism of many teachers discovered by Griffiths and Williams, the challenge for Venezuelan revolutionary teachers to continue their counter- hegemonic struggle against capitalism, racism and imperialism remains paramount.

As noted earlier in this chapter, the overall societal reforms with respect to the "missions" and the other ameliorative measures are precisely that—*reforms*. However, just as these societal reforms need to be seen in the context of the country having had a revolutionary socialist president and millions of pro-Chávez workers, who are *or have the potential to become* revolutionary socialists, so do the reforms at the level of education in general, and at the level of the alternative school in Barrio Pueblo Nuevo.

In the same way that the societal reforms are reminiscent of those of the post–World War II Labor governments in the United Kingdom, the educational reforms being carried out in Barrio Pueblo Nuevo recall those that took place, for example, in the Inner London Education Authority (ILEA) and other progressive authorities. Indeed, in some ways these UK-based educational reforms were more progressive, particularly with respect to equality policies, as are equality policies embedded in UK equalities legislation today (see chapter 4 of Cole, 2011, for a discussion). In Mérida, there are, however, revolutionary teachers fostering, in Freire's terms, a deepening awareness of the sociocultural reality that shapes their students' lives. To reiterate, unlike the United Kingdom and the United States, either historically or contemporaneously, the promotion in future workers of the consciousness that they have the capacity and the power to transform that reality is supported in Venezuela by a revolutionary movement and a revolutionary president.

Chávez's death is a tragedy of immense proportions for the Bolivarian Revolution. However, as stressed in this chapter, socialist revolution must be first and foremost a revolution of the people.

In the words, spoken before Chávez's death, of one woman resident in the Caracas barrio of Baruta, who joined the hundreds of thousands of people, maybe a million, descending from the barrios around Caracas, successfully demanding the reinstatement of Chávez after the military coup in 2002:

> We love our president, but this is not his revolution. This is our revolution and it will always be the revolution of the people. If President Chávez goes, we will miss him dearly but we will still be here. We are revolutionaries and we will always be here. We will never go back! (Cited in Blough, 2010)

Capitalism is a failed system. Workers throughout the world need to be awakened to the possibility that another world is possible.

Notes

1. This chapter develops and draws on parts of chapter 5 of Cole, 2011 (see also Cole, 2014a, b).
2. The Venezuelan working class should not be viewed as constituting a traditional industrial proletariat, akin to the working class that constituted the driving force of much of 20 cs (see Cole, 2011, chapter 1, for a discussion). Some 60 percent of Venezuelan workers are involved in the informal economy (street vendors and so on), primarily in the barrios from where Chávez drew his support (Dominguez, 2010).
3. Liberation theology began as a movement within the Catholic Church in Latin America in the 1950s, achieving 2011, in the 1970s and 1980s. It emphasizes the role of Christians to be aligning themselves with the poor and being involved in the struggle against economic, political and social inequalities. In Chávez's view, "[t]he people are the voice of God" (cited in Sheehan, 2010). Chávez was referring to the Venezuelan revolutionary masses.

4. Stalinism refers to political systems that have the characteristics of the Soviet Union from 1928 when Joseph Stalin became leader (his leadership lasted until 1953). The term refers to a repressive and oppressive from of government by dictatorship, which includes the purging by exile or death of opponents, mass use of propaganda and the creation of a personality cult around the leader.

5. It must be stressed that in terms of getting rid of corruption there is still much to do. Disturbingly, there was corruption and self-aggrandizement within the supposedly pro-Chávez national and local state apparatuses. Grassroots organizers have described this as a "bureaucracy," "the endogenous right," "the Fourth Republic within *Chavismo*," "the Boli-bourgeoisie" (Martinez et al., 2010, p. 23). As Luis Perdomo has argued, many government officials, on becoming ministers or heads of a department in an institution, act as if they own that institution. As he puts it, "[b]eing a revolutionary is modelled by the attention given to the people…We don't want to be a deck of cards shuffled by someone else…we want to shuffle the deck. We want to construct along with the president and the assembly representatives, and the ministers as well" (cited in Martinez et al., 2010, pp. 230–231). Greg Wilpert (2010, p. viii) has also described the practices of "clientelism patronage" and "personalism," the former referring to politicians' use of government resources such as jobs or material benefits to favor their own supporters against political opponents; the latter to the tendency among both citizens and political leaders to place greater importance on loyalty to politicians than to political programs. It should be pointed out that Chávez showed awareness of these major impediments to the revolutionary process on a number of occasions.

6. Vladimir Illyich Ulyanov (commonly known as Lenin), one of the founders of the Russian Revolution, characterized capitalist democracy as the process by which oppressed workers are allowed once every few years to decide which particular representatives of the oppressing class will represent them and repress them in parliament ([1917]2002, p. 95).

7. "Barrio" is a Spanish word meaning district or neighborhood. In the Venezuelan context, the term commonly refers to the outer rims of big cities inhabited by poor working-class communities.

8. The fieldwork at this school was carried out on my behalf by Edward Ellis. I am most grateful to him for this. The subheadings in this section of the chapter reflect the main issues and concerns that arose in Ellis's interviews. The issue of racism was also raised (see Cole, 2011, chapter 5). Cole, 2011 as a whole specifically addresses racism, and chapter 5 of that volume also considers racism and antiracism in Venezuela.

9. Venezuelanalysis.com, in its own words, is an independent website produced by individuals who are dedicated to disseminating news and analysis about the current political situation in Venezuela. The site's

aim is to provide ongoing news about developments in Venezuela, as well as to contextualize this news with in-depth analysis and background information. The site is targeted toward academics, journalists, intellectuals, policy makers from different countries and the general public.

10. For Paulo Freire, learning environments, as democratic spaces, entail an absence of authoritarianism (Freire, 1987, p. 102, cited in Freire and Shor, 1987). Such an absence is not to be confused with a lack of authoritativeness. As Peter Ninnes (1998) points out, Freire explains the importance of teachers being authoritative, rather than being weak and insecure or being authoritarian. In addition to democracy, dialogic education centralizes the need to develop an open dialogue with students, and requires a balance between "talking to learners and talking with them" (Freire, 1998, p. 63, cited in Ninnes, 1998). Freire maintains that only through talking with and to learners can teachers contribute to the "[development of] responsible and critical citizens" (Freire, 1998, p. 65, cited in Ninnes, 1998). Freire makes a distinction between the progressive and democratic teacher, on the one hand, which he favors, and the permissive or authoritarian teacher, on the other, which he rejects.

11. Participation Action Research (PAR) involves respecting and combining one's skills with the knowledge of the researched or grassroots communities; taking them as full partners and co-researchers; not trusting elitist versions of history and science that respond to dominant interests; being receptive to counter-narratives and trying to recapture them; not depending solely on one's own culture to interpret facts; and sharing what one has learned together with the people in a manner that is wholly understandable (Gott, 2008).

References

Althusser, L. (1971), "Ideology and Ideological State Apparatuses," in *Lenin and Philosophy and Other Essays,* London: New Left Books, http://www.marx2mao.com/Other/LPOE70NB.html (accessed December 19, 2009).

Artz, L. (2012), "Making a 'State for Revolution'—The Example of Community and Public Media," *Links international Journal of Socialist Renewal* (May 1), http://links.org.au/node/2849.

Au, W. (2009), "Obama, Where Art Thou? Hoping for Change in U.S. Education Policy," *Harvard Educational Review* 79(2), Summer: pp. 309–320.

Beckman, A., Cooper C. and Hill, D. (2009), "Neoliberalization and Managerialization of 'Education' in England and Wales—A Case for Reconstructing Education," *Journal for Critical Education Policy Studies* 7(2), November, http://www.jceps.com/PDFs/07-2-12.pdf (accessed April 16, 2010).

Blough, L. (2010), "Bolivarian Republic of Venezuela: It Is Not Chavez. It Is the People," *Axis of Logic* (April 14), http://axisoflogic.com/artman /publish/Article_59344.shtml.

Chávez, H. (2010), "Coup and Countercoup: Revolution!" http://venezuela -us.org/2010/04/11/coup-and-countercoup-revolution/April11(accessed April 14, 2010).

Cole, M. (2008), *Marxism and Educational Theory: Origins and Issues*, London: Routledge.

———— (2009), *Critical Race Theory and Education: A Marxist Response*, New York: Palgrave Macmillan.

———— (2011), *Racism and Education in the U.K. and the U.S.: Towards a Socialist Alternative*, New York and London: Palgrave Macmillan.

———— (2012), "'Abolish the white race' or 'transfer economic power to the people'?: Some Educational Implications," *Journal for Critical Education Policy Studies* 10(2), http://www.jceps.com/?pageID=article&articleID =265.

———— (2014a) "The Alternative School of Community Organisation and Communicational Development, Barrio Pueblo Nuevo, Mérida," in S. C. Motta and M. Cole, *Constructing Twenty-first Century Socialism in Latin America: The Role of Radical Education*, New York and London: Palgrave Macmillan.

———— (2014b) "The Bolivarian Republic of Venezuela," in S. C. Motta and M. Cole, *Constructing Twenty-first Century Socialism in Latin America: The Role of Radical Education*, New York and London: Palgrave Macmillan.

Contreras Baspineiro, A. (2003), "Globalizing the Bolivarian Revolution Hugo Chávez's Proposal for Our América," http://www.narconews.com /Issue29/article746.html (accessed April 7, 2010).

Correo Del Orinoco International (2011), "Chavez Campaign Prepares Nationwide Grassroots Coalition for 2012 Elections," venezuelanalysis. com/news/6544 (accessed October 17, 2011).

Dominguez, F. (2010), "Education for the Creation of a New Venezuela," Paper delivered at *Latin America and Education*, Marxism and Education: Renewing Dialogues XIII, Institute of Education, University of London, July 24.

Freire, Paulo (1998), *Teachers as Cultural Workers: Letters to Those Who Dare Teach* (trans. Donaldo Macedo, Dale Koike and Alexandre Oliveira), Boulder: Westview Press.

Freire, P. and Shor, I. (1987), *A Pedagogy for Liberation: Dialogues on Transforming Education*, London: Macmillan Education.

Gott, R. (2008), "Orlando Fals Borda: Sociologist and Activist Who Defined Peasant Politics in Colombia," *The Guardian*, August 26, http://www .guardian.co.uk/world/2008/aug/26/colombia.sociology (accessed October 17, 2011).

Griffiths, T. G. (2008), "Preparing Citizens for a 21st Century Socialism: Venezuela's Bolivarian Educational Reforms," Paper presented at the

Social Educators Association of Australia National Biennial Conference, Newcastle, Australia.

Griffiths, T. G. and Williams, J. (2009), "Mass Schooling for Socialist Transformation in Cuba and Venezuela," *Journal for Critical Education Policy Studies* 7(2): pp. 30–50, http://www.jceps.com/index.php?pageID =article&articleID=160 (accessed April 12, 2010).

Kachur, J. L. (2012), "The Liberal Virus in Critical Pedagogy: Beyond 'Anti-This-and-That' Postmodernism and Three Problems in the Idea of Communism," *Journal for Critical Education Policy Studies* 10(1), http://www.jceps.com/PDFs/10-1-01.pdf.

Lee, F. J. T. (2005), "Venezuela's President Hugo Chavez Frias: 'The Path Is Socialism,'" http://www.handsoffvenezuela.org/chavez_path_socialism _4.htm.

Lenin, V. I. ([1917]2002), *On Utopian and Scientific Socialism*, Amsterdam: Fredonia Books.

Martinez, C., Fox, M. and Farrell, J. (2010), *Venezuela Speaks: Voices from the Grassroots*, Oakland, CA: PM Press.

MercoPress (2009), "To School for Reading Classes with Karl Marx and Che Guevara," MercoPress, May 17, http://en.mercopress.com/2009/05 /17/toschool-for-reading-classes-with-karl-marx-and- che-guevara (accessed February 10, 2011).

McGill, S. (2012), "Grassroots Interviews from Venezuela: Developing the Power of the Community," http://links.org.au/node/3064.

Ministerio del Poder Popular Para la Educación (2007), "Currículo Nacional Bolivariano: Diseño Curricular del Sistema Educativa Bolivariano," http://www.me.gov.ve/media.eventos/2007/dl_908_69.pdf.

Motta, A. C. (2010), "Populism's Achilles' Heel: Popular Democracy beyond the Liberal State and the Market Economy in Venezuela," *Latin American Perspectives* 38: p. 28, originally published online October 6, 2010, http://lap.sagepub.com/content/38/1/28.

Ninnes, P. (1998), "Freire, Paulo," *Teachers as Cultural Workers: Letters to Those Who Dare Teach* (trans. D. Macedo, D. Koike, and A. Oliveira), Boulder: Westview Press, *Education Review*, August 4, http://www .edrev.info/reviews/rev28.htm (accessed September 12, 2010).

Pearson, T. (2009), "Venezuela Opens National Art Gallery and Launches National Reading Plan," Venezuelanalysis.com, http://venezuelanalysis .com/news/4402 (accessed April 7, 2010).

——— (2011), "Venezuela's Dreams and Demons: Has the Bolivarian Revolution Changed Education?" venezuelanalysis.com, March 18, http:// venezuelanalysis.com/analysis/6072.

——— (2012), "Planning the Next 6 Years of Venezuela's Bolivarian Revolution," venezuelanalysis, July 6, http://venezuelanalysis.com/analysis /7091.

Piper, S. (2007), "The Challenge of Socialism in the 21st Century: Some Initial Lessons from Venezuela," International Viewpoint, http:/interna tionalviewpoint.org/spip.php?article1269.

Rikowski, G. (2012), "Monthly Guest Article (September): Critical Pedagogy and the Constitution of Capitalist Society," September 15, http://www.heathwoodpress.com/monthly-guest-article-august-critical-pedagogy-and-the-constitution-of-capitalist-society-by-glenn-rikowski/.

Sheehan, C. (2010), "Transcript of Cindy Sheehan's Interview with Hugo Chavez," March 30, http://venezuelanalysis.com/analysis/5233 (accessed August 1, 2010).

Socialist Outlook Editorial (2007), "Chavez: 'I also am a Trotskyist,'" *Socialist Outlook* 11, Spring, http://www.isg-fi.org.uk/spip.php?article430.

Suggett, J. (2010), "Chávez's Annual Address Includes Minimum Wage Hike, Maintenance of Social Spending in Venezuela," http://venezuelanalysis.com/news/5077 (accessed August 5, 2010).

Victor, M. P. (2009), "From Conquistadores, Dictators and Multinationals to the Bolivarian Revolution," Keynote speech at the Conference on Land and Freedom, of The Caribbean Studies Program, University of Toronto, October 31, venezuelanalyis, December 4, 2009, http://www.venezuelanalysis.com/analysis/4979 (accessed April 9, 2010).

Wilpert, G. (2010), "Prologue," in Martinez, C., Fox, M. and Farrell, J., *Venezuela Speaks: Voices from the Grassroots*, Oakland, CA: PM Press.

Interlude: Some, Our Leaves of Fall

Angela Martinez Dy

When I teach I am the wind.
I know this.

You cannot see the wind
but you'll always feel its presence
    if you don't listen
    you'll miss it

When I teach I am the wind.

My children
    they be fireflies
afraid to shine their lights in the darkness of the ghetto
for fear of being singled out:
Semhar, self-described, a short black building,
a whale. Tony, a television set, Chucky, a gun,
Reesie, a charm bracelet made of gold, but in fact
an iron lung; Zamaya, the razor hidden
under her tongue, flashes her smile at us
but once—then it's gone. She hides it quick,
the dangerous weapon that it is
    Rosemary, since her school days began,
was bussed from her home to lower Queen Anne for her parents'
hopes of a better education, one far from
the Holly Park projects. Tamica, despite the gift
of an innate stage presence, frets each day
about her appearance, though she sees herself mostly
as "a child of God."
    My children be rocket launchers,
government-issue grenades—pride their pins, exploding when pulled
like Shy's hair—and temper—on her natural days.
To Shykeisha, everythang come natural, Nicole, a small caged animal
bent and hateful from years of being prodded at
with roughened, too-sharp sticks
    beat-up running shoes pointed outward
    toes hanging over the precipice

My children been pushed
to the edge and some of them
prepare to slip
into lives of labor
after years of public education
have prepared them for nothing but

My kids done shut their eyes and ears
to this "learning" business
and learned to take matters into
their own—not-quite-grown—hands

I let Chuck down the way a rock falls.
Plunked down an "unsatisfactory" on the grade chart
without warning, in the way one chucks a rock
'cross the water to watch it skip—
but it plops and lets you down,
an upturned edge missing an intended leap.
         I let him down like a falling leaf
whose bright summer hues fade quickly
come fall. Come fall, the new school year
brings nothing for him. Cracking jokes
'bout bricks of weed, I ask him for an image. He says:
"What, bricks of weed ain't images?"
         When I ask for a simile, he writes
"People twist like tornadoes" and even though
I know he's right, he can't tell me why
then when we cover metaphor he writes
"*I AM THE SKY*"   but with no faith in his words

never once have you had something in which to believe

the worst mark i could give him
was no fair warning. "Unsatisfactory" smacked him
cross the face like the cops did, the ones on his block,
accosting young men who look just like him.
         no fair warning
Come fall, the new school year brings nothing
no reason to trust his teachers
why would I be any different
Ain't no one sparked the match
under the pilot light of his conscious mind
or blown him away with the power of words
and **now it seems the only thing he's learned**
is not to care

"Schools these days are teaching
antiquated information, preparing students for a world

that no longer exists."
—Robert T. Kiyosaki

My students—
They be dreams of one day
owning black Range Rovers
and stories of pregnant teenage baby mamas

"that's their friend"
gangs and big dogs on the block, family drama and sometimes
suicides in the neighborhood, with funerals on Saturdays
or maybe mid-week if the mortuary
is all booked up
or maybe mid-week if the mortuary
is all booked up...

When I teach them,
      I'm the wind.
They won't know I've been there till I'm gone
and there is no more gentle pressure
constant at their backs, wishing waves into the sands
of their youthful desert dreams

      My students?

      they're the soft fleshy part on the inside of your cheek
      it's too easy to bite down on
but they're also the razors, glinting, solid, sharp
      hidden under tongue
            pushed to the edge
            minds reeling at the precipice
be clammy palms
be seashells
be shadows of their future selves
be all their shallow calls for help
      be but numbers to the school district
          but butterflies to me
      be the iron lungs that live to let
      each other breathe
      be present moment
          poetry
exploding,
like Shykeisha's hair
           on her natural days.

Part III

Education and Pedagogy from Below

Chapter 9

Movement Methodologies and Transforming Urban Space

Jennifer L. Martinez

> *[The popular education methodology] is a political instrument…because you participate and you are the generator of a politics…It's from the common people. I mean, you put your knowledge here and from your knowledge we are going to see how to improve all of our knowledges…First, you plan from the people, with the people, for the people…And using another method someone else plans for you. They are planning your life. They are planning your development in the world. They are completely dominating you.*
>
> Marcelo, Urban Land Committee Activist[1]
> (personal interview, May 29, 2010)

This chapter raises an example of how popular education is used by movements to construct collective power and to transform their environment. The chapter examines the popular education methodology used by the Venezuelan movement *Comites de Tierra Urbana* (CTU, Urban Land Committees)[2] and argues that this is a practice that has helped the movement to produce what Henri Lefebvre (1991) called "lived space." Though at times the CTU movement has struggled to preserve its national unity and force, the strength of the movement is premised on differences within and between barrios (shantytowns). Such a mode of organization is somewhat unique in Venezuelan history and signals the construction of new urban social relations in the country. In this chapter I argue that the production of *collective* lived space, a term that will be defined through the discussion, and the movement's capacity to shape a national urban agenda can be attributed, at least in part, to the popular education methodology that the CTUs have adopted. The methodology has over time expanded the movement's understanding of urban power relations and the manner in which those power relations must be reworked across urban space—not just in the barrio—in order to transform the city. The first part of the chapter will discuss who the CTUs are. The second section describes the popular education methodology (from here The Methodology), discussing its origins and the principles upon which it is based. The third section will explain where and when The Methodology is used and will touch on some of the more obvious outcomes of the process. The chapter then develops the argument that this methodological process constitutes the construction of collective lived knowledges, a powerful tool for popular movements in the struggle to transform the city. The discussion unfolds by taking up the issues of difference and collectivity. The importance of these two elements for the transformation of urban space will be clarified through an engagement with popular education theory and Henri Lefebvre's idea of "lived space." The chapter will conclude with the movement's need to continually reproduce collective lived space in order to overcome historically fragmented social relations and its own internal contradictions.

The Venezuelan Urban Land Committees

Five weeks before the 2002 coup against Venezuelan president Hugo Chávez—which famously saw his return to the presidency two days later—another important but lesser-known event happened in Venezuela. On February 4, 2002, President Chávez issued Decree 1666 to begin "the process of regularizing urban land tenancy occupied by barrios and poor urbanized areas" (Decree No. 1666, Art. 1, 2002). The decree instructs state institutions to issue land titles to barrio residents who inhabit state-owned land. In a country where almost 95 percent of the population lives in urban cities and towns, and 60 percent of those live in barrios with no prior legal claim to the land, the potential impact of the decree is significant. In fact, according to Gregory Wilpert (2003, p. 113), the decree and the 2006 law that followed have the potential to affect more Venezuelans than any other national legislation, with the exception of education laws.

According to the decree, in order to obtain land titles barrio residents must form an Urban Land Committee (CTU). The CTUs are meant to

- foster public participation in the development of the Special Law for Comprehensive Regularization of Land Tenancy of Popular Urban Settlements (which was passed in 2006);

- identify the boundaries of their territory (usually 200–400 households) and compile an inventory of housing;
- write a Barrio Charter, which includes a list of residents, a barrio history and a vision for the barrio;
- discuss how to improve the barrios (Decree 1666, Art. 8, Section 3).

Once formed, a CTU can then apply for land titles for each of its member households.

Since the implementation of the decree, the CTU movement also participated in the writing of the 2006 Urban Land Regularization Law, one of the first laws that were "hammered out with those actually affected" (Wilpert, 2003, p. 113). Then in 2011, the reform of the Urban Land Regularization Law was passed, in which the CTUs also played a significant role. This latter law includes the creation of a Land Bank and implementation of popular oversight of the land regularization process; it expands the legal understanding of private property ownership to include collective ownership and facilitates the titling of privately owned land.

With over 7,000 registered Urban Land Committees, the CTUs comprise one of the most significant popular organizations in the country. Indeed, since their creation the CTUs have become what scholars and activists recognize as "one of the few expressions that we can see of an autonomous popular organization [in Venezuela]" (Gerardo, Pobladores Movement activist, personal interview, May 6, 2010; see also García-Guadilla, 2006; Wilpert, 2007). What makes the CTUs particularly interesting is that unlike other Venezuelan state-born organizations, such as the Bolivarian Circles (see Hawkins and Hansen, 2006), the *misiones* (see Wilpert 2007), or even the now-famous Communal Councils, at their inception many CTUs organized themselves independent of state institutional mediation, instead putting into practice the principles of self-organization and the mutual exchange of local knowledges and experience (see Martinez, 2011). This relative organizational independence has since given rise to a politics that goes beyond the remit of the decree,[3] at times challenging state institutions and questioning the very premise upon which the CTUs were established: private property ownership.

The Popular Education Methodology of the CTU Movement

Key to the CTU movement's articulation at a national scale and the evolution of the movement's political agenda is the popular education methodology that it uses. The Methodology is one of the defining practices of the CTU movement, something for which the movement is recognized. It has been used during or in preparation of every major national meeting of the movement since 2004. Dozens of CTU activists go on to utilize The Methodology in other organizations, such as the Communal Councils. Additionally, the principles of The Methodology permeate the movement's other local and regional spaces of articulation.

The origins of The Methodology can be traced to Chile during the presidency of Salvador Allende where a group of rural community activists developed The Methodology in order to collectively negotiate with the state. After the assassination of Allende, many of the activists lived in exile but continued to develop their popular education methodology, finally bringing it to Venezuela (Methodology Workshop, April 24, 2010). Those who worked with The Methodology came to be known as "Churuatas," the name of the distinctive indigenous communal housing of Venezuela's southern region. The contemporary form of The Methodology, which has evolved over several decades, also draws on the work of Brazilian educator Paulo Freire and Venezuelan educator Simón Rodríguez (Marcelo, CTU activists, personal interview, May 29, 2010).

Several CTU activists had previously worked with the Churuatas, so in 2004, they were invited to teach The Methodology to CTU members from across the country (Cristóbal, CTU activist, personal interview, June 5, 2010). This group became known as the *Equipo de Formación* (Training Team), which during its first two years of existence was a paid team of CTU activists who organized local *encuentros* and facilitated The Methodology for CTUs across the country.[4]

While similar to popular education work across Latin America (see Kane, 2001), it is notable that the Churuatas specifically designed The Methodology for use by people engaged in community work, rather than for educators in schools. This has several implications. First, activists and not outside "experts" learn and facilitate The Methodology. The CTU movement over the years has trained new facilitators within their own ranks. This both democratizes the popular education process and attempts to renew the informal leadership and coordination of the movement, a common oversight of Venezuelan popular organizations that has often led to their failure (Fadda, 1987, p. 368).

Second, The Methodology's purpose is to transform lived practices. Similarly, Brazilian popular educator Paulo Freire (1972) argued that in order to overcome oppression, one must develop critical consciousness, a process that he referred to as "conscientization." "To surmount the situation of oppression, men [*sic*] must first critically recognize its causes, so that *through transforming action they can create a new situation*—one which makes possible the pursuit of a fuller humanity" (p. 24, emphasis added).

If analysis of practice is the focus of The Methodology, then the content utilized in the process is actually highly varied depending on what practice is being analyzed. The *process*, then, is what is essential and generalizable and is worth sketching out here. The Methodology involves five steps:

(1) Accumulation of information: telling each participant's story or experience, elicited through a guiding question.
(2) Coding the information into themes.
(3) Analysis: debating the content of each theme.
(4) Synthesizing the debate into an agreed upon assessment of practices and proposals for moving forward.
(5) Evaluation.

Key to this process is an "open registry" of everything that is said. That is, one person or a team of people writes what is said on butcher paper, which is then posted on walls. This serves as the material from which to debate and write a collective synthesis of the discussion. The whole process may take several hours or several days.

To illustrate the process, during a ten-day Pobladores Movement School for Activists in 2009, the guiding questions, or what Freire (1972) calls "generative questions," were: "What are we doing [as CTUs in our community]? Why are we doing it? With whom are we doing it? How are we doing it?" The school was divided up into groups of 15–17, where each person shared his or her response to these questions. Over the course of four mornings, for a total of almost 20 hours, local stories were shared and written. By the end of the morning on the fourth day, people's stories covered the walls of the small rooms that the school occupied.

Then the stories were codified into four themes: ideas that suggested more *research* was necessary in order to understand the problem; ideas that implied *organizational articulation* was necessary; ideas for *organizational planning*; and *other*. Within the small groups each theme, informed by the stories, was then debated in turn.

The debates produced a variety of discussions that commonly recur for the CTU movement. They included the ongoing struggle to build and preserve dignified housing; the expanded understanding of "habitat" to go beyond housing and include living environment; analysis of relationships with different state institutions; how and why the state was different in distinct regions; how successes were achieved and what could be tried in other localities; what kind of city people wanted to create; how the culture of capitalism made creating socialism difficult; and ideas about future plans for the movement and the Bolivarian Revolution more broadly. This debate was also captured on paper.

Finally, each group put together a "synthesis": all the statements of analysis and ideas for future action that all the participants agreed upon. Those statements that could not be agreed upon were marked for continued debate and left out of the "synthesis." The synthesis was eventually typed up and sent around to CTU activists, as is also done after every National *Encuentro* (the biannual meeting of all CTUs). At the end of the ten days, the whole process was evaluated.

The Methodology's analysis of practice is also guided by a number of principles:

- The three "inters": *interdependencia, interconexión*, and *intercambio* (interdependence, interconnection, exchange).
- The three "mutuos": *apoyomutuo, conocimiento mutuo, respeto mutuo* (mutual support, mutual knowledge, mutual respect).
- The three "autos": *autogestión, autonomia, autosustentación* (self-management, autonomy, self-sustainability).

These principles are also reflected in other meeting spaces of the movement, such as the Caracas Metropolitan Assembly of CTUs. These assemblies are organizational spaces where information is exchanged and issues are debated. Both the Caracas Metropolitan Assembly and the movement's monthly National Meeting are guided by the "right to speak" (*derecho a la palabra*), which permits everyone to speak for as long as they need to, in the order that they raise their hand, regardless of who they are or what formal credentials they have. Each item on the agenda is debated in this way until some kind of consensus is reached or a proposal for moving forward is developed. The debates can be loud and heated, and they often endure for many hours, especially when the issue is polarizing or hundreds of people are in attendance.

This strategy for popular organization and the development of popular politics is not new to Latin America (Kane, 2001). Popular education of the kind that the CTUs use is a widespread practice among popular movements throughout the region, the most recognized of which is the Landless Worker's Movement (MST) in Brazil (Kane, 2001). The use of such a practice involves the critique of traditional, expert-oriented epistemologies, an examination of the relationship between knowledge and power, and the use of knowledge production to create alternative spaces that challenge dominant power relations (Torres, 1990, p. 22; hooks, 1994).

Encuentro y Re-encuentro

The methodological process and the principles that underpin it are central to the CTU movement's efforts to construct popular power at various scales of articulation (barrio, city, state and nation). Most importantly, the movement regularly organizes National *Encuentros* (2004, 2006, 2008, 2010) where The Methodology is used as the process by which a national political agenda is set. The National *Encuentros* usually last 3–4 days, and attendees have first participated in a local *encuentro*, where they will go through the same popular education process.[5] Since its adoption by the CTU movement, The Methodology has been used in hundreds of local CTU *encuentros* in preparation for the larger national events. Spokespeople are selected to bring the "synthesis" of their local *encuentro* to the national event, where as many as 500 (2006) have been in attendance. Consequently, the synthesis that comes out of the National *Encuentro* should reflect an accumulated discussion of the various scales of the movement from the local to the national (see also Motta, 2011). The syntheses from National *Encuentros* then serve as the movement's national political agenda until the next one is convened.[6]

Out of these National *Encuentros* have come several concrete proposals. One was to create the National Meeting as a monthly meeting point for all CTUs through which political projects could be coordinated. The reform bill for the Urban Land Regularization Law came out of the 2006 National *Encuentro* where streamlining the land titling process was deemed necessary. The beginnings of the Pobladores Movement were also proposed at the same *Encuentro*, though it had no name at the time (*Síntesis, II Encuentro Nacional de Comités de Tierra Urbana, Los Teques*, Miranda State, November 3–5, 2006). Other proposals that have been realized include the national Land Bank and several marches to demand passage of the urban land reform bill (*Síntesis, III Encuentro Nacional del Movimiento de Pobladores, Maracaibo*, Zulia State, 2008).

Many of the most important outcomes of the National *Encuentros*, however, are less tangible. On the one hand, the simple act of meeting to hear other people's experiences is a unifying and motivating activity for CTU activists. As Francesca says, "I like to go to the [national] *encuentros* because you learn a lot from the experiences of people. They share what they are doing, the projects, the issuing of the land titles…it makes me happy to hear that others are getting titles" (Francesca, CTU activist, personal interview, May 20, 2010). Similarly, other national meetings have spurred local CTUs to become more active, to reexamine their relationship with state institutions, or to develop a deeper understanding of how to construct popular politics (Evaluation, Pobladores Movement School for Activists, August 8, 2009; group interview, Bolívar State, May 30, 2010).

Other intangible outcomes require a view of how the movement is developing over time. That is, the *encuentros* result in a period of self-reflection for the movement and the debate itself is a meaningful experience that affects how individual CTUs understand their political environment and take action in their local territory. The analysis of local practices that The Methodology facilitates allows participants to put their experiences into a larger context, revealing difficulties, successes, systems, or opportunities that might have been previously hidden. From a popular education perspective, this active engagement with lived experience is a more powerful form of knowledge and learning than that which is simply told to you (a form of learning that Freire, 1972, called "banking"). Participants in the process often experience an "ah-ha moment" that affirms that "you must discover truth and knowledge for yourself or it will not be your truth or your knowledge" (Campbell, 2003, p. 130).

In addition, the *encuentros*, supported by The Methodology, are concerned with seeking truth where "[t]ruths are events that no longer allow us, in good faith, to see as we previously saw and to be as we previously were" (Pithouse, 2006, p. 27). Hence, from this meeting and truth discovery, practice is transformed. While there is clear evidence that transformation of practice at a local scale occurs (various personal interviews with CTU activists), for the national CTU movement this transformation of practice is also evident in the phases that the movement has undergone since its emergence in 2002. Each "moment" of *encuentro* has shifted the political agenda of the national movement to where it is now: developing the "right to the city" under the broader umbrella of the Pobladores Movement.

Two other issues stand out as evolving debates that have grown with intensity in each *encuentro*. The first is the relationship with other popular organizations, which includes those that make up the Pobladores Movement, but also includes other barrio organizations, especially the *Consejos Comunales* and the *Comunas*. Analysis of these organizations and the CTUs' relationship to them has been difficult, requiring CTU activists to confront not just the fragmentation in the barrios but also their own failures to support the political develop-ment of what are becoming the most important popular organiza-tions in the country.

Perhaps the most important revelations that the analysis draws out are the nuances of the movement's relationship with the state. Hence, despite the fact that most CTU activists supported the Chávez gov-ernment, recurring analysis spurs proposals for greater autonomy and self-governance. In short, the analysis and transformation of practice has increasingly led to the movement's ability to understand and "to master its own conditions of existence" (Lefebvre, 2009, p. 134).

Producing Collective Lived Space: Unity through Difference

What is additionally profound and meaningful about The Methodol-ogy's process is expressed in the words of Marcelo who was quoted at the beginning of this chapter. Marcelo's summary of what makes The Methodology valuable to the movement—the lived knowledges of participants and the rejection of top-down power relations in favor of collective political construction—are also the characteristics that allow The Methodology to be a tool for producing what this chapter calls collective lived space.

Drawing from the work of Henri Lefebvre (1991), "lived space" is produced by people's lived knowledges and practices, referred to here as *conocer*.[7] The central attribute of lived space is difference. According to Lefebvre (1991) and Scott (1998), this presents a chal-lenge to dominant social relations (e.g., the state and capital), which exert power to fragment, homogenize and absorb difference. They do this, in part, "by means of epistemology and seek to institute a supposedly absolute knowledge [*saber*] which is in fact no more than a pale imitation of divine wisdom" (Lefebvre, 1991, p. 414). The per-vasive belief that *saber* is absolute—that it is the only form of legiti-mate knowledge—reflects an attitude that attempts to "[exclude] the necessary role of local knowledge and know-how" and seeks instead to impose order and control (Scott, 1998, p. 6). Where this manifests most acutely is in the production of the modern city.

Of course, in thinking about cities it is already apparent that these two types of knowledges are not mutually exclusive. Even within the experience of the CTU movement, the very formation of an

Urban Land Committee is premised on both the *conocer* of barrio inhabitants and the technical skills of *saber*; the process of marking the territory of the CTU, mapping the barrio and numbering the houses depends on the lived knowledges of residents who are familiar with the peculiarities of each place and technical know-how. Yet, it should instead be recognized that the concern mounted by Lefebvre and others is around the exercise of power (see Scott 1998; Slater 2004; de Souza 2006), or the "collusion between [a certain kind of] 'knowledge' and [a certain kind of] 'power'" (Lefebvre, 1991, p. 415) that seeks to eliminate, or at least control, lived space. Orin Marcelo's words: "They are planning your life. They are planning your development in the world. They are completely dominating you." The Methodology, like many popular education practices, seeks to expose these power relations and equip practitioners with their own sense of power.

And it goes further. Lefebvre's idea of "space," and "lived space" in particular, opens up a way of seeing the knowledge production that the CTUs engage in as more than exposing power relations—a particular concern of popular education traditions that, though important, misses how practitioners are also weaving together new social relations between themselves, and *in so doing* how they are transforming the political and physical conditions of their place.

As explained above, The Methodology starts from knowledges that come from the lived experiences of CTU activists, which are often place-specific and, accordingly, infused with idiosyncrasies. In this way, the political development of the national CTU movement is informed by the local experiences and knowledges of barrio communities. CTU activist Carlos explains,

> Our fundamental organizational seed begins in the local, in the barrio, with all the difficulties [that it brings]. And from there it begins to progress. It wasn't that it was first created at the national level and then later addressed the local. It was born in the reverse...
>
> At first...the land committees were only local in the barrio and they only saw establishing conditions for their communities, the small stuff. But out of the small, as my father says, is born the large. And from there the local begins to develop experiences...in transformation, in involving the people, mobilizing, above all organizing, and getting others involved...
>
> [Expectations] aren't constructed by...what happens to occur to an intellectual. No, it has to do with popular knowledge, with the communities' own knowledge. (Carlos, CTU activist, personal interview, April 10, 2010).

Through the use of The Methodology the CTU movement is turning what has historically been a limitation to popular organization in Venezuela—localized and fragmented social relations between the barrios—into a launching pad for the construction of what is often called "popular power." Hence, rather than only engaging at a single scale (e.g., the local barrio) and "treating the differences at that scale as *the* fundamental line of political cleavage" (Harvey, 2000, p. 79, emphasis in original), as was historically the case, these diverse lived knowledges are used to collectively construct popular power.

Importantly, The Methodology explicitly builds on the specific experiences and unique identities of each locality. The local territory is acknowledged as the starting point and those experiences are then shared across localities in order to co-construct a collective political identity and a macro-analysis of what the CTU movement across the country is experiencing. This has helped the CTUs to articulate a national movement while still preserving (even honoring) local identities and differences. For example, "take it back to the local" is a common refrain within the movement, reflecting the national movement's attempt to be driven by local decision-making.

It is this dialectical relationship between local, self-determining organizations (individual CTUs) and articulation at wider scales that makes the CTU movement unique in the Venezuelan experience. This type of articulation signals the constitution of new urban social relations, which in turn has implications for transforming the city: popular movements are able to transform the city *through the very act of producing new, collective knowledges.*

In particular, what is suggested by the above discussion is that in stitching together the multiple, heterogeneous local knowledges (*conocer*) of barrio inhabitants, the CTU movement is producing another scale of lived space, thus reshaping how the urban is conceived of and produced by barrio residents across Venezuela.

Producing Collective Lived Space: Collectivity

An aspect of this wider scale of lived space that is not readily addressed by Lefebvre's concept is its collectively produced nature. Evident in the process and principles of The Methodology is a commitment to the construction of *collective* knowledge, identity, analysis and solutions. It is both an orientation toward the collective as the agent of social transformation and the construction of that agent. As Carlos says, "We generate expectations that are collectively constructed" (personal interview, April 10, 2010). Again and again, CTU activists talk about the need to build a popular politics and change the urban by thinking and acting collectively. Carlos goes on:

> We have a politics that we think is important, that has weight and that we want to share in other spaces with people who are in the same struggle…Organization is what permits you to have an impact in those spaces. You could be alone and have ideas but you don't have anyone behind you. If the ideas come from debate and mutual construction they have more weight.

This suggests that more than "difference" is necessary to provoke urban transformation. Another CTU activist, Pedro, explains his understanding of the movement's orientation toward the construction of popular power.

> I am going with the majority, even if the majority is wrong and I'm the one who is right…But I will never go alone…I'll go in community…Three or four is a lot—alone nothing. Where are we going [as a movement]? Where the majority decides. What are we going to construct? What the majority decides. Ah—am I going to influence it? Yes. Am I going to give my opinion? Yes. Am I going to have criteria? Yes…But listen, we construct it in consensus. (Personal interview, May 18, 2010)

Popular education practices that aim to transform the world also emphasize the connection between individual transformation, the development of new individual subjectivities and collective transformation (Kane, 2001, p. 221). Peter McLaren (2000, p. 118) describes the potential revolutionary agency that such a process fosters as

> an agency that helps to forge among the oppressed themselves a sense of the authority to act concretely and with specific social outcomes in mind, a praxis that connects power to meaning, thought to action, and *self-empowerment to social empowerment*, and that joins the confidence of controlling one's own destiny to a larger collective power of reclaiming history for the poor and the powerless. (Emphasis added)

Latin American popular educator activist Maria Clara Bueno Fischer adds to this by emphasizing that the collective is *the key actor* in the transformation of society. About this she says, "even conscientisation—on its own does not change reality and people need to organise collectively to be 'subjects' of change, to be able to take action and put forward proposals" (quoted in Kane, 2001, p. 232).

This is further expressed in the process of collective debate and consensus that the CTU movement strives for at their assemblies and *encuentros*. Richard Pithouse (2006) has argued that the meetings of the South African Abahlali movement are "central to radical process." He reiterates the importance of arriving at consensus and argues that for "a hugely diverse group of vulnerable people with profound experiences of marginalization and exploitation in multiple spheres of life," it is necessary that the synthesis, or outcome, is not determined elsewhere but that "the meeting produces a result we are all committed to" (p. 28).

As Marcelo suggests in the epigraph of this chapter, the process of collective knowledge production that the CTUs have adopted is itself a political strategy to rupture traditional power relations premised on hierarchical knowledges *and* to produce new collective subjectivities founded on the principles mentioned earlier. By helping to produce this *collective* lived space, The Methodology has directly contributed to the articulation of the movement at a national scale and to the evolution of the movement to go beyond land titling.

The emphasis on a collective politics that is constructed through the participation of many individuals is also critical to understanding the Bolivarian Revolution. This is a politics that does not look toward the state for its articulation. Instead, a collective politics, of the kind that Pedro and Carlos talk about, turns toward the knowledges of inhabitants for direction.

The Continuous Production of Collective Lived Space

The production of collective lived space, however, is uneven, unstable and at times contested. For example, while The Methodology continues to be used and invoked in almost all of the regional and national spaces of the movement, it is not an uncontested strategy for developing the movement. For example, in 2006, the spokespeople from the state of Monagas did not approve of The Methodology as a suitable model for popular organization (Juana, CTU activist, personal interview, April 26, 2010). Several other regions raised this concern and sought a more regimented organizational structure, in part to offset the strong influence of the Caracas-based CTUs (Sofia, CTU activist, personal interview, May 19, 2010; National Liaisons Meeting, May 22, 2010).

Rootedness in difference, on the one hand, and the push to form a national identity with a common vision, on the other, have always existed in tense balance for the CTU movement (Cristóbal, CTU activist, personal interview, June 5, 2010). This is clearly exemplified in the debate about adopting the identity of the Pobladores Movement, which was a move to expand the movement's agenda and would result in negotiating organizational space with other interests, such as renters' rights. As Gillian Hart (2002, p. 28) suggests, "the 'unities' constructed through practices and processes of articulation are almost always contradictory, and must be continually renovated, renewed, and re-enacted." Likewise, the question of whether or not the CTU movement should become part of the Pobladores Movement reflects the apparent contradiction between *difference* and *collective* that this chapter has suggested is the foundation of how the CTU movement is able to transform the urban in Venezuela.

What is important to recognize both in Hart's comments and in the CTU's commitment to ongoing analysis and transformation of practice is the sense of process. That is, the production of collective lived space and, in turn, the transformation of the urban must be continuous. Yet one must remember that for *pobladores*, enacting the process is not always easy. In the early years of the movement's organization, the Venezuelan National Technical Office made possible both the development of the Training Team and the completion of hundreds of *encuentros*. Since the office lost much of its funding and changed directorship several times, the ability for the CTUs to organize *encuentros* on a large scale has become more and more difficult. Ricardo explained, "Before we did 150 local *encuentros* but we had funding then and there was a team who went around supporting the others. This time [in 2010] there weren't resources and each had to do how it could and they couldn't" (Ricardo, CTU activist, personal interview, April 14, 2010). The result was the lowest participation in a National *Encuentro* since the movement was born and significant logistical problems in bringing the national movement together.

The material limitations of a popular movement, such as the CTUs, should not be overlooked as the act of *encuentro*, as explained earlier, is fundamental to the analysis of practice and, ultimately, the transformation of the oppressive systems that barrio communities face. The concern here is the extent to which these limitations and the dependence on state resources might undermine the popular movement's capacity to develop a transformative politics that is based on lived experiences and knowledges and not on the technocratic interests of state institutions. This concern lurks in the shadows of many of the debates within the CTU movement and is at times the explicit topic of debate. This concern speaks to a concrete reality in the daily practices of Venezuelan popular movements in general.

Conclusion

At the beginning we only fought for land tenancy, for the transfer of urban land. [Then] we started to grow, to mature, and to have a political vision further out, not just of land transfer and land tenancy. Precisely I think that this had to do with the maturity of the movement insofar as it is articulating with different actors, insofar as there is debate, there is studying, to the extent that it begins to have a greater perspective, (Carlos, CTU activist)

As Carlos's words illustrate, this chapter has focused on the movement's practice of exchanging lived knowledges through the use of a popular education methodology. For the CTU movement, lived knowledge and the collective, critical analysis of it constitutes the basis from which the movement can organize itself, claim its legitimacy and power, and seek to transform the urban. In particular, The Methodology has been the backbone of how the movement has forged (and continues to construct) a collective identity at a national scale and has evolved a political agenda that seeks to transform the social relations of the city in a more profound way. Despite the material struggles that the CTUs face in practicing The Methodology, the emphasis that the movement places on producing local knowledges and facilitating the exchange of those knowledges so as to construct a collective national agenda is one of the aspects that sets the CTU movement apart from other barrio-based organizations in Venezuela's history.

Notes

1. All quotes are anonymous.
2. This chapter is based on seven months of fieldwork in Venezuela over a two-year period, April 2008–June 2010. Thanks to the School of Politics and International Relations, the Centre for the Study of Social and Global Justice and the Graduate School at the University of Nottingham for funding this research. Thank you to the editors for their thoughtful feedback. Special thanks to the Venezuelan people who opened their lives, joys and sorrows to my inquisitive presence. All mistakes and omissions are, of course, my own.
3. The CTUs now form part of the larger *Movimiento de Pobladores y Pobladoras* (Urban Settlers' Movement, from here the Pobladores Movement), an alliance between various urban popular movements, including the CTUs, who are calling for "the right to the city," which includes but is not limited to barrio-specific concerns.
4. Due to a change in directorship, and the subsequent reduction of funds for the OTN, the team is now entirely voluntary.

5. "Local" is a word, in this instance, used by the CTU movement to describe any *encuentro* smaller than the national *encuentro*, which could mean anything ranging from an individual CTU or the meeting of all CTUs in a state.

6. Other spaces, such as the National Meeting and the Caracas Metropolitan Assembly, are also important in advancing the political agenda of the movement. The point being made here is that the moment of *encuentro* crystallizes the politics of the movement and clarifies where the movement is in its national development.

7. In Spanish, *conocer* and *saber* both mean "to know." However, the former suggests a subjective knowledge derived from direct experience and therefore not completely knowable to anyone else, while the latter is a form of objective knowledge that can be easily replicated, interpreted and transferred.

References

Campbell, T. (2003), *My Big TOE: Awakening*, Lightening Strike Books.

de Souza, M. L. (2006), "Together with the State, Despite the State, Against the State: Social Movements as 'critical urban planning' agents," *City* 10(3): pp. 327–342.

Decree No. 1666, *Mediante el cual se inicia el proceso de regularización de la tenencia de la tierra en los asentamientosurbanospopulares* (2002), Official Gazette of the Bolivarian Republic of Venezuela, No. 37,378, February 4, 2002.

Fadda, C. G. (1987), *Discurso, Político y Praxis Urbano: Caracas 1973–1983*, unpublished PhD thesis, Universidad Central de Venezuela.

Freire, P. (1972), *Pedagogy of the Oppressed*, Middlesex: Penguin Books.

García-Guadilla, M. P. (2006), "Ciudadanía, inclusión y autonomía en lasorganizacionessocialesbolivarianas: los comités de tierraurbana," paper presented at the Latin American Studies Association International Congress, San Juan, Puerto Rico, March 15–18, 2006.

Hart, Gillian (2002), *Disabling Globalization: Places of Power in Post-Apartheid South Africa*, Berkeley: University of California Press.

Harvey, D. (2000), *Spaces of Hope*, Edinburgh: Edinburgh University Press.

Hawkins, K. A. and Hansen, D. R. (2006), "Dependent Civil Society: The Circulos Bolivarianos in Venezuela," *Latin American Research Review* 41(1): pp. 102–132.

hooks, b. (1994), *Teaching to Transgress: Education as the Practice of Freedom*, New York and London: Routledge.

Kane, L. (2001), *Popular Education and Social Change in Latin America*, London: Latin America Bureau.

Lefebvre, H. (1991), *The Production of Space* (trans. D. Nicholson-Smith), Malden, MA and Oxford: Editions Anthropos.

—— (2009), *State, Space, World: Selected Essays* (ed. Neil Brenner and Stuart Elden), Minneapolis and London: University of Minnesota Press.

Martinez, J. L. (2011), *Comites de Tierra Urbana (CTUs) and the "Right to the City": Urban Transformation in Venezuela's Bolivarian Revolution*, unpublished PhD thesis, University of Nottingham, UK.

Motta, S. C. (2011), "Notes towards Prefigurative Epistemologies," in Motta, S. C. and Nilsen, A. G. (eds.), *Social Movements in the Global South: Dispossession, Development and Resistance*, Basingstoke: Palgrave Macmillan.

Pithouse, R. (2006), "Our Struggle Is Thought, On the Ground, Running: The University of Abahlali Basemjondolo," *Center for Civil Society Research Reports* 1(40), http://ccs.ukzn.ac.za/files/RReport3a.pdf (accessed May 12, 2011).

Scott, J. C. (1998), *Seeing Like a State: How Certain Schemes to Improve the Human Condition Have Failed*, New Haven and London: Yale University Press.

Slater, D. (2004), *Geopolitics and the Post-Colonial: Rethinking North-South Relations*, Oxford: Blackwell.

Torres, C. A. (1990), *The Politics of Nonformal Education in Latin America*, London: Praeger.

Wilpert, G. (2003), "Collision in Venezuela," *New Left Review* 21: pp. 101–116.

——— (2007), *Changing Venezuela by Taking Power: The History and Policies of the Chávez Government*, London and New York: Verso.

Chapter 10

Which Education for Which Democracy?: The Case of the Penguins' Revolution in Chile*

Ivette Hernandez Santibañez

In October 2011, I joined a student march called by the Confederation of Chilean Students (CONFECH), the Coordinating Assembly of Secondary Students (ACES) and the National Coordinating Committee of Secondary Students (CONES) in a street near the Alameda Avenue in the city of Santiago de Chile. While marching I encountered an old man holding a small banner with two little penguins drawn on it. I asked him why he held a banner with this drawing. He replied that what Chile witnessed in 2011 had been a process that secondary students, called the Penguins because of their school uniform, had begun in 2006 when they demanded education is a right and not a privilege.

The Penguins' Revolution emerged between April 20 and June 9, 2006, when social protests led by hundreds of thousands of students aged between 13 and 17 marked the appearance of the largest social protests of the post-Pinochet democratic era. The students demanded structural changes in the education system and questioned the neo-liberal agenda implemented under the Concertación (center-left) governing political coalition in power since the return to democracy in 1989. They made visible the failure of these reforms by making public the crisis of inequality of opportunity for quality education that mostly affected students from the most disadvantaged socio-economic sectors. Their demands included improvement of schools' infrastructure, more and better school meals, the elimination of fees for national college exam (PSU) and free student public transport. The students also called for structural demands by demanding the elimination of the *Ley Organica Constitucional de Enseñanza*, known as the LOCE; the end of municipalization; and reform of the Full-School Day, known as the JEC. The Penguins' Revolution legitimized social mobilization by encouraging a society—characterized by social and political demobilization—to mobilize and participate in what the secondary students defined as "the major restructuring of the Chilean model of education (Diaz, 2008)."[1] Their protest also revealed the emergence of new political subjectivities and democratic structures of participation that put in question the quality of the democracy political elites had consolidated since the beginning of the 1990s.

Thus far there have been various attempts to explain and theorize the impact of the Penguins' Revolution in the field of education policy analysis (see Bellei et al., 2010; Inzunza, 2009; Kremerman, 2007; OPECH, 2009; Redondo and Munoz, 2009). Nevertheless such attempts have often left underanalyzed or even unanalyzed (1) the political activism that the Penguins' Revolution expressed; (2) the processes through which this political activism emerged and what role such political articulation had in the "massive and well-articulated critique of Chilean schooling" (Pinkney Pastrana, 2010, p. 32); and (3) the emergence of new political subjects and projects that challenge not only neoliberal education and neoliberal hegemony in Chilean society.

This essay aims to map, understand and conceptualize the reconstruction and building of youth political activism in the emergent spaces and subjectivities of resistance of the Penguins' Revolution. It is based upon a number of unstructured interviews with Chilean students carried out in 2011 (see table 10.1).

Table 10.1 School geographic categories of secondary students from 2006 and 2000/2001

Secondary students	2000/2001	2006
1) Municipal elite school/ Santiago centre	3	12
2) Municipal non-elite school/ Santiago centre	1	3
3) Municipal school/Metropolitan region/Other region		2
4) Subsidized school/ Metropolitan region		5
5) Private school/Metropolitan region/Other region		3

The Emergence of Social Movements in the Latin American Region

As Motta (2009, p. 32) explains, "With the advent of democracy, it is argued, social movement activity declines" and yet across the region we have seen the rise of social movements that are "arguably reimagining politics and social and political change." Across the continent processes of neoliberal reform occurred and were responded to by social movements who struggle against "privatization processes, structural adjustment programs and dismantling processes of national states" (Zibechi, 2006, p. 221). As a result of their social mobilization and public protest, the political scenario in the region has gradually been transformed and made visible at the governmental level through the emergence of the "so-called progressive or left-wing governments" (Zibechi, 2010) in countries such as Bolivia, Venezuela, Ecuador and to some extent Argentina. However, in the often less visible realities of popular organizations there has also been an emergence of a plethora of Latin American Social Movements (LASMs). They are diverse and characterized by multiplicity (Melucci, 1996) with daily life, a major focus around which, cultural, economic, political and social struggles are articulated. As Motta argues (2009, p. 36), they "do not separate economic struggle from a struggle to create social relations based on dignity and human realization."

Their increasing systemic differentiation allows them to locate oppression beyond traditional relationships of production since they emphasize new forms of oppression based on excesses of regulation of modernity that affect ways of work and production, ways of life, poverty and asymmetries of social relations (see Santos, 2001). LASMs are reinventing the spaces of politics by relocating them in their everyday experiences. They move toward a territorialization of their demands. The latter implies that they are involved in a new political praxis of place-based subjectivities of "localised, yet linked self-governing communities" (Denis, 2006; Motta, 2006).

In positioning politics in everydayness and territoriality, the LASMs construct new political praxis and subjectivities through horizontal structures in which assemblies became a commonplace form of organization. In such horizontal structures, the LASMs break with traditional forms of participation and hierarchies by emphasizing principles of *horizontalidad or horizontalism* as a way of "social relationship, a way of being and relating" (Sitrin, 2010) and equal democratic participation in order to avoid fragmentation, exclusion, atomization and unequal access to information.

The Rise of the Neoliberal Chilean
Education Model

In this scenario Chile appears as a paradoxical case: since the return to democracy politics has been demobilized by a center-left government that actively displaced the role of social movements by developing a strategy of "growth with equity," which continued the neoliberal economic and political reforms implemented under the Pinochet military dictatorship (1973–1989).

Such a neoliberal reform, referred to as the "Chilean model," was ideologically designed by a group of Chilean economists known as the Chicago Boys because of their attachment to Milton Friedman's neoliberal economic theories at the University of Chicago. After a military coup overthrew the democratically elected leftist government of Salvador Allende in 1973, the Pinochet regime adopted the Chicago Boys neoliberal economic ideas as its own ideological and economic program with the purpose of transforming and modernizing welfare institutions and welfare policies through introduction of a free-market economy as the main regulator mechanism of health, education and pension systems.

Since the beginning of the 1990s the new democratic governments of the Concertacion embraced the legacy of Pinochet's neoliberal economic reform, which was acknowledged as the second trajectory of the Chilean experiment of a neoliberal state. The governments of the Concertacion (1990–2010) initiated a development strategy of "growth with equity" as a political program that stood between social democracy and free-market capitalism and as a "potential Third Way option for Latin America" (Taylor, 2006, p. 5).

In the field of educational policies, the development strategy of growth with equity was argued to be the optimal route to make quality education available for all. Such an approach reflected a new focus by the Concertacion on social democracy and economic policies as "equality of opportunities rather than of outcome" (Keaney, 2005, p. 30) in a mixed educational policy paradigm of "market or choice models and state or integration models" (Cox, 2003, p. 19).

Yet, the nature and impact of such a reformed second-generation neoliberal trajectory began to be questioned in 2006 when high school students mobilized against the lack of equal opportunities to quality education. The emergence of the Penguins' Revolution publicly revealed that such a reformed template of neoliberalism had failed. It had deepened both unequal opportunities for quality education and socioeconomic stratification of schools to the extent that inequality and segmentation had acquired an "institutionalized character" (Garcia Huidobro, 2006) in the Chilean education system.

The Secondary Student Movement: Undertaking a Political Diagnosis

The reconstruction of the Chilean secondary student movement took place in such a political scenario. The process was mainly led by political groups, known as colectivos; left-wing political groups such as some militants from the Communist Youth; some political groups linked to factions of the MIR;[2] students from the MJL;[3] autonomous students and anarchist students. The political aim of these groups was to enlarge the student movement beyond the frontiers of what they called "the historical emblematic schools located in the centre of city of Santiago" to politicize those students and those families who were deeply non-politicized and who did not represent what was known as a traditional left-wing family in Chile. As Julio, president of the FESES[4] 2000, explained in 2011:

> We were very concerned about doing politics for the same people. In fact we saw each other in all marches [. . .] we wanted to see other faces and when we imagined those other faces, we thought about common and ordinary families who were deeply non-politicized.

This was also underlined by Ursula, former spokesperson of ACES 2001:

> We should deal with a new reality and a new actor we would like to engage in the movement. This new actor will not be willing to participate in a march about justice for the missing detained people, because of he or she may not even have an idea about missing detained people in Chile. You should understand that the dictatorship was taken away from history in the curriculum. I remember that the history of Chile went as far as the military coup and there was nothing about the dictatorship in the curriculum.

Important for the new emerging movement and colectivos was transformation of traditional ways of building and doing politics within the secondary student movement so that it would become more than, as Julio continues, "a small circle of political leaders the student movement has always transformed into." Thus a bottom-up process was led by the colectivos and students who were not involved in existing spaces of political participation such as the FESES or institutional invited spaces as the Association of Students Representative Bodies from Santiago known as ACAS.[5] The students argued that both formal student organizations lacked representativeness and legitimatization because of the bureaucratic machine they had become and the political clientelism involved. In reconstructing the student movement, the secondary students aimed to build a new political movement and subject by politicizing the social and socializing the political.

Such political practices facilitated the emergence of a political actor who recognized his own political construction as one that did not carry ties to an inherited political identity or culture. As Patricia highlighted in 2011:

> We are very abandoned by politics; I think we are an orphan generation. We have made ourselves loners, step by step. It was because of…what the closest political reference is for us? I think it is the Surda from the 1990s perhaps, but the Surda was destroyed by the Communist party […] so we do not have any inheritance, we do not have anyone to ask. It makes us lack political expertise. However I think that after a social construction period like Chile experienced during the military dictatorship and civil governments it would seem normal that there is a missing generation such as ours.

This student's narrative makes visible a dilemma for those of us trying to understand this emergent student movement. On one hand the movement shares some of the common tendencies already identified in existing social movements in Latin America (see Motta, 2009; Sitrin, 2010; Zibechi, 2003) but on the other, it came about through a process in which the political and social had been disarticulated and atomized through a political transition that turned Chile into the most neoliberal Latin American country.

In the following I hope to deepen our understanding and engagement with this emergent political actor and new forms of politics. I focus on the historical development of the movement to then conceptualize three areas of its development: territoriality, subjectivity and participation.

Emergence of the Penguins' Revolution

In a mixed educational paradigm characterized by "market or choice models and state or integration models" (Cox, 2003, p. 19), the Penguins' Revolution emerges from and within. Through their political protests of 2006, the students demanded education as a right not a privilege. Their social protest prompted an exponential social debate concerning what education, the right to education and freedom to education meant by repositioning education in its political dimension. The students also relegitimized social mobilization and protest by redefining what democracy means for a generation that had grown up in a post-democratic demobilized transition era, as Maria Huerta, spokesperson of the Political Committee of AES, described in an interview in 2006:

> Democracy means that we have the right to think, to speak, to criticize and others should do the same, etc. So obviously, in my opinion this is what a person must do. That is, you have to understand that we are exercising a right.

Their protests challenged and broke down the dominant structures of participation and representation that had been sustaining democratic rule in Chile. As Patricia explained in 2011:

> Most left wing people did not know the colectivos and they did not understand the Assembly. So these forms of participation challenged those traditional forms of political and social participation.

Emerging from a depoliticized and disarticulated social and political context this raises questions about how the Penguins' Revolution learnt this sort of knowledge about democracy and participation. It also raises questions about what new political subjects and subjectivities are emerging in this rearticulation of politics. To examine these questions involves focusing on the dynamics of the micro-politics of everyday interaction and organization (Motta, 2009).

In research about the emergence of LASMs, it is acknowledged how territoriality constitutes one of the most distinctive features of new forms of popular politics. The role of territoriality does not just mean physical appropriation of a place but also the symbolic appropriation of a territory, as a social construction intertwined with new social relationships and political subjectivities. So while social movements such as the Landless Movement, the autonomous piqueteros or the Ecuadorian indigenous are recuperating their lands, territories and factories (Caldart, 2000; Davalos, 2001; Zibechi, 2003), similarly Chilean students began to occupy schools. The students reappropriated this space as a territory in which they positioned themselves as new political actors that attempt to transform the modes of domination of a neoliberal (education) system.

The Generative Past of New Political
Subjectivities in the Penguins' Revolution

The Chilean secondary student movement, as with many LASMs, reflects new forms of politics that challenge existing modes of domination and enact a distancing from centralized and hierarchical structures that marked modes of participation, grassroots organizing and decision-making (Foweraker, 2001) of social movements and popular politics in the past. The contemporary LASMs practice autonomy from traditional forms of political power by organizing spaces of participation in which horizontalism and direct democracy are the cornerstone of their democratic decision-making processes.

The reconstruction of the secondary student movement was modeled and fashioned by the Coordinating Assembly of Secondary Students (ACES) and the Coordinating of Revolutionary Autonomous Students (CREA). Such a process was led by colectivos, nonformal political groups, who created spaces as spaces of horizontalism and direct democracy—both practised in Assembly work and independent from institutional power. The colectivos became spaces for alternative politics, populated, as Victor explained in 2011, "with anarchist ideas but they were also politically led by some far-left political groups, such as Groups of Popular Action known as GAP," who were inspired by the revolutionary ideas of Guevarism. In the secondary student movement, the colectivos emerged by focusing neither on becoming a political structure like a political party nor a social organization. As Lucas explained in 2011:

> They came to be formed as spaces that developed and replaced the lack of political leadership and orientated and systematized the political lines in the secondary student movement.

The emergence of colectivos also occurred as Victor described in 2011 "because of the political and cultural crisis the left was involved in." In a bottom-up process the colectivos instilled the need to transform the FESES and its traditional vertical spaces of politics. As Julio explained in 2011:

> There were an important group of militants at the Communist Youth who understood the need of reforming the FESES. So, in implementing this reform we opened the organization up to those student organizations which did not respond to the most structured profile that the FESES had had.

The ACES displaced the FESES as the leading secondary student organization. The ACES endorsed a new logic of democratic participation based on principles of horizontal participation, direct democracy and representation led by a spokespersons' committee instead of a leadership group. Student mobilizations in March and April 2001, known as the rucksack or *el mochilazo*, led to an exponential increase in the number of high schools that adopted the Assembly as their main space of democratic participation and came to participate in the ACES. Such an expansion constituted a pivotal step in the task of transmitting this experience and continuing with the construction of the secondary student movement. These created the conditions of possibility out of which the Penguins' Revolution emerged.

From this time the ACES and the CREA prioritized articulation of the movement with schools from the peripheral areas of Santiago as these were seen as pivotal in expanding the participation and legitimization of the student movement. The inclusion of periphery schools whose participation in the student movement came from their daily life struggles rather than from a politically well-structured critique of education was given value by the newly emerging student organization. As Julio explains, in the student movement students from peripheral schools became a political actor by not "politicizing reality from the politics, it is an actor that has followed a different way that is, this actor has politicized his own reality."

In 2004, existing colectivos joined the Rebel Cordon of Autonomous Students (CREAR) to assign colectivos the task of developing politics, leading political debates, making political propaganda and developing political organization at schools. The CREAR played a key role in building the political and organizational conditions for the emergence of the Penguins' Revolution in 2006 by fostering political reflection within the movement and expanding its political articulation to schools from peripheral communes in Greater Santiago (Metropolitan Region).

The Penguins' Revolution linked its own political construction to the heritage of the ACES and the CREA. It is reasonable to think that such a contribution has not been static. Rather it came about as a process in which inherited political identities, understandings of old politics and the production of new alternative politics have contributed in different ways to the construction of a novel student movement, as Pablo reflected in 2011:

> At that time we still maintained some traditions from the left and dictatorship like being and acting clandestinely; it was more common in the past years [...] We were quite clandestine for everything ... e*h*m in 2006 we broke up with this; I mean we went to streets with our bare hands and unveiled faces; it was quite interesting too.

Table 10.2   Work proposal of secondary students from metropolitan region

Commissions	Subcategories
Public education and state role	Municipal education
	Private guarantors
	Corporations
Full school day reform (JEC)	
Sports and Arts	
Students' Centers	Lack of information
	School councils
	Dialogue with the Ministry of Education
	Modifications of Decree 524
Community and environment	
Sexuality	
Technical and vocational education	
Transport	Loss of student pass
	Internship student pass
	Students from Province of Talagante

Source: Estudiantes Secundarios de la R.M. (2005) (Author's translation).

In 2005 various student organizations, such as ACAS, ACES, CREAR and the Public Education Front led by the Communist Youth, gathered and created the Coordination of Secondary Students from the Metropolitan Region (CEREM). In April 2005, they accepted an invitation from the regional secretary of the Ministry of Education from Metropolitan Region (SEREMI) to schedule a work agenda. Between April and November 2005, secondary students worked on and elaborated a document in which they identified what issues needed to be addressed and changed in the Chilean education system (table 10.2).

The work agenda and the final document later turned into what was known as the short and long agenda of education. This was the first attempt by the secondary school students to put forward their demands at an institutional level. This experience taught the students to politicize their demands and to be mobilized beyond conjectural issues, as Pablo explained in 2011:

> We planned mobilizations in 2006 involving different zones from Santiago and some students from the regions. In this assembly we reaffirmed what we talked about in 2005. That is, we are not going to be concerned about the conjuncture. It will not be our main concern. And we are not going to leave mobilizations although the conjuncture is resolved. This time we will attack from other sides, we will touch the system.

The Assembly as an Expansion of the Politics of Horizontalism and the Politics of Difference

Lefebvre (1991) contends that every space is a social product constructed by its own history and woven in this process with "the traces of other histories, in other spaces, its own generative past" (p. 110). In the Penguins' Revolution the Assembly of Secondary Students (AES) expanded largely in high schools in the city of Santiago and in some cities across the country. Such an expansion seemed to disclose a "generative past" (p. 110) interwoven with the role played by colectivos and other political groups in the building of new spaces for social and political participation and the articulation of new types of politics and political actors.

The AES came to be recognized as the main political structure upon which the secondary students articulated their participation and deliberation in the decision-making process in 2006. As Juan Carlos highlighted in 2008, expansion of AES in 2006 aimed at installing methods of democratic participation developed by the colectivos since 2001, "inside schools, inside schools and to articulate responsibilities among secondary students by following the principle of revocability based on their peer evaluation."

In the Penguins' Revolution, the principle of horizontalism aimed to develop the equal participation of students as Estefania pointed out in 2011 "without giving more importance to one actor over the other." This meant that the Assembly was opened to everyone who wanted to participate without excluding students who did not participate or run student groups at their schools. The movement believed, as Estefania argued, that "horizontal participation was the way through which discussion could be spread in order to develop political consciousness about education in Chile." Horizontalism seemed to contribute to the development of solidarity and cohesion among secondary students participating in assemblies in different territorial zones in Greater Santiago. Equal participation in the Assembly allowed students to share their everyday experience of lack of equal opportunity and to recognize their experiences in others as Maria Jesus explained to Domedel and Pena y Lillo in 2008:

> 95% of the secondary students share an absolutely common reality. It is the reason why the assembly has come to acquire so much relevance for them. It is due to the fact that the assembly is a horizontal and open space. It would not matter if all students are Marxist or from other political backgrounds because, what is allowing our unity with those of different existing views within the assembly, is the way in which we are living.

In a process that "expanded the horizons of the political" (Motta, 2009. p. 43) the Assembly became a space for producing an ethics of politics as a model of political youth activism displayed in 2006 as Maria Jesus emphasized:

> That day, there was a demonstration and the government attempted to put down mobilized students. I think they invited us to that house to see if they could arrange with us something that would put down the mobilizations. But they did not recognize yet that we were an assembly, the spokespersons were the Assembly and the Assembly had "vocerias" or committees that were just one thing. (Diaz, 2008)[6]

The division of the Assembly into six territorial zones[7] played a key role in spreading information, giving voice to the voiceless and challenging "power relations and the ways things are commonly done" (Cleaver, 2007), as Estefania expressed in 2011:

> The assembly was mainly led by three or four voices. These students always came to the assembly, they always talked and most of them were students from the most prestigious state schools or emblematic schools. So, if a student talked about a different reality to that of the emblematic schools, his or her opinion was disregarded. Nevertheless, it changed when the Assembly was divided into four territorial zones. Through its division, new educational territorial unities emerged. Much more of these territorial unities shared common educational realities which allowed demands of these sectors to be made visible.

Participation as a produced space is always a site for appropriation and reconstruction. Thus it "may be created with one purpose in mind, but used by those who come to fill them for something quite different" (Cornwall, 2002, p. 9). In the Penguins' Revolution, the division of the Assembly allowed schools from different territorial units to autonomously lead their decision-making processes and to infuse production of these spaces with meaning and demands that derived from the different daily life struggles they were engaged in. For example, secondary students from elite state schools in the center zone defined student conflict as the result of a lack of equal educational opportunities and social mobility. Yet, secondary students from peripheral communes from Greater Santiago identified the conflict as one about imposed ways of constructing life and social relationships that do not allow the development of a human being. Thus, students from peripheral communes identified their political struggle against ways of life imposed by neoliberalism rather than against the exclusion it creates. As Juan Carlos explained in 2008: "The majority of organizations on the left, they do not like to be included (...) they work upon idea of transforming ways of life, did you get it? And it is because of this political understanding: it is clear that capitalism is not just about economy, did you get it? It is also about culture and in this way it produces ways of life upon which it is based on."

The emergence of territoriality and the key role it played in defining student struggles in 2006 underscored the fact that these new political subjects neither came from a traditional left-wing family nor had been politicized by traditional left-wing political discourse and culture. They came from the periphery and became politicized because of the contradictions that an uneven geographical development of neoliberalism had brought into their lives.

Occupations as Places and Spaces for Producing Politics in the Penguins' Revolution

Occupations of high schools turned into a key space to expand the horizons of politics in the Penguins' Revolution. On May 19, 2006, students occupied the two most prestigious municipal high schools in Santiago: the Liceo de Aplicacion and the Instituto Nacional. The occupations were planned in January 2006 as a political strategy to install structural demands within mobilized schools and to change negative public opinion about student mobilizations. As Pablo explained:

> We planned occupations in January 2006 as a political strategy in the movement [...] as we were always hit in streets we decided to occupy schools; it was a discourse of victimization...yet it allowed us to legitimize occupations [...] of course occupations constituted a stronger administrative pressure as schools stop working; we occupy spaces [...] and occupations allowing us to develop activities [...] through occupations we could debate and talk in depth about our demands; they became a space for reflection [...] thus our demands encouraged an important debate e*h*m...and at level of political debate they become stronger.

After May 19, 2006, the secondary students started progressively occupying their schools. As a consequence, on June 3 about 520 schools were occupied and 172 schools went on strike across the country. Occupations allowed the emergence of alternative narratives that reappropriated schools as territories with different social relationships and meanings. As a secondary student explained in 2006:

> The experience of spending the time together has been excellent...the same, thinking like in the future, after this, did you get it?...ehm...getting back to the school for those who have been here, sacrificing themselves for the movement, this won't be the same again [...] now it is our home...now...school will really be our second home...now yes, it will be a different story.[8]

Such a notion constitutes "places as social relations" (Massey, 1993), which endow students with "self-affirmative forms" (Zibechi, 2003) in producing politics. As Patricia explained:

> I learnt we could do things; I do not how to explain it in words but somehow the political work gives results and one is able to get involved...every one of us is able to build herself through a political reflection which has to be based on involving people in my own reflection rather than to attempt to convince them. Moreover, it may also imply being united to do something and it also implies being part of a collective process. Then the occupation meant this.

Moreover, such an expansion of "the horizons of the political" (Motta, 2009) entailed transformations of *power-geometry* (Massey, 1993) of politics and how it was a process that developed. As Pablo reflected in 2011:

> I remember we received a call from an occupied school in the commune of San Bernardo; they call us quite dissatisfied as they did not have an answer from the Assembly and nobody had talked to them; they wanted an answer about...I do not remember what exactly the issue was [...] we came to the school; it was in a vulnerable neighbourhood [...] ehm drugs trafficking; when we arrived all students were waiting an answer from us; they listened to us quietly; nobody threw us a paper or nobody was disrespectful; you would think that it could not happen in a school like this; I mean a teacher probably could not manage to have a quiet class; yet we achieved this. I thought what is this? What is going here?...We can. It was tremendously important for me.

In a sense to argue for new power-geometries of politics in the Penguins' Revolution is to recognize the contributions these new political actors have made in expanding the horizons of politics. In becoming politicized from their daily life struggles rather than from formal politics they have opened the possibilities for multiplicity, radical difference and interconnections across differences to the extent that as Nicolas explained in 2011, the Penguins' Revolution constitutes "a historic breakthrough of a new student movement."

Concluding Remarks

The most frequent question I am asked regarding the Penguins' Revolution is: what can be learnt from this student movement from 2006?

Probably, the answer places the Penguins' Revolution as a student movement that spoke out before they announced what was "taking shape and before its direction and content had become clear" (Melucci, 1996, p. 1). As Patricia reflected in 2011: "Most of us were not aware that by questioning the end of profit-making education we were attacking the essential axis of neo-liberalism in Chile."

There is a strong focus on a process that builds upon the intrinsic contradictions that neoliberalism generates by reappropriating territories as places and spaces for producing new political subjectivities.

The Penguins' Revolution challenged the hegemony of the Concertación when students demanded that education is a right and not a privilege, and when they called for more participation in the Chilean education system and in the post-transition democracy. The question about which education for which democracy disclosed that the mixed educational paradigm of the 1990s was designed by political elites in conformity with a negotiated democratic transition and the neoliberal development model for a generation that did not carry ties with the traumas. Yet for the students their histories were neither defined by political defeat and dictatorship nor often by past political identities. So, they not only questioned the Chilean model of education, they also demanded and practiced a redefined democracy. The redefinition and reinvention of politics, as they argued, marks them as the sons and daughters of democracy who were not afraid to raise their political voices.

The secondary student movement in 2006 made public new political subjectivities that on the one hand put in question the idea of youth as socially and politically indifferent to everything and on the other expanded the horizons of politics by placing at the center of these new political subjectivities, the role the colectivos played as "submerged networks" (Melucci, 1996) and political spaces upon which students made themselves into political subjects.

Territoriality became central in the Penguins' Revolution in 2006. As Motta (2009, p. 43) highlights, expanding the horizons of the political encompasses "re-conceptualization of the nature of structure and the relationship between place and space." In the Penguins' Revolution such reconceptualization emerged through occupations at high schools in which mobilized secondary students reappropriated places and spaces through new narratives and practices of social relations.

In 2006, the secondary students took a step further when they challenged dominant narratives of the marketization of education. They positioned their struggle as one that represented a sign of hope and solidarity and that opened a new political horizon. As Maria Huerta explained in 2006: "Education is a matter that is present in all aspects of life. There is no place in society where education is not present. As students we are conscious of it as it involves our own lives and the lives of future generations." This opens discussion regarding to what extent social movements, such as the Penguins' Revolution, have made a step forward in placing their demands as an intergenerational responsibility that some authors have exclusively attributed to ecological movements or rather what the Penguins' Revolution seems to bring into discussion was the need to reexamine analytical tools to analyze the capacity social movements have to speak before they announce what was taking shape and processes in which they are constantly reinventing "the meaning and practice of the political" (Motta, 2009, p. 49).

Notes

*Analysis and interpretation addressed in this chapter is based on emerging research findings from interviews conducted in Santiago de Chile in 2011 as part of field studies for a doctoral thesis on the Chilean student movement.

1. Spokesperson of the Secondary Student Assembly (AES) and the National Assembly of Secondary Students (ANES). Available at http://www.youtube.com/watch?v=cnxXyzvjTbk&feature=channel.
2. MIR (Revolutionary Left Movement).
3. Movimiento Juvenil Lautaro (MJL; Lautaro Youth Movement)
4. Federación de Estudiantes de Santiago (FESES; Students' Federation from Santiago).
5. Asociacion de Centros de Alumnos de Santiago (ACAS; Association of Student Representative Bodies from Santiago).
6. Available at http://www.youtube.com/watch?v=cnxXyzvjTbk&feature =channel.
7. In May 2006, secondary students divided the AES into six territorial zones: north, south, eastern, western, center and regions.
8. Available at http://www.youtube.com/watch?v=ZvyHZYBdzOM &feature=channel.

References

Bellei, C., Contreras, D. and Valenzuela, J. P. (2010), *Ecos de la Revolucion Pinguina: Avances, debates y silencios en la reforma educacional*, Santiago de Chile: Universidad de Chile.

Caldart, R. (2000), *Pedagogia do Movimento Sem Terra*, Petropolis: Vozes.

Cleaver, F. (2007), "Understanding Agency in Collective Action," *Journal of Human Development and Capabilities* 8(2): pp. 223–244.

Cornwall, A. (2002), "Making Spaces, Changing Pplaces: Situating Participation in Development," http://www.powercube.net/wpcontent/uploads/2009/11/making_spaces_changing_places.pf (accessed April 29, 2010).

Cox, C. (2003), "Las políticas educacionales de Chile en las últimas dos décadas del siglo XX," in Cox, C. (ed.), *Políticas educacionales en el cambio de siglo La reforma del sistema escolar*, Santiago de Chile: Editorial Universitaria.

Davalos, P. (2001), "Fiesta y poder: El ritual de la toma en el movimiento indígena," *Boletin ICCI* "Rymay" 3(37), http://icci.nativeweb.org/boletin/23/davalos.html (accessed, August 30, 2012).

Denis, R. (2006), *Las claves teóricas del proyecto Nuestra America*, Caracas: Nuestra America.

Diaz, L. J. (Director) (2008), *La Revolucion de los Pinguinos*, DVCam, Chile: Santiago de Chile.

Domedel, A. and Pena y Lillo, M. (2008), *El Mayo de los Pinguinos*, Santiago de Chile: Ediciones Radio Universidad de Chile.

Estudiantes Secundarios de la R. M. (2005), "Propuesta de Trabajo de Estudiantes Secundarios de la R.M.," http://www.opech.cl/bibliografico/doc_movest/finalccaa.pdf (accessed, January 23, 2008).

Foweraker, J. (2001), "Grassroots Movements and Political Activism in Latin America: A Critical Comparison of Chile and Brazil," *Journal of Latin American Studies* 33: pp. 839–865.

Garcia Huidobro, J. E. (2006), "La reforma educacional chilena y la educación pública," in Bonal, X. (ed.), *Globalizacion, Educacion y Pobreza en America Latina ¿Hacia una nueva agenda politica?* Barcelona: CIDOB.

Huerta, M. (2006), Interview with Maria Huerta, student leader: "El derecho a la educación es lo primero," Programa Interdisciplinario de Investigacion en Educacion, PIIE, http://www.piie.cl/entrevistas/maria_huerta.htm (accessed, September 4, 2011).

Inzunza, J. (2009), *La construccion del derecho a la educación y la institucionalidad educativa en Chile*, http://www.opech.cl/Libros/doc2.pdf (accessed September 4, 2011).

Keaney, M. (2005), "Social Democracy, Laissez-Faire and the 'Third Way' of Capitalist Development," *Review of Radical Politics Economics* 37(3): pp. 357–378.

Kremerman, M. (2007), *Radiografia del Financiamiento de la Educacion Chilena: Diagnostico, Analisis y Propuestas. Por una Educacion Universal,*

Gratuita y de Calidad, http://www.opech.cl/inv/investigaciones/Kremer man_Radiografia_Financiamiento_Educacion.pdf (accessed September 4, 2011).

Lefebvre, H. (1991), *The Production of Space*, London: Verso.

Massey, D. (1993), "Power-Geometry and a Progressive Sense of Place," in Bird, J., Curtis, B., Putnam, T., Robertson, G. and Tickner, L. (eds.), *Mapping the Futures Local Cultures, Global Change*, London: Routledge.

Melucci, A. (1996), *Challenging Codes: Collective Action in the Information Age*, Cambridge: Cambridge University Press.

Motta, S. (2009), "Old Tools and New Movements in Latin America: Political Science as Gatekeeper or Intellectual Illuminator?" *Latin American Politics Society* 51(1): pp. 31–56, http://onlinelibrary.wiley.com/10.1111/j.1548-2456.2009.00039x/pdf (accessed February 4, 2011).

Motta, S. (2006), "Utopias Re-imagined: A Reply to Panizza," *Political Studies* 54(4): pp. 898–905.

Observatorio de Politicas Educativas (OPECH) (2009), "Documentos de Trabajo OPECH: La búsqueda de un sentido común no privatizado," http://www.opech.cl/Libros/doc1.pdf (accessed July 4, 2010).

Pinkney-Pastrana, J. (2010), "A Wolf in Sheep's Clothing or a Sheep in Wolf's Clothing: Resistance to Educational Reform in Chile," in Macrine, S., McLaren, P. and Hill, D. (eds.), *Revolutionizing Pedagogy. Education for Social Justice Within and Beyond Global Neo-Liberalism*, New York: Palgrave MacMillan.

Redondo, J. and Munoz, L. (2009), "Juventud y Ensenanza Media en Chile del Bicentenario. Antecedentes de la Revolucion Pinguina," http://www.opech.cl/Libros/doc4.pdf (accessed July 4, 2010).

Santos, Boaventura de Sousa (2001), "Los nuevos movimientos sociales," http://www.boaventuradesousasantos.pt/media/pdfs/Los_nuevos_movimientos_sociales_OSAL2001.PDF (accessed April 29, 2010).

Sitrin, M. (2010), "Horizontalism," http://marinasitrin.com/?page_id=108 (accessed April 29, 2012).

Taylor, M. (2006), *From Pinochet to the "Third Way," Neoliberalism and Social Transformation in Chile*, London: Pluto Press.

Zibechi, R. (2010), "Interview with Raul Zibechi," http://bibliotecavirtual.clacso.org/ar/libros/osal/osal21/Zibechi.pdf (accessed April 29, 2012).

Zibechi, R. (2006), "Movimientos sociales: nuevos escenarios y desafíos inéditos," http://bibliotecavirtual.clacso.org.ar/ar/libros/osal/osal21/Zibechi.pdf (accessed April 29, 2010).

Zibechi, R. (2003), "Los movimientos sociales latinoamericanos: tendencias y desafíos," http://bibliotecavirtual.clacso.org.ar/ar/libros/osal/osal9/zibechi.pdf (accessed May 17, 2012).

Chapter 11

Experiential and Relational Dimensions in the Pedagogical Practice of Solidarity Economy: Insights from Brazil

Ana Margarida Esteves

On the Importance of "Border Pedagogies" and "World-Traveling" Identities

Giroux (1991) claims that a basic trait of an effective popular educa-tion methodology is that of being a "border pedagogy," a pedagogical practice that de-centers participants from their own taken-for-granted realities, leading them to transform their identities and remap norms, meanings, social relations and subjectivities in an emancipatory manner. Adriana Hernández (1997) argues that at the core of such transformative process is the development of the capacity for "world-traveling," to mediate between the mainstream and oppressed groups, as well as to empathically understand the worldview and living condi-tions of the "other." A basic question arising from Hernández and Giroux's claims is how, and in what circumstances, do participants in popular education initiatives gain the skills necessary to become world-travelers. So far, the focus of analysis has been on the skills and attitudes necessary for educators/coordinators to assume such a role (Darder, 2002). It is therefore important to develop empirical, case study-based analyses of the kind of life histories and dynamics between what Paulo Freire calls "coordinators" and "educatee-educators" that contribute to the development of world-traveling identities.

This chapter analyzes the construction of a "border pedagogy" by the Brazilian Solidarity Economy movement, and how it contributes to the construction of world-traveling activist identities and counter-hegemonic economic practices. It calls attention to the need for tak-ing into account the impact of differentials in knowledge, experience and worldviews among participants, as well as of personal relationships based on affinity and affect established in the framework of popular education initiatives. This chapter is illustrated with fieldwork data, collected between July 2008 and July 2009, on the activities of one participant network: The Cooperative Network of Women Entrepreneurs (CNWE), based in Rio de Janeiro.

Toward a Socioeconomic Pedagogy of Liberation

The Brazilian Solidarity Economy movement has been developing strategies and institutional forms that are unique and understudied. It combines the institutional support to noncapitalist economic initiatives with the setting up of participatory public spaces—the Solidarity Economy forums—aimed at promoting collaboration between production units and civil society organizations, as well as the co-production and implementation, in partnership with the state, of public policies for the sector. Gadotti (2009) claims that popular education is a central aspect of the movement, since one of its core goals is to build empowered subjectivities that are able not only to build sustainable alternatives to capitalism, but also to assert and exercise their social and political rights. One can identify two dimensions in the pedagogy practiced in the Brazilian Solidarity Economy movement. The first is that of economic empowerment, that is, the development of the knowledge, skills and abilities necessary for the creation of noncapitalist self-managed production units, commercialization mechanisms and community-based and grassroots-controlled financial institutions. The second dimension is that of political empowerment, that is, the development and sharing of knowledge about socioeconomic oppression and oppressive structures, as well as the promotion of the collective action necessary to change them. The pedagogical praxis promoted within the Cooperative Network of Women Entrepreneurs of Rio de Janeiro (CNWE) is a representative example of the application of that pedagogy.

The CNWE was created in the framework of the earlier articulations of the Brazilian Solidarity Economy movement. It was founded in 1997 by ASPLANDE—*Assessoria e Planejamento para o Desenvolvimento* (Technical Assistance and Planning for Development), a community development NGO based in Rio de Janeiro. The purpose of CNWE is to gather women from the popular classes, who work as members of units of cooperative production or microentrepreneurs, in a network of economic collaboration, with the purpose of developing a production and commercialization collective. This network meets monthly to promote the sharing of knowledge between participants about the management of their production units. CNWE works in tandem with the state-level Solidarity Economy Forum of Rio de Janeiro, of which ASPLANDE is a part.

Structuring Aspects of CNWE's Pedagogy: Contributions to Theory

The ASPLANDE team, together with other grassroots NGOs participating in the Solidarity Economy Forum of Rio de Janeiro, developed what the coordinator of this institution calls a "Methodology of Integral and Harmonic Development." The goal of this methodology is to promote the development of sustainable noncapitalist economic initiatives. This methodology is participatory and dialogical in nature, in a way that links back to Freirean methodology and its promotion of a rereading the world as the foundation of an emancipatory educational praxis. It is based on the collective construction of pedagogical materials, as well as on the sharing of what Motta (2011a) calls the "immanent knowledge and understanding" of oppression and emancipation that is developed in the everyday experience of participants. This shared "immanent knowledge" is not taken at face value, being instead the objective of a collective critical analysis of aspects that may be the outcome of internalized oppression.

This methodology is applied in the regular monthly meetings of CNWE, as well as in workshops and seminars organized within the network and in the framework of the Solidarity Economy Forum of Rio de Janeiro. Workshops and seminars are organized around topics related to the development of noncapitalist economic initiatives, such as "Price Definition" and "Management of Cooperatives," as well as more general themes such as "Women and the Economy." The sessions, workshops and seminars are generally structured around three phases: they begin with a general exposition of the subject by CNWE coordinators, open to discussion by participants; then participants form small subgroups and each of them debate a specific topic brought up in the initial exposition/discussion; and in the final phase all participants reassemble, with the purpose of sharing and discussing the conclusions reached by each subgroup.

The key pedagogical material used in CNWE workshops on topics related to the development of noncapitalist economic initiatives is a collection of texts on how to start and manage a workers' cooperative, microenterprise or commercialization collective. This collection includes texts written by staff from ASPLANDE and other NGOS participating in the Solidarity Economy Forum of Rio de Janeiro.

At the time of fieldwork, this collection was considered to be "in construction," since it is constantly being reviewed in order to incorporate feedback from participants, as well as new knowledge created during meetings.

During the second trimester of 2009, the collection added a document on the legal procedures necessary for registering a workers' cooperative or microenterprise, written by a participant, hereafter referred to as "Laiz." This participant is the coordinator of a seamstresses' cooperative located in a shantytown in the southern borough of Rio de Janeiro. She started the cooperative as a result of her participation in CNWE. According to Laiz, the whole process encouraged her to finish high school and take a bachelors' degree in Law. When she finished her degree, she became the legal expert in CNWE, as well as a part of ASPLANDE's team of popular educators. Laiz claims that the everyday challenges of managing her cooperative showed her the need for furthering her knowledge of economic and management law. From fellow participants in CNWE, she found the encouragement necessary to further her goals. She also found role models among the staff of Asplande, who are university-educated and have a solid trajectory in grassroots activism. Although they have a middle-class background, they are world-travelers in the sense that they identify themselves with grassroots struggles and contribute to them by mediating between their language and that of dominant social groups.

The Personal Is Economic and the Economic Is Political

The construction and sharing of knowledge on oppression is an aspect of the "Methodology of Integral and Harmonic Development" that is present in workshops related to the development of noncapitalist economic initiatives, as well as to those on general themes. In line with the Freirean approach to knowledge construction, participants of both types of workshops are encouraged to relate the material discussed with their own personal experiences of oppression.

The sharing of knowledge on oppression and the discussion of strategies of resistance were a central aspect of the workshop on "Women and the Economy," which took place during the second trimester of 2009. The topics of discussion, which were directly related to gender- and race-based oppression in the private and public spheres, led to the sharing of personal stories of workplace discrimination, sexual harassment and intimate violence, as well as beliefs and assumptions resulting from internalized oppression. In this workshop, the coordinators promoted discussions, supported by audiovisual material, that show the connections among class, gender- and race-based oppression and the structural mechanisms of capitalism. The material traces the relegation of women to reproductive labor back to the emergence of modern industrial capitalism and its impact on the gendered division of labor. It also connected racial stereotypes and everyday experiences of racism and classism to the legacy of colonialism and slavery in Brazilian society. The promotion of sustainable noncapitalist production units, as well as relationships of mutual support among participants, was presented and discussed as the key strategy of emancipation from such circumstances, since it promotes a material and organizational autonomy from capitalism. A significant part of each workshop session was spent discussing possible options for dealing with specific circumstances of discrimination and violence, such as taking refuge in a women's shelter and using the legal aid resources offered by feminist organizations.

Institutional oppression is a topic that often comes up in debates at CNWE meetings, especially those that focus on the relationship between the Solidarity Economy movement and the state. The key topic on the agenda of the monthly meeting of December 2009 was the setting up of a meeting between a delegation of the CNWE and members of the Legislative Assembly of the state of Rio de Janeiro. The purpose was to discuss the pending regulation of the state-level law of Solidarity Economy, which guarantees the availability of public funds for public policy programs for the sector. A participant started a debate on how public policy programs may help break the clientelistic ties of dependence that many shantytown microentrepreneurs have on patrons in political parties, corporations or other private economic and political interests. Following this debate, another participant shared how a corporate-funded charity tried to co-opt her workers' cooperative, and how she responded to this attempt:

> We thought that the arrival of [name of the charity withdrawn] would give our project a boost. However, since we didn't want them to control us, they ended up not giving us any support. They tried to smother our project. […] [The charity] likes to take pictures with people, look good and give the idea that they support the projects. They think that the people from the shantytown are ignorant, that they accept everything they want to give them, regardless of their agenda. But I was not educated to be that that way. I was brought up to fight for what I want, not for what other people want to give me.

This aspect of CNWE's pedagogy identifies another dimension of the construction of world-travelling identities, what Motta (2011b) identifies as the overcoming of the dualism between intellect and emotion, mind and body, thought and action, subject and object that characterize knowledge production within capitalism. That happens through two concomitant processes. One of them is the sharing of everyday "immanent knowledge and understanding" on oppression. The emotional dimension plays a central role in this process, since the knowledge shared takes the form of descriptions of personal, embodied experiences of oppression, mainly from the standpoint of the experience of the participant. Another is the attribution of political meaning to the experiences shared, as well as the collective construction of strategies of resistance.

Relational Aspects of CNWE's Pedagogy

On Affection, Authority and Projection

At the time of fieldwork, economic transactions among participants were still minimal. Most participants produced handcrafted food products or decorative goods. There was little room for the establishment of supply chains because the goods produced by each participant could not be used as production materials by others. The "glue" that kept CNWE together and promoted the collective construction of emancipatory knowledge was the relationship of affinity and affection established among the participants. However, the web of friendships established between them does not have the shape of a "grid," in which everybody related to everybody else in the same way and at the same level. Instead, it took the form of "concentric circles" surrounding the staff of ASPLANDE, and especially the coordinator of the NGO, "Leticia," who also coordinated the CNWE meetings.

Leticia, among the staff of ASPLANDE, is the person whose identity and life experience fits the concept of world-travelers proposed by Hernández (1997). Leticia is a white, queer woman who started her activism during the authoritarian regime, in the framework of the opposition to the dictatorship promoted by the Ecclesial Base Communities. In the 1980s, she emigrated to Sweden, where she did a master's degree on the management of workers' cooperatives. In the early 1990s, after her return to Brazil, she founded ASPLANDE and organized the first articulations that led to the emergence of the Brazilian Solidarity Economy movement. The research she did in Sweden contributed to the intellectual foundations of the movement. In the same period, she also became active in feminist and queer circles.

Leticia's knowledge and life experience, as well as her position of authority as one of the founders of ASPLANDE, make the participants in CNWE regard her a mentor, if not a kind of "owner" of the group. During fieldwork, I very often heard participants refer to CNWE as "Leticia's group." The fact that Leticia enjoys socializing with CNWE participants outside of meetings, often entertaining them in bars, restaurants or her own residence, very much contributes to what Bowler (1999) would call her "pastoral power," meaning the power to share knowledge and shape perceptions due to a combination of caring and authority. Such pastoral power was evident at the conclusion of the first session of the workshop on "Price Definition." Leticia wanted to make a statement about the necessity to question institutional authority and technical knowledge when she said: "Big companies have hordes of consultants to help them do this. We have the power of own minds and common sense."

At the end of the session, an elderly microentrepreneur who produces handmade jewelry and knitted goods approached her and said:

> Thank you so much [Leticia]! If it wasn't for you and your way of communicating, we would never be able to understand these things.

The effusive declaration of this participant indicates a self-denying attitude that is shared by other participants and poses challenges to the border pedagogy practiced by CNWE, as well as to the egalitarian aspirations of popular education in general. In *Pedagogy of the Oppressed*, Freire claims that one of the major obstacles to emancipation is the internalization of the oppressor by the oppressed. Such internalization may express itself by a more or less conscious desire to "be" like the oppressor, to embody his power and personal characteristics, to attain the same position in the social hierarchy instead of changing it. Even if a member of an oppressed group knows that the attainment of such goals is most likely very difficult or impossible, the oppressor is still held as a reference for "success" "beauty," "culture" or the embodiment of the qualities deemed necessary to become what the mainstream culture considers to be a fulfilled human being. It may also express itself through attitudes like that of the elderly microentrepreneur in CNWE. They indicate a tendency by people who were socialized in the framework of capitalism and complex hierarchical bureaucracies of regarding those that play the role of educator or coordinator as "hierarchically superior." Such an attitude is accompanied by unconscious projection onto them of their own innate abilities. This happens despite the focus on the part of educators on the "immanent knowledge and understanding of participants," with the purpose of exposing them to a more emancipatory model of learning than that promoted by "banking education." Participants often have a tendency of seeing educators and coordinators as "more in the know" or "more able" than themselves. In CNWE, this happens despite the conscious effort that Leticia and other educators/coordinators make of following the Freirean principle of using authority in a non-authoritarian way, by keeping the space open for critical reflection and constructive criticism by participants. "Adelia," a popular educator from an NGO that collaborates with ASPLANDE in the setting up of the courses and workshops offered in CNWE, claims:

> One of the major difficulties that we face is that we were all educated in hierarchical institutions—schools. When the students have to obey the teacher because he or she "knows best," what do you expect? [...] The thing continues in adulthood. You sell your labor to a capitalist firm. There is a hierarchy there. The boss. The manager. They are the ones who "know." You just obey them, you have to follow orders. Then there is the state bureaucracy. [...] The police. The politicians who try to "buy" the support from local organizations. [...] The know-it-all public officials who give you all those complicated forms to fill if you want to have access to any kind of support from the state, or even to register your firm. They patronize you. [...] People end up internalizing that. It is one of the major difficulties we face in the Solidarity Economy movement—that people where socialized within capitalism and act according to the "place" that was assigned to them by capitalism. [...] It reflects itself in the way people act in the courses and workshops, the way people act in the [Solidarity Economy] forum, the way people act in their production units. [...] It is very difficult to change mentalities and attitudes that people are often not aware of. It takes a lot of time and effort. We are still finding out how to deal with that.

One of the major challenges of the pedagogy promoted by CNWE is to make participants aware that the technical and personal empowerment they experience is the result of their own ability and effort, as individuals and a collective. The "Methodology of Harmonious and Integral Development" does not include measures that specifically address the tendency for participants to "project" their qualities and capacities on the coordinators. However, the relationships of affect established between coordinators and participants, between participants themselves and between these and other members of their communities promote a deconstruction of that tendency in their everyday interactions. That happens because they create incentives and opportunities for participants to become active participants of their own empowerment, as well as of emancipatory political projects. They do that, for example, by eroding the division of labor between coordinators/educators and other participants by promoting a closer collaboration among them and creating incentives for the latter to increase their civic engagement in their communities.

The "Inner Circle": "Emerging Organic Coordinators"

Leticia's pastoral power is reflected in the fact that she is constantly surrounded by an "inner circle" composed of close friendships—a category of participants that can be defined as "emerging organic coordinators." This category includes two types of participants in CNWE that have several traits in common. A key characteristic is having had previous experience in activism or civic engagement, which contributed to the development of leadership abilities. Such skills ended up facilitating their integration as active participants within CNWE, as well as the Solidarity Economy forums. Some assumed "coordinator" roles in the courses and workshops organized within the network, as well as having a relatively more visible role in the co-production of pedagogical material. Some also became active participants in the state-level Solidarity Economy Forum as representatives of the municipal-level forum of Rio de Janeiro.

Those that had been working with ASPLANDE for a considerable period of time as partners in community development programs generally began their engagement with ASPLANDE and CNWE as a result of their activism as grassroots leaders and community organizers. A significant example is that of Laiz, who started participating in ASPLANDE's courses when the NGO opened its first headquarters, which were located in the shantytown where she lives and works. At that time, she was an active participant in her neighborhood association, as well as a community organizer in a local church. She got to know about ASPLANDE through pamphlets about a course on the formation and management of cooperatives, sent by the then recently formed NGO to the neighborhood association. After the course, Laiz started working with Leticia and another ASPLANDE's staff member in the development of a seamstresses' cooperative for women in the neighborhood who lost their jobs as the result of the closure of a nearby textile factory. This collaboration led her to become one of the founding members of CNWE. It also introduced her to the Solidarity Economy movement and its forums. At the time of fieldwork, Laiz was one of the coordinating members of the municipal-level forum of

Rio de Janeiro, as well as one of its representatives in the state-level forum. When interviewed, Laiz described how her collaboration with ASPLANDE in the creation of the cooperative, as well as her activity as its coordinator, presented her with challenges that motivated her to further her education by enrolling in a university to obtain an equivalent to a B.A. degree in Law.

> When we [Laiz and the other women in her cooperative] started working together, we realized that making sure the cooperative would be successful required more, much more that rolling up our sleeves and getting ourselves to work. We have to deal with a lot of bureaucratic, legal stuff: receipts, permits, taxes etc. [...] We first started as an informal association, but then we became formal. [...] [The person referred to here as Leticia] helped us with those issues [...] [W]e became aware of how important it is for us to learn how to solve them [...] That's why I decided to enroll at the university and take a degree in Law.

By gaining that certification, Laiz was able to participate in the elaboration of pedagogical materials, namely by elaborating leaflets that explain, in a language accessible to nonexperts, the legal procedures necessary for formalizing cooperatives and workers' associations, regularizing their tax status and getting the permits necessary for the production and commercialization of their products. Laiz's law degree also contributed to her being hired by ASPLANDE as one of its collaborators. Besides, it also enabled her to expand the reach of her activism. In 2009, Laiz became a leading member of a squat in downtown Rio de Janeiro, part of Movimento *Nacional de Luta pela Moradia*/National Movement for Dignified Housing (MNLM). Her law expertise became an important asset in the struggle for the recognition of the right of members to live and work in empty public buildings like the one occupied by Laiz and other members of MNLM.

Another type of participant tends to have joined the network not because of participation in community development projects that had partnerships with ASPLANDE but as a result of activism in movements related with the causes espoused by this NGO. This is the case, for example, with "Teresa," who in early 2008 started participating in the meetings, courses and workshops of CNWE, as the result of a suggestion made by an acquaintance from a feminist organization that she has been collaborating with for a considerable period of time. Before joining CNWE, Teresa was already a seasoned feminist activist, associated with "Associação das Mulheres Brasileiras"/Association of Brazilian Women (AMB) and "Associação das Mulheres Negras

Brasileiras"/Association of Black Brazilian Women (AMNB). It was in the framework of rallies, protests and workshops organized by AMB and AMNB that she met other women with whom she started an association of embroiderers/artists in her neighborhood. Teresa describes how her feminist activism together with the challenges presented by the management of her production group made her aware of the necessity of furthering her education:

> Above all, I identify myself as a Black feminist, as well as a shantytown inhabitant. We [Teresa and her fellow workers] got together because we needed to find solutions for the problems we were facing in our shantytown. Problems of unemployment, of violence perpetrated by the drug gangs, problems related with health, with the lack of access that people in our community, especially women, have to information about health, as well as healthcare. [...] For example, there is a lack of access to information about reproductive health and sexually transmitted diseases. [...] The purpose of our association is not only to produce embroidery and make money, but also to empower women in our shantytown, to share information about health and to search together for solutions to the violence that we face in our everyday lives. [...] I realized that, in order to make that possible, I needed to learn about how to manage the association, how to make it in this economy, because our work as embroiderers is the support of our work in empowering women in our community.

When she joined CNWE, she had just completed a university degree with a double major in marketing and business administration. Joining CNWE stimulated her to develop her political knowledge through a "learning-by-doing" process:

> I realized that it is not enough to learn how to manage your source of livelihood. It is necessary to have a political voice. Before I joined CNWE, I became a militant of the Workers' Party. [...] When I joined CNWE, I realized that I needed a more active political voice. To join forces with other people in order to better defend my interests, to have access to policy-makers and put pressure on them. [...] In order to transform the lives of women, especially the lives of poor women, you need to transform the economy. But you can only achieve that if you join forces to make your voice heard, to have political power. [...] That's why I joined the [Solidarity Economy] Forum.

After joining CNWE, Teresa quickly became an active participant in the Solidarity Economy forums, becoming a representative of the municipal-level forum of Rio de Janeiro in the state-level forum.

During fieldwork, I participated in informal socialization activities that included Leticia, other ASPLANDE staff members and "emerging grassroots coordinators." During these activities, I noticed how the shared feminist worldview contributed to develop a sense of camaraderie and friendship. Here there was a "bracketing" of the role of "coordinator" and "educatee-educator" between them. NGO technicians and emerging grassroots coordinators would debate issues related with the agenda of CNWE and the Solidarity Economy forums. ASPLANDE technicians asked emerging grassroots coordinators for opinions and advice regarding technical issues related not only with the movement, but also with the functioning of the NGO and its projects. Treating emerging grassroots coordinators as peers and including them in educational activities as "coordinators" and contributors to the elaboration of pedagogical material seems to be in line with the goal, expressed by an ASPLANDE technician when interviewed, of promoting the "ownership" of the NGO by the community.

The fact that emerging grassroots coordinators had leadership skills developed in their previous civic engagement contributed to the development of those friendships. However, there was another factor that strongly contributed to the development of those relationships: The emerging organic coordinators all lived inside the city of Rio de Janeiro. This fact facilitated their socialization outside CNWE meetings. It also helped ASPLANDE to obtain grassroots information necessary for the development of its community development projects in the city. Besides, ASPLANDE, like Laiz, was part of the coordination of the municipal-level Solidarity Economy Forum of Rio de Janeiro. Their informal socialization outside of CNWE meetings were occasions to discuss issues related with the forum and debate possible strategies to deal with them.

My observation of the informal socialization between Leticia, other CNWE coordinators and emerging organic coordinators left me with no doubts that the friendships developed between them were based on true affection and caring. Verbal and physical expressions of affect were very frequent. The use of humor and friendly teasing between them denoted an intimacy that is only possible between true friends. It was obvious that they all greatly enjoyed each other's company and derived emotional satisfaction from it. However, one should not exclude the possibility that they were also based on pragmatic motivations, like accessing information or deepening the debate of issues related with the municipal-level Solidarity Economy Forum. Regardless of whether or not those friendships had a pragmatic dimension, it is clear that they created incentives and opportunities for pro-activeness and leadership from the part of participants. From this, one can extrapolate that another dimension of the construction of world-traveling identities is the overcoming of the dualism between affect and pragmatism. Pragmatic motivations may contribute to bring people together and create opportunities for the development of affect between them. In its turn, affect may contribute to facilitate the attainment of pragmatic goals. This perspective fits with the overall perspective of overcoming the duality between the private and the public sphere, as well as between intellect and emotion, mind and body, thought and action that underlies not only Solidarity Economy, but also the pedagogy developed by other popular movements in Latin America (Motta, 2011a).

The "Outer Circle": "Emancipatee-Emancipators"

Surrounding the inner circle of emerging organic coordinators is a category of participants that can be called "emancipatee-emancipators." This category includes participants in CNWE that lacked previous experience in activism or any other kind of civic engagement, but ended up developing political consciousness and leadership skills that turned them into agents of their own economic, political and personal emancipation, as well as that of other fellow participants. Most participants that fit this category lived in the suburban area of Rio de Janeiro, a fact that made it difficult for them to socialize with Leticia and other coordinators/educators outside CNWE meetings. A significant example of an emancipatee-emancipator is "Isabel," member of a family-based collective of handicraft producers who, during the courses I observed during fieldwork, made several interventions on how Solidarity Economy can contribute to change the balance of power between the genders in the household in a way that is favorable to women.

Isabel entered the Solidarity Economy movement through technical courses for artisans organized by grassroots NGOs in her municipality, located in the suburban region of Rio de Janeiro known as "Baixada Fluminense." This respondent claims that at the time she was experiencing domestic violence from her husband. As a result of her participation in meetings, courses and workshops in the framework of the Solidarity Economy forums and CNWE, she became aware of how the constraints experienced by women in the capitalist labor market promote their economic dependency vis-à-vis their domestic partners, leading many of them to remain in abusive situations for the sake of ensuring their survival. Isabel claims that her initiative of starting a family-based handicraft production unit contributed to change the balance of power between her and her husband, which reversed the abusive situation she was experiencing. Isabel gained technical knowledge that gave her a significant level of economic authority in the household, in the sense that she trained the rest of the family, including her husband, to produce the goods that her unit commercializes. The fact that she was not working outside the home turned out to be an asset, as it gave her time flexibility to commercialize her own handicraft products. Besides, the thematic CNWE meetings on gender politics and women's rights increased her knowledge of the Brazilian legal system, a fact that made her confront her husband about the possible legal consequences of his behavior.

> I started gaining economic independence, as well as knowledge about my rights. [...] I started speaking up in public, as well as at home. All this came together. [...] All this increased my confidence, my awareness of the right I have to take control of my own life.

These positive changes in Isabel's family life made her take the initiative to reach out to other educatees-educators that were experiencing similar circumstances and provide them with emotional support, legal information and technical knowledge, as they tried to improve the balance of power in their private lives. Isabel's participation in the educational activities of the movement also contributed to the development of leadership skills. Although she didn't have any previous experience in activism or civic engagement of any kind, Isabel became a regular and active participant in her municipal-level Solidarity Economy Forum, as well as one of its representatives at the state-level Solidarity Economy Forum of Rio de Janeiro. She also became a card-carrying member of "Associação das Mulheres Brasileiras"/ Association of Brazilian Women, one of the major networks of feminist organizations and activists in Brazil. As a result, Isabel became a well-known activist in her suburban region and formed close relationships with participants in CNWE that live in the area.

The trajectory of Isabel is illustrative of the emancipatory potential of mutual and respectful engagement between the human experience of participants in popular education initiatives. The fact that she was not directly involved in the production of pedagogical materials in CNWE does not mean that her role was secondary, either within the group or the Solidarity Economy movement as a whole. The relationships she formed with other participants and her engagement with the Solidarity Economy forum in her municipality show otherwise. Although she came from a position of intense oppression and had no previous experience in civic engagement, the collective construction of knowledge within CNWE prompted her not only to gain control of her home life and terminate an abusive situation but also to become engaged in the economic and personal emancipation of other people in her community. This indicates that the most fundamental source of incentives for personal empowerment and activism in these types of initiatives is the shattering of the boundaries between what is considered public and private. That happens by bringing into public discussion aspects of one's life that are seen as "private" or "intimate." The sharing of life stories allows participants to find commonalities between their own experience and that of others. It also contributes to a process of collective construction of knowledge on the structural causes of oppression in the private sphere. Such processes decrease the sense of isolation and self-blame that is often experienced by oppressed people and develops solidarity between those in similar situations of oppression.

Conclusions

The analysis of the pedagogy carried out in the framework of CNWE contributes to the theoretical goals of this chapter by providing insights on the role of what Giroux (1991) calls a border pedagogy in the construction of what Hernández (1997) refers to as world-traveling identities, capable of communicating between dominant social groups and subaltern realities, languages and knowledge. The development of such identities is deemed a central aspect of the pedagogy and political practice of the Solidarity Economy movement. It aims not only to deconstruct and criticize the multidimensional power relations that sustain capitalism but also to promote alternatives in the here-and-now, in the form of noncapitalist economic initiatives based on principles of worker ownership and control, cooperation and priority of the satisfaction of social needs over the attainment of profit.

The construction of world-traveling identities happens through two concomitant processes. One of them is the sharing of everyday "immanent knowledge and understanding" on oppression. The second process is the attribution of political meaning to the experiences shared, with the purpose of collectively elaborating strategies of resistance. Affection and emotion play as much of a central role in this process as intellectual analysis, since the knowledge shared takes the form of descriptions of personal, embodied experiences of oppression, expressed from the perspective of the emotional experience of the participation. Such sharing promotes and is promoted by the development of intimacy among participants over time, based on a shared condition and shared goals that promotes the openness necessary for sharing personal stories and engaging in a critical dialogue regarding that of others.

This indicates that the most fundamental source of incentives for personal empowerment and activism promoted by the popular education initiatives of the Solidarity Economy movement is the shattering of the boundaries between what is considered public and private. That happens by bringing into public discussion aspects of one's life that are seen as "private" or "intimate." The sharing of life stories allows participants to find commonalities between their own experience and that of others and promotes the development of relationships based on affinity and affection. Such friendships also have a pragmatic dimension, because they contribute to the personal empowerment and civic engagement of participants, as well as to the promotion of the goals of ASPLANDE and the other NGOs that coordinate CNWE. Regardless of the weight that pragmatism may have in the establishment of those relationships, it is clear that it is generally tied to affinity and the development of mutual and genuine affection. It is also clear that those friendships create incentives and opportunities for pro-activeness and leadership in the community from the part of participants. They do that by eroding the division of labor between coordinators/educators and other participants and creating incentives for the latter to increase their civic engagement in their communities.

References

Bowler, M. (1999), *Feeling Power: Emotions and Education*, New York: Routledge.

Darder, A. (2002), *Reinventing Paulo Freire: Pedagogy of Love*, Boulder, CO: Westview Press.

Gadotti, M. (2009), *Educar para a Sustentabilidade* [Educating for Sustainability], São Paulo: Instituto Paulo Freire.

Giroux, H. (1991), *Postmodernism, Feminism and Cultural Politics: Redrawing Educational Boundaries*, Albany, NY: State University of New York Press.

Hernández, A. (1997), *Pedagogy, Democracy and Feminism: Rethinking the Public Sphere*, Albany, NY: State University of New York Press.

Motta, Sara C. (2011a), "Pedagogies of Resistance and Anticapitalist Creation in Latin America," *Reimagining the University—Roundhouse Journal,* http://roundhousejournal.org/2011/05/08/reimagining-the -university-journal/ (accessed on September 29, 2012).

——— (2011b), "Populism's Achilles' Heel: Democracy beyond the Liberal State and the Market Economy in Venezuela," *Latin American Perspectives* 38(28): pp. 28–46.

Chapter 12

Colombia: Education and Gender Equity in Context

Glory Rigueros Saavedra

This essay will take a broad view of education and gender equity in Colombia, which will help to show how they are constrained, or enabled, by the context within which they are practiced. It will also therefore show that education and gender policies cannot merely be self-contained but are supported or hindered by policies in other sectors (e.g. see Holmes, 2010; UNESCO, 2007). Education and gender issues permeate day-to-day activities, ranging from family life through to social movement activities and embody the wider aims of the economy and a nation's vision of itself. Various social movements in Colombia have had a key role in resisting the erosion of educational standards and values and in promoting nondiscrimination. These movements are now important actors in redesigning national education policies and as a consequence also wider national development policies. The discussion will also, inevitably, highlight the weakness of the main education and gender indicators in use: the EFA-EDI (Education for All—Education Development Indicator) and the GII (Gender Inequality Index) used in the Human Development Report (HDR, 2011).[1]

Context

With the relentless backdrop of more than 50 years of continuing civil war and more recently in the climate of global recession, what has education and overall efforts at gender equity offered women and men in Colombia, over the past decade? To understand this, it is necessary to consider the socioeconomic and political milieu in which education and gender are lived.

In 2002, Colombia emerged into the twenty-first century with the election of one of its most retrograde governments, under the helm of far-right ex-president Alvaro Uribe Velez. With an emphasis on "democratic security"—which those in opposition dubbed "undemocratic insecurity"—the eight years of this regime had extremely negative impacts on all human rights and on the provision of public services (CINEP, 2010). In August 2010, Juan Manuel Santos, Uribe's ex-minister of defence, was elected as president, and has presided over an administration of continuity. But since Santos' election, and particularly in 2011, there have been massive student and social movement mobilizations, indicating deep discontent with this administration. The protests continue, despite the welcome peace dialogues set in motion, in 2012, with the largest guerrilla group in the country, the Fuerzas Armadas Revolucionarias de Colombia (Revolutionary Armed Forces of Colombia or FARC). The situation is indicative of a divergence between the plans for education and development the government wishes to implement and fund and those that citizens desire, particularly those excluded from the "miracle" of marketized development.

Both the Uribe and Santos governments hold a view of education solidly bound to the neoliberal edicts of increased privatization and deregulation within a framework of free trade agreements (FTAs), which, it was said, would increase foreign investment and GDP. Yet, the country remains one of the most unequal in the world as indicated both by its income inequality (Gini at 0.56) and its land distribution (Gini of 0.86), making it one of the top three most inequitable countries and the worst at land distribution (INDH, 2011, p. 47; World Bank, 2010a). Thus the healthy GDP figures are really a reflection of the national gains made by those *few* already in possession of the greatest amounts of wealth.

Analysts point out that education is being turned into a commodity whose content and delivery are to be largely determined by the whims of big foreign and local business concerns, which do not represent the more rounded future educational needs, or requirements, of the varied constituencies they serve (Robledo, 2006, pp. 49–51). In this scenario, the role intended for education has been a utilitarian and impoverished one, in which, as its proponents have said, it "probably does not pay" to educate the vast majority (of those destined for cheap labor?) and in which demands by the business sector are increasingly allowed to determine the supply and content of education, as the state obligingly retreats. Privatization has proceeded apace, buoyed by the intensified public finance cuts of 2001 quickly followed by those of 2007 (Tribuna Magisterial, 2012). The attendant civil war is not incidental, as the average spent on *defence and security* was over 6 percent GDP per year over the 2002–2008 period (Otero Prada, 2008)[2] compared to education expenditure, which rose from only 4.3 percent in 2002 to 4.8 percent GDP with lows of 3.9 percent GDP in both 2006 and 2008 (World Bank, 2010b). More recent figures show the continued difference in investments made by the state to particular public sectors. In 2011 public expenditure per year was: USD 1,900 per student, USD 6,432 per prisoner and USD 10,000 per member of the armed forces[3]—indicating that investment in education is still of less importance than war for the Colombian state.

Paradoxically, during this decade of wholesale dismantling and underfunding of the public sector, international gender statistics for Colombia by UNDP show a steady improvement in the Gender Inequality Index (GII), which is said to have decreased from 0.53 in 2003 to 0.48 in 2010 (HDR, 2011). With respect to education alone, however, according to UNESCO, between 2002 and 2008, Colombia's position on gender parity in education "marginally" deteriorated, notwithstanding the rise in overall educational development (UNESCO, 2006; 2011).[4]

How did this occur and what is behind the official figures? It is important to note that the pervasive effects of the civil war and generalized violence are not generally conducive to a climate of either sound education or improved equality. Studies have indicated the serious effects of violence on education, educators and those educated, but also how this violence in Colombia can be directly linked to the adoption of neoliberal and militaristic policies, which have transnational links (Novelli, 2009; 2010). Other studies have pointed to the negative effects of conflict on gender equity (United Nations Commission on the Status of Women, 2005) and to the fact that more gender equal societies are less likely to experience conflict (Hvistendahl, 2012; Melander, 2005). In Colombia, unsurprisingly, with its continued civil war, investment in education has also decreased in conflict areas, and the effects on those living in these conditions are long term (Barrera and Ibáñez, 2004; Wharton and Uwaifo Oyelere, 2011). All this, added to the continued violence against teachers and students in educational institutions and outside them (Villar-Márquez and Harper, 2010), would seem to make present EDI and GII indicator levels questionable. Can the state really have achieved these improvements in overall gender and education, under the unfavorable conditions described above? Why had the gender index "marginally" slipped in education? It is hoped that this overview will help to contextualize and clarify the complexity of this picture.

Education under the Uribe Administration

Education policy, in Uribe's government, was included within a "social cohesion policy" that purported to promote equal opportunities and reduce poverty. The program had seven strands: *the education revolution, the promotion and expansion of social security, the promotion of an economy based on solidarity, the social management of public services, the social management of rural areas, urban quality of life and the idea of private ownership* (DNP, 2002–2006). However, the government obediently followed a neoliberal, World Bank supported, enthusiasm for wholesale privatizations and public private partnerships (PPPs). In the education sector the already existing involvement of the private sector was frequently cited, by ministers and bank analysts, as a good reason to spread its involvement even further. According to Patrinos and Sosale: "The private sector share in education in Colombia is high: approximately 20% of students in primary, 35% in secondary and 65% in higher education" (2007, p. 43). By 2010, the government's own upbeat assessment of its *education revolution* was accepted by expert observers as having "increased coverage at elementary and high school from 80% to 100% and from 57% to 80%, respectively, while university coverage has gone from less than one million students to close to 1.7 million, a figure that includes degrees granted at the technical and technological levels" (CINEP, 2010, p. 10).

On closer inspection, however, the seeming favorable spread of education had very high hidden costs. Quality, resources and staff-to-student ratios were sacrificed for the sake of greater coverage, plunging many institutions into a funding crisis, from which they have, as yet, not recovered. The private sector that had been invited to make investments in education, was, in effect, unable—or unwilling—to meet the variety of shortages, resulting in redundancies and over-crowded classrooms and lecture halls (desde abajo, 2011). Even some of the World Banks's own analysts describe the uneven coverage reproduced by this approach, in the disadvantaged areas of Colombia, with improvements in privately subsidized schools, unsurprisingly not reliably spilling over onto nearby surrounding unsubsidized schools. Despite the cited improvements in dropout rates and test scores, the quality of wider coverage, under these arrangements, has forcibly remained patchy (Barrera-Osorio, 2006, p. 27). Meanwhile, in higher education, the increase in coverage was achieved by the Uribe Ministry of Education (MEN)[5] via a spate of dubious certification upgrades of a variety of educational institutions and the SENA,[6] which came under severe criticism from the academic community.

Gender, Education and the Uribe Years

What happened to gender equality in education, under the conditions delineated above in the previous sections?

At the start of the Uribe period, in 2002, at primary level enrolment, the gender gap had been small and both boys and girls completed at least an average of 7.5 years of schooling. Despite overall equality, however, boys and young men lagged slightly behind. Girls were less likely to withdraw and repeat years and also more likely to subsequently enroll for secondary education, the ratio of girls to boys being 100:111, according to the United Nations Development Fund for Women (UNIFEM) (Garces de Eder and Marulanda Herran, 2005]. Poverty and class discrimination, however, maintain an inequitable transition to tertiary education. Only 6 percent of the poorest enrolled for higher education compared to 40 percent of the richest sectors, but of those who did enroll, women again outnumbered men. At tertiary level, 52 percent of students were women (IBRD, 2003, pp. 2–6). By the end of 2008, gender parity levels were overall still maintained for primary education, with a welcome improvement in boys intake and completion rates, but, at secondary level and tertiary level, young men's enrolment and completion rates continued to be worse than those of women. According to the Colombian Ministry of Education's Career Observatory for Education, between 2001 and 2010, 54.7 percent of women and 45.3 percent men graduated from tertiary education as shown by figure 12.1. At doctoral level, on the other hand, women began to lose out, as only half their number graduated with doctorates, as compared to men (see figure 12.1) (Observatorio Laboral para la Educacion, 2011). UNESCO thus reports that 2015 gender parity goals for secondary education are unlikely to be met (UNESCO, 2010).

Discrimination toward women in tertiary education also exists in *qualitative* terms. According to Tovar Rojas: "micro discriminative practices" are very common in traditional male fields such as science and engineering (2008, p. 1). These discriminative practices unfortunately have been shown to also become full-blown via their action in other sectors. In the field of work, increasing numbers of women get sidelined into traditionally "feminine" careers and increasingly casualized and lower-paid work, despite leaving higher education with equivalent qualifications to men and mostly in greater numbers (Observatorio Laboral para la Educacion, 2011). These were exacerbated, by the Uribe administration, through regressive reforms to labor conditions, in 2002, including flexible contracts, cuts to

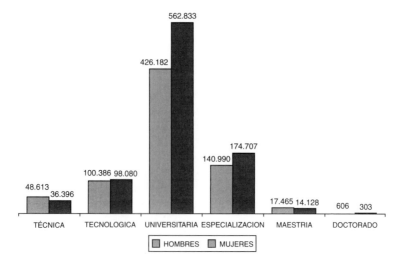

Figure 12.1   Distribution of graduates by sex at an advanced level (2001–2010)

Note: Numbers allude to total number of graduates from various advanced institutions, as follows: Tecnica, Vocational Technical; Technologica, Technological; Universitaria, University level; Maestria, Master's level; Doctorado, Doctoral level; Hombres, Men; Mujeres, Women.

Source: Adapted from *Observatorio Laboral para la Educacion* (Career Observatory of Education), http://www.graduadoscolombia.edu.co/html/1732/article-195404.html.

overtime pay, reduced severance pay and a lengthening of the working day, which affected both men and women, but with women's well-being increasingly paying a higher price throughout their life cycle (ENS, 2008; 2011).

Studies indicate that sustainable overall gender equality is a multifaceted process, which should include changes in the education system *as well as* changes in ingrained cultural perceptions, family policies and social policies (Pathways of Women's Empowerment, 2011). Gains in gender equality for women, and LGBT rights to non-discrimination, were won gradually throughout the 1990s via the 1991 Colombian Constitution and the achievement of rights and welfare provisions (Garces de Eder and Marulanda Herran, 2005). But they have not been sufficient to prevent various crises in education brought about by neglect of social protection from the increased violence and disregard during the Uribista government. Every sector of society, but especially women and LGBTI people, experienced higher levels of violence (Amnesty, 2011; Colombia Diversa, 2011).[7]

The social and educational circumstances affecting internally displaced persons (IDPs) in Colombia also illustrate the limitations of gender and education indicators. The IDP population ballooned from 2 million in 2002 (Meertens, 2002, p. 3) to an unprecedented 4.1 million in 2010 (UNHCR, 2010)—a doubling of this humanitarian crisis—precisely because of the Uribista emphasis on a military solution to Colombia's internal problems.[8] Over half of the IDP population is under 18 and female (57 percent). Further, 70 percent of this population is indigenous and Afro-Colombian women and children. The neglect of their wellbeing was such that, in 2004, during the first term of the Uribe regime, the Constitutional Court was forced to rule that government was "required to address the problems facing displaced people" in their many social needs, but particularly those of education. The judicial measure brought "a steady increase in the proportion of IDPs aged 5 to 17 attending school, from 48% in 2007 to 86% in 2010" (UNESCO, 2011, p. 216). This was then an achievement of justice and equality via the judiciary against the state—one example of the type of victory that the Colombian state often presents as its own achievement, in the international arena.

Gender and education indicators, then, within their narrow parameters, cannot hope to illustrate what women and members of other genders experience, overall, on the ground, and are therefore deficient as alerts to the severity of the situation in Colombia.

Education under the Santos Administration

In August 2010, Uribe was irrevocably barred from re-election by the Constitutional Court, due to substantial violations of democratic principles, and the government of neoliberal president Juan Manuel Santos came to power. As will be seen, the deepening of the neoliberal program has proceeded apace but social movements have created quite a stir in their legitimate demands for change.

In 2010, the first year of the Santos "National Unity" administration, education spending in Colombia dropped even further to 13 percent of public expenditure, below the average of 15.9 percent for Latin American countries. Gross expenditure on education rose just 0.9 percent while expenditure on military and security services rose by 9.98 percent in 2009. This continued the trend of increases on military expenditure during the Uribe government, which were between 17–18 percent during 2000–2009 (MANE, 2012, p. 41). War continues to be prioritized over education.

State schools and colleges remain underfunded, with increased patchy privatization favored in lieu of increased redistribution of wealth. Goals are missed by the *segregation* of these impoverished students into schools in poor areas, that is, by *generalized social poverty and inequality,* which therefore implies the urgent need for redistribution (Rangel and Lleras, 2010) and a solution to the civil war, which exacerbates and reinforces these conditions. Higher education, which was consistently underfunded under Uribe, at 0.292 to 0.112 percent GDP during 2002–2008, despite the growth of the Colombian economy by over 5 percent in that period (Garzón, 2010 in Bula, 2011), still struggles with a wide variety of chronic problems, such as the severe financial constraints and persistent lack of coordination between different providers.

Santos' government has therefore continued the shift of public goods yet further, from public rights to utilitarian tools in the service of national and international markets. The starkest example of this were the draconian transformations, proposed for higher education in 2011 by Maria Fernanda Campo, Santos' Minister of Education, which would deepen, even further, all the weaknesses in the original education funding Law 30 of 1992 (desde abajo, 2011). This Law already limits university budgets to the rise in inflation, which does not allow for expansion or improvement of facilities nor further development of research. In summary, Campo's proposed reforms sought to:

- shift the function of education from a social good to a tradable market commodity—to an ossifying rather than transforming power;
- regain control of the educational curriculum;
- stamp out the student movement;
- throw public institutions to the market to compete for funds;
- feed an increasingly casualized free-market economy. (Funcomisiones Modep, 2011)

Unsurprisingly, academics and communities rejected this view of education as a "privileged commodity." They declared education a worthwhile investment and right that, in parallel with other policies, promotes delivery and rewards (Munera Ruiz, 2011; Gomez de Mantilla, 2011). The Colombian students' movement shone in late 2011 as they joined academics, parents, trade unions, political parties and social movements in opposition to Santos' proposed reforms of Law 30 (see box 1). The choice is, as Left senator Enrique Robledo pointed out, whether Colombia is to be a country made up of unskilled workers in subservience to international capital or one with a highly skilled labor force, creating added value and innovations for a sovereign future.

Box 12.1 History of the MANE—Social
Movements in Action

The Colombia nation-wide student movement began to come together over the years 2009–2011 as the different student groups in existence realized the importance of joint action. The groups at its inception were the Federación de Estudiantes Universitarios (FEU), the Asociación Colombiana de Estudiantes Universitarios (ACEU), the Federación Universitaria Nacional (FUN), the Organización Colombiana de Estudiantes (OCE) and the Proceso Nacional Identidad Estudiantil (PNIE).

Through steady work, the groups finally consolidated as the MANE on August 21, 2011. The threat of the Santos' reform to Law 30 was a powerful motivator to unite but also the catalyst to a movement deeper and wider in its scope than just student affairs. In organizational terms, the movement was strengthened by clearly defined goals and the delegation of work through regional committees. Strong alliances were formed not only with the obvious stakeholders such as academics and students' families, but also with other workers' struggles.

As David Florez, one of the MANE founding leaders, has said: "We did not want to be narrow in scope and only concern ourselves with issues affecting students. We linked struggles against neo-liberalism, not just in different regions of Colombia, but across sectors. This was particularly effective in drawing comparisons with health sector workers' struggles, as nearly everyone in Colombia has been shocked and outraged at the effects of privatisation of the public health sector: corruption, wasted resources, sacked workers, deteriorating health care and unnecessary suffering for ordinary citizens. In this way we managed to bring many on-board, including our fellow students and academics from the private tertiary sector, and widen solidarity throughout Colombia" (Florez, pers. comm., April 26, 2013).

The level of activism, dedication and commitment of the MANE movement is impressive and includes solidarity with other student groups in the region, such as those in Chile, who have also been at the forefront of similar powerful opposition against the further privatization of their education system.

In early November 2011, after initially dismissing the evidently well-supported protests and patronizing its critics, the Santos' government finally gave in and withdrew the reform to Law 30. The students' move-ment: the *Mesa Amplia Nacional Estudiantil* (MANE or Nationwide Students' Platform) has been extraordinarily successful in creating a broad solidarity movement for a publicly funded education as a right for all. The MANE is now part of a nationwide consultation toward reform of education from the grassroots (Mane, 2012). The propos-als are pertinent to current peace process negotiations, since, for new generations of Colombians, it is more preferable to improve one's lot via educational opportunities than via obligatory conscription into a war that has lost its purpose and must definitely end.

Gender, Education and the Santos Years

Women's involvement in all spheres of life is encouraged by the Santos' government, and in 2012, for the first time after the Uribe decade, the UN special representative for the office of Conflict and Sexual Violence, Margot Wallström, was invited to visit[9] (DNP, 2010–2014: Chapter IV). But goodwill on paper and state visits have not translated into practical action by the state. Institutionally, therefore, the picture for gender equity remains very poor (Sanchez, 2011; Waldmann, 2007). Despite Colombia having a presidential adviser for Women's Equity since 1999, UNESCO figures show that for the two indicators that together make up the *empowerment* dimension of the gender inequality index—*education* and *representa-tion in parliament*—Colombia still has one of the lowest scores for representation of women in parliament in Latin America (CEPAL, 2010). Also, crucially, 39 percent of Colombian women acknowledge having experienced physical and sexual violence on a regular basis and the situation is recognizably serious for women leaders of social, educational and political movements (Amnesty, 2011; UN Women, 2011). The 1991 Colombian Constitution and resulting instruments of law act as bulwarks against these continued infringements, but impunity for these crimes persists at 98 percent.[10]

Therefore, as in the Uribe years, during this present government, there is a definite dissonance in the positive outlook provided by offi-cial national indicators seeking to show "overall" improved educa-tion and gender equality and the experience of Colombian people in their everyday lives. What is noted is that while improvements in GII measurements do represent some of the singular aspects they seek to quantify, they do not yet manage to *contextualize* or capture the *depth and range* of uneven gender inequality, which is *additionally criss-crossed by generalized violence* and *economic inequality*.

Evaluation of Present Education and Gender Policies in Colombia

The Santos government is not radically altering the status quo left by Uribe. However, this latest administration has a self-conscious awareness of the damage done to perceptions of Colombian governance, and of the need to improve the country's international image, if only for the sake of Free Trade Agreement approvals. Even entrenched elites are unlikely to prosper in a climate of gender inequality and extreme human rights abuses, as evidence in other countries shows (Schober and Winter-Ebmer, 2011). Outwardly, it therefore appears to be seeking to isolate the narco-military mafia from everyday affairs and to minimize a few of the many gross inequities that have characterized Colombian everyday lives. But the present government's neoliberal sympathies have entrenched marketized and compartmentalized policies in both education and gender equality, which consistently fail the majority of Colombians, due to a proliferation of self-generated internal contradictions. It is evident that all manner of policies undermine each other. In education, patchy privatization in increasingly economically polarized communities leads to exclusion and underachievement. National increases in coverage are instigated with ever-decreasing budgets leading to drops in quality, inefficiency and high dropout rates. There are national gender policies that are immediately invalidated by a national policy of militarism. There is a parallel peace process without a ceasefire, so that the conflict continues to pervade the whole of society, including the conditions and quality of educational provision, and, of course, the safety and wellbeing of both men and women. And beyond education, there are national gender policies for work, while, simultaneously, market deregulation and "flexibility" policies contribute to cut backs in the very work women do, and a national rate of 68 percent casualization of employment (ENS, 2008; Vásquez, 2011).

Indicators therefore do not manage to capture what citizens experience throughout their lives, as they navigate through the pervasive violence and make transitions from school to higher education or from education to work, for example, or as they move through different life stages and ages. The examples in this chapter show that the *inter-sectorial effects* of education and gender equity are, not yet, efficiently captured by merely integrating sectorial indicators. Atomized indicators, which may in themselves be flawed due to incomplete data or assumptions, only point to discrete aspects of social progress and, even when integrated, still miss out the essential horizontal fabric of social wellbeing. In sum, though unitary official indicators throughout the Uribe-Santos period illustrate apparent improvements in both education and gender equality, they give incomplete compartmentalized and de-contextualized snapshots that skim over the surface and hide the coarser realities and the trade-offs, which have been deemed acceptable and politically necessary to achieve the rise in indicators. Successive Colombian governments have progressively commodified education and gender equality, including its indicators, via policies that neuter their transformative and developmental potential. Education and a life with dignity and non-discrimination are social rights, which will only be achieved through taking markedly different routes to those at present traced by neoliberal and elite agendas.

The greatest impetus for positive social change in education and gender is consistently being knitted at the grassroots, in the convergence of different social movements supported by organized progressive politics, as demonstrated by the MANE. These are already effectively being scaled up to regional level, as shown by the cited example of developments instigated by the student movement nationally and in many other sectors, such as the new Bogota center-left administration, which cannot be elaborated on here. International social movements and pro-equality politics also have positive effects on improvements in Colombia at the national level. The international ideals of gender equality (and other equalities) cannot be ignored as nondiscriminatory practice becomes the norm rather than the exception, worldwide. However, the Colombian state and its encrusted elites remain stuck in a neoliberal frame (interlaced with what can only be termed a pseudo-colonialist paternalism), which is already failing in Western economies, and which is also, even now, being quietly abandoned by some of its own international proponents in social policy (Mahon, 2010). Much therefore remains to be done.

Colombia is at an interesting juncture, therefore—and its political and developmental moment is best captured at the national and international levels by the influence and scope of its social movements rather than the circumscribed data described by indicators in gender and education alone. These movements—student, women, LGBTI, indigenous, afro, campesino—are a strong clue as to how Colombian society has managed to survive and innovate despite years of the worst forms of capitalist and militarist onslaught. In education, as previously mentioned, they have salvaged and lobbied for the best that pedagogy has to offer through local organizing and intense networking at both national and international levels. Inclusive workshops and assemblies are part of the very fabric of Colombian society and they have gained increasing impetus—both as a response to the rabid repression of the Uribe regime as well as to the subtler but increasingly noxious neoliberalism practiced by Santos and his present government. As the attempts at a peace process indicate—social movements are the key toward the building of a new and more humane Colombia.

Abbreviations

CINEP   Centro de Investigación y Educación Popular
DNP   Departamento Nacional de Planeacion
UNHCR   United Nations High Commissioner for Refugees
UNRISD   United Nations Research Institute for Social
          Development

Notes

1. The *Human Development Report* (HDR) is an independent publication commissioned by the United Nations Development Programme (UNDP) from http://hdr.undp.org/en/reports/. The discussion in this chapter concerns the HDR-GII indicator used in the HDR. There are now a total of five gender indicators, three of which have emerged since 2010. For a discussion on this, see van Staveren (2011).
2. According to the Stockholm International Peace Research Institute, defence spending portions were 3.4% GDP in 2002 to 3.6% GDP in 2010 (latest available figure) with a maximum of 3.8% in 2009 (SIPRI, 2012). However if defence spending *as well as* attendant security spending (e.g. police, secret services, etc.) are taken into account the average expenditure in 2004 was over 6 % GDP per year over this period (Otero Prada, 2008, pp. 16–17).
3. COP (Colombian Pesos) 3.5 million = USD 1,900/student, COP 12.5 million = USD 6,432/prisoner and COP 18 million = USD 10,000/student. At exchange rate COP 1,942 = USD 1 on December 1, 2011.
4. In this period Colombia rose from position 81 to position 76 out of 127 countries according to UNESCO's Education for All Development Index (EFA-EDI). The EDI *includes* four easily quantifiable goals: universal primary education, adult literacy, *gender parity* and quality of education. The closer the EDI is to 1 the higher a country's ranking. In 2008, for Colombia the EDI was measured at 0.929 as compared to 0.867 in 2002. However, this included the gender-specific index at 0.967 in 2008, which had dropped from the 2002 figure of 0.969 (UNESCO, 2006, p. 257; 2011, pp. 262–263).

5. MEN, Ministerio de Educacion (Ministry of Education).
6. SENA, Servicio Nacional de Aprendizaje (National Learning System public institution).
7. The number of LGBTI homicides increased nationally between 2006 and 2009. The figures are likely underestimated due to a large degree of underreporting, which is improving.
8. Meertens explains the figure in her 2002 report for UNHCR. The 2010 figure is 4.1 million total displaced persons, which includes IDPs, international refugees and asylum seekers. The figure of concern for UNHCR is given as 4.3 million (UNHCR, 2010). This is on a par with the numbers occurring in Afghanistan and Iraq. The numbers of displaced are now more than 5 million, the largest in the world, according to the reputable NGO Consultoria para los Derechos Humanos y el Desplazamiento (Consultancy for Human Rights and Displacement, CODHES) (CODHES, 2011).
9. http://www.eltiempo.com/justicia/experta-dice-que-la-violencia -sexual-es-el-lado-oscuro-de-colombia_11848151–4.
10. Margot Wallström, UN Special Representative on sexual violence in armed conflict, insisted after her visit to Colombia, in May 2012, that "Colombia should increase its efforts to combat impunity for crimes of sexual violence."

References

All internet sources were accessed during November and December 2012
Amnesty (2011), *Colombia: "This Is What We Demand, Justice!" Impunity for Sexual Violence against Women in Colombia's Armed Conflict*, http://www.amnesty.org/en/news-and-updates/report/colombian-authorities -fail-survivors-sexual-violence-2011-09-21.
Barrera, Felipe and Ibáñez, Ana María (2004), *Does Violence Reduce Investment in Education?: A Theoretical and Empirical Approach*, http://ideas.repec.org/p/col/000089/002382.html.
Barrera-Osorio, F (2006), *The Impact of Private Provision of Public Education: Empirical Evidence from Bogotá's Concession Schools—Contracting Private Providers to Deliver Public Education for the Poor: A Successful Experiment from Colombia*, Policy Research Working Papers, World Bank.
Bula, Jorge Iván (2011), *En Riesgo Financiamiento de la Universidad Publica*, May 9, http://universidad.edu.co/index.php?option=com_content &view=article&id=2023:en-riesgo-financiamiento-de-la-universidad -publica&catid=36:ensayos-acadcos&Itemid=81.
CEPAL (2010) *Naciones Unidas, El Progreso de América Latina y El Caribe hacia los Objetivos del Milenio, Desafíos para lograrlos con Igualdad*, Santiago de Chile: Comision Economica para America Latina y el Caribe (ECLAC), http://www.eclac.cl/mdg/GO03/#; http://www.eclac.cl /cgi-bin/getProd.asp?xml=/MDG/noticias/paginas/7/35637/P35637 .xml&xsl=/MDG/tpl/p18f-st.xsl&base=/tpl/imprimir.xsl.

CINEP (2010), *El Legado the las politicas de Uribe—retos para la adminis-tracion de Santos. Reporte Especial—agosto 2010* (The Legacy of Uribe's Policies: Challenges for the Santos Administration), Special Report—August 2010, http://cinep.pasosdejesus.org/node/1083.

——— (2012), "Cien Dias—vistos por CINEP/PPP," *La Paz: tan cerca, tan lejos* 72 (Mayo–Julio).

CODHES (2011), "CODHES Informa: De la Segurida a la Prosperidad Democratica en Medio del Conflicto," *Boletin* 78(17), September 19, http://www.codhes.org/index.php?option=com_docman&task=cat_view&gid=64&Itemid=50.

Colombia Diversa (2011), "All the Responsibilities, Not Many Rights, The Human Rights Situation of Lesbians, Gays, Bisexuals, and Transgenders in Colombia" International HIV/AIDS Alliance, 2011, http://www.eldis.org/go/home%26id=58937%26type=Document.

desde abajo (2011), 169 (Mayo 20–Junio 20), *Suplemento Educacion y Economia No 1*.

DNP (2002–2006), *Plan Nacional de Desarrollo 2002–2006*.

——— (2010–2014), *Plan Nacional de Desarrollo 2010–2014*, Capitulo III—Crecimiento Sostenible y Competividad and Capitulo IV—Igualdad de oportunidades para la prosperidad social, http://www.dnp.gov.co/PND/PND20102014.aspx.

ENS (2008), *La discriminación laboral tiene cara de mujer Panorama de la situación laboral de las mujeres colombianas—Informe preparado por el Área Mujer Trabajadora de la ENS*, Escuela Nacional Sindical (ENS) 2008.

——— (2011), *Informe nacional de coyuntura económica, laboral y sindical en 2010*, Escuela Nacional Sindical (ENS), http://www.ens.org.co/index.shtml?apc=ba – ;1;-;-;&x=20166447.

Funcomisiones Modep (2011), Hacia donde apunta la nueva ley de Educacion Superior *desde abajo* 168(Abril 20–Mayo 20): pp. 16–19, http://www.desdeabajo.info/ediciones/item/17614-hacia-d%C3%B3nde-apunta-la-nueva-de-educaci%C3%B3n-superior.html.

Garces de Eder, Elena and Herran, Adriana Marulanda (2005), "Women in Colombia: 'you forge your path as you walk,'" in Billson, Janet Mancini and Fluehr-Lobban, Carolyn (eds.), *Female Well-Being—Towards a Global Theory of Social Change*, London and New York: Zed Books, pp. 133–158.

Garzón, Carlos (2010), "Educación Superior Pública en Colombia: ¿Escasez de recursos o de voluntad política?: Ascun, Pensamiento Universitario N° 20. Estudios de base sobre la Ley 30 de 1992, Bogotá," in Bula, Jorge Iván, *En Riesgo Financiamiento de la Universidad Publica*, pp. 129–151, 9 Mayo 2011, http://universidad.edu.co/index.php?option=com_content&view=article&id=2023:en-riesgo-financiamiento-de-la-universidad-publica&catid=36:ensayos-acadcos&Itemid=81.

Gomez de Mantilla, Luz Teresa (2011), *De las dicotomias a las contradic-ciones en la propuesta de reforma a la Ley 30. Una lectura sobre la extension universitaria* in desde abajo No 169, May 20—June 20, *Suplemento Educacion y Economia* (1): pp. 14–19.

Holmes, Rebecca (2010), *The Role of Social Protection Programmes in Supporting Education in Conflict-Affected Situations*, Paper prepared as part of UNESCO Research Background Papers for the EFA Global Monitoring Report 2011: "The Hidden Crisis: Armed Conflict and Education," Overseas Development Institute (ODI), June 2010, unesdoc. unesco.org/images/0019/001913/191354e.pdf.

Hvistendahl, Mara (2012), "Gender and Violence," *Science*, May 18, 2012: pp. 839–840.

HDR (Human Development Report) (2011), http://hdr.undp.org/en /reports/.

IBRD (2003), *Tertiary Education in Colombia: Paving the Way for Reform*, World Bank Country Study, Washington DC: World Bank, pp. 2–6.

Mahon, Rianne (2010), "After Neo-Liberalism?: The OECD, the World Bank and the Child," *Global Social Policy* 10, p. 172, http://gsp.sagepub .com/content/10/2/172.

MANE (2012), *Documentos de trabajo*, Primer encuentro social y popular: Por una nueva educación para un país con soberanía, democracia y paz Bogotá 8, 9, 10 y 11 de junio de 2012, Equipo Dinamizador Comisión Académica Nacional, MANE, Colombia.

Melander, Erik (2005), "Gender Equality and Intrastate Armed Conflict," *International Studies Quarterly* 49: pp. 695–714.

Mancini Billson, Janet and Fluehr-Lobban, Carolyn (2005), *Female Well-Being—Towards a Global Theory of Social Change*, London and New York: Zed Books.

INDH (Informe Nacional de Desarrollo Humano, National Human Development Report) (2011) *Colombia Rural—Razones para la esperanza*, UNDP, http://hdr.undp.org/en/reports/national/latinamericath ecaribbean/colombia/name,23256,en.html.

Meertens, Donny (2002), *Colombia: Internally Displaced Persons and the Conditions for Socio-Economic Reintegration*, WRITENET Paper No.12, UNHCR October 2002, www.unhcr.org/refworld/pdfid/3de62e427 .pdf.

Munera Ruiz, Leopoldo (2011), *Algunas notas sobre la reforma de la Ley 30 de 1992—Espejismo del Mercado y autonomia heteronoma* in desde abajo, No 169, May 20—June 20, Suplemento Educacion y Economia (1): pp. 10–13.

Novelli, Mario (2009), *Colombia's Classroom Wars: Political Violence against Education Sector Trade Unionists*, Brussels: Education International.

——— (2010), "Education, Conflict and Social (In)justice: Insights from Colombia," *Educational Review* 62(3): pp. 271–285.

Observatorio Laboral para la Educacion (2011), Government of Colombia Labour and Education Information System, http://www.graduados colombia.edu.co/html/1732/channel.html.

Otero Prada, Diego (2008), *Experiencias de investigación: las cifras del conflicto Colombiano* INDEPAZ (Instituto de Estudios para el Desarrollo y la Paz) Bogotá, junio de 2008, http://www.setianworks.net/indepazHome /index.php?view=article&id=191%3Aexperiencas-de-investigacion-las -cifras-del-conflicto-colombiano&option=com_content&Itemid=99.

Pathways of Women's Empowerment (2011), "Empowerment: A Journey Not a Destination," Institute of Development Studies (IDS), UK, http:// www.eldis.org/go/home%26id=62744%26type=Document.

Patrinos, H. A. and Sosale, S. (eds.) (2007), *Mobilising the Private Sector for Public Education: A View from the Trenches—Can Public Private Partnerships Work in Different Education Systems around the World?* World Bank.

Rangel, Claudia and Lleras, Christy (2010), "Educational Inequality in Colombia: Family Background, School Quality and Student Achievement in Cartagena," *International Studies in Sociology of Education* 20(4) December: pp. 291–317.

Robledo, Enrique (2006), *El TLC recoloniza a Colombia—Acusación a Álvaro Uribe Vélez*, Bogotá, septiembre de 2006, www.moir.org.co /IMG/pdf/tlc.pdf.

Sanchez, Natalie (2011), "Mujeres en la Ley de Victimas," in CINEP (2012) *Cien Dias—vistos por CINEP/PPP, La Paz: tan cerca, tan lejos* 72 (May—July): pp. 20–22.

Schober, Thomas and Winter-Ebmer, Rudolf (2011), "Gender Wage Inequality and Economic Growth: Is There Really a Puzzle?—A Comment," *World Development* 39(8): pp. 1476–1484.

SIPRI (2012), *Military Expenditure of Colombia*, Data from the Stockholm International Peace Research Institute (SIPRI), http://milexdata.sipri .org/result.php4.

Tovar Rojas, Patricia (2008), "la mujer colombiana en la ciencia y la tecnología ¿se está cerrando la brecha?" (Colombian Woman in Science and Technology, Is the Gap Closing?) Arbor Ciencia, *Pensamiento y Cultura* CLXXXIV(733 September-October): pp. 835–844.

Tribuna Magisterial (May 20, 2012), Radio Programme from the education sector of MOIR (Movimiento Obrero Independiente Revolucionario, Independent Revolutionary Worker's Movement) with Maria Antonieta Cano, http://www.moir.org.co/IMG/mp3/tribmag_may20_12.mp3.

United Nations Commission on the Status of Women (2005), Chapter 13: "The Impacts of Conflict on Women," in *Gender Equality: Striving for Justice in an Unequal World*, New York and Geneva: UNRISD/UN Publications, http://www.unrisd.org/80256B3C005BCCF9/%28Look upAllDocumentsByUNID%29/1FF4AC64C1894EAAC1256FA3005E 7201?OpenDocument.

UNESCO (2006), *Education for All (EFA) Global Monitoring Report 2006 Report—Literacy for All*, http://www.unesco.org/new/en/education /themes/leading-the-international-agenda/efareport/reports/2006 -literacy/.

———— (2007), *A Human Rights-Based Approach to EDUCATION FOR ALL—A Framework for the Realization of Children's Right to Education and Rights within Education*, unesdoc.unesco.org/images /0015/001548/154861e.pdf.

———— (2010), http://www.uis.unesco.org/FactSheets/Pages/default.aspx? SPSLanguage=EN.

———— (2011), *Education for All (EFA) Global Monitoring Report: 2011 Report—The Hidden Crisis: Armed Conflict and Education*, http:// www.unesco.org/new/en/education/themes/leading-the-international -agenda/efareport/reports/2011-conflict/.

UNHCR (2010), *UNHCR Global Trends 2010*, http://www.unhcr.org /4dfa11499.html.

UN Women (2011), *The Violence against Women Prevalence Data: Surveys by Country*, http://www.unifem.org/gender_issues/violence_against_women /facts_figures.php.

van Staveren, Irene (2011), *To Measure Is to Know? A Comparative Analysis of Gender Indices*, International Institute of Social Studies (ISS), Working Paper No. 2011–02, ISS September, http://www.indsocdev.org/resources .html.

Vásquez F, Héctor (2011), *Agencia de información laboral Las cifras de empleo y modelo de desarrollo*, ESN, February 22.

Villar-Márquez, Eliana with Harper, Caroline (2010), "School-Based Violence in Colombia: Links to State-Level Armed Conflict, Educational Effects and Challenges Background," Paper prepared for the Education for All Global Monitoring Report 2011—The *Hidden Crisis: Armed Conflict and Education*, ODI.

Waldmann, Peter (2007), "Is There a Culture of Violence in Colombia?" *Terrorism and Political Violence* 19(4): pp. 593–609.

Wharton, K and Uwaifo Oyelere, Ruth (2011), *Conflict and Its Impact on Educational Accumulation and Enrollment in Colombia: What We Can Learn from Recent IDPs*, Discussion Paper Series No. 5939, August 2011, Bonn: Institute for the Study of Labour (IZA), http://ideas.repec.org/p /iza/izadps/dp5939.html.

World Bank (2010a), Gini Index, http://data.worldbank.org/indicator /SI.POV.GINI.

———— (2010b), *Public Expenditure on Education Total (% of GDP)*, http:// data.worldbank.org/indicator/.

Chapter 13

Cali's Women in Collective Crossing for Three Worlds: Popular Education, Feminisms and Nonviolence for the Expansion of the Present, Memory and for Nurturing Life

Norma Lucía Bermúdez

Introduction

My reflection[1] presented here is based on an educational and emancipatory practice made by many hands, minds and hearts in one autonomous learning space of women in Cali, Colombia: the Pazíficas Women's Political School. This is an experience that has been lived like a journey that has nurtured connections between the individual and collective lives of its participants.

Thus I have decided to tell our history as a journey; a journey that begins on earth, in the deep roots of who we are, from where we come from which emerges the possibility of flying (the air), the motivations for doing so and the fears that arise when we want to fly away and transform our realities. The journey continues by water, sailing and flowing through calm and turbulent waters, finding tributaries and streams that feed our voyage. Finally our journey completes itself with fire and its transformational capacity, with the alchemy to transform ourselves and the new ports and landscapes we reach and create.

Connection with the Earth: Exploring Our Roots.

Colombia occupies a "privileged corner of the planet." With coasts on the Caribbean Sea and the Pacific Ocean, it is one of the most biodiverse places on the planet. It has all the ecosystems, from desert to rainforest, from perpetual snow to warm beaches, countless species of fruit and flowers and produces foods, metal, oil, gas. Colombia also has a rich cultural history and heritage with more than 80 indigenous peoples, Afro-descendant communities, gypsy communities, Arabs, European, Japanese colonies. All of these groups come together to make a country full of languages, customs, knowledges, a country of multiple colors and flavors.

Nevertheless, the history of inequality in the distribution of wealth, in the making of political decisions and the history of dispossession, humiliation and violent conflicts makes us a society and a country full of sorrows, inequalities and injustices.

As a consequence of this history, we live an internal armed conflict—fed by drugs, weapons and human trafficking—which has lasted more than six decades. It ravages people's life through the actions of legal and illegal armed actors that disrespect human rights and impoverish the lives of the majority

As with any place in the world, the main protagonists of war are men, its main logic is patriarchal and its main victims are women.

However, in the midst of the barbarism and inequality that war generates, thousands of initiatives arise that confront violence, poverty and patriarchy. They are the practices and voices of hope and humanity and they stand resolutely on the side of care for life, developing creative ways to deal with conflicts, create other social relationships of respect through which to reconstruct themselves (ourselves) as subjects and citizens.

One of these experiences can be found in Pazíficas Women's Collective, a network that emerged in 2000 in the city of Cali, with the aim of developing nonviolent pacifist and feminist proposals and practices within Colombian society, in order to denounce and make visible the violence experienced by women. This collective is composed of different groups, such as the Drama Company "The Mask," the Cultural House "Weaving Sororities," Foundation "Mavi," Fundación "Peace and Good," the Cultural House Chontaduro, the Foundation "Yes Woman" and the Broad Women's Group. The collective also includes independent women.

We formed at a moment when the broader political context in the country seemed to be offering hope that the armed conflict would be resolved. There was a process of political negotiation between the Colombian government and the FARC (Revolutionary Armed Forces of Colombia). However it was a negotiation between leaders in which the voice of civil society was silenced. Later, when public hearings were established to hear these voices, we, women prepared our intervention. From Cali we decided to send a letter to the "guerrilla" women who were also absent from the negotiations. In the letter we asked them to recount their experiences in the midst of war. How do they love and how do they stop loving, how do they live their menstruation, how do they face their pregnancies, what do they think about the country, about other women, about their lovers? With this letter we opened a space for debate, not only outside but also inside the women's movement. We made visible what is radically different in our positions, practices and proposals. We challenged the content and the traditional ways of making politics, which assumes war as a continuation of politics and vice versa.

We knew that the debate and dialogue that we had opened would have major consequences for us and for moving beyond the old formulas of politics We were facing something deeper: to question the meaning of politics, of its objectives and of its means, to question the sense of power, that power is enacted not only in parliaments and battlefields, but also in social relations, on the streets, in the square, at home and in the bedroom (see Motta, 2009[2] for a more generic discussion of this new politics).

This is the context from which the Pazíficas Women's Collective began. We convened a series of monthly reflexive workshops over 18 months for women of the Valle del Cauca. Out of this experience emerged the initiative to create and consolidate the Pazíficas Women's Political School.

The Air under Our Wings: The Desire to Fly and the Fear of Doing So

Our experience began with a question, as does the beginning of any project. Every flight begins with the meeting of two opposing forces: the intuition that beyond the horizon there are landscapes and climates that deserve to be known and enjoyed and, on the other hand, the fear of leaving the known, the usual benchmarks, the illusion of certainties.

Some of the questions that helped us decide to take flight and launch our school were as follows: How do we want Colombia's history to be told to our future generations? Do we want it only to be remembered for its barbarism and injustice? Do we want our grandchildren to believe their country killed hope while we remained silent?

Or do we want that they know that even in times of increased polarization, inequality and barbarism there were always voices that arose with other ideas and hands of solidarity that tried to build upon what had been destroyed, "planting food in the bomb craters"?[3]

Is it possible to build dialogues among diverse knowledge of so many women that everyday reproduce their lives with their practices without any recognition of their work and often unaware of the political dimension of their contribution and resistances?

Is it possible to make a double rethinking of politics in the sense of making visible everyday life as deeply political and, simultaneously, to connect the public and private spheres in a continuum that challenges hegemonic ideas and practices and rescues it from the individualism and disarticulation of today's reality?

Pazíficas Women's Political School collects many dreams and individual and collective attempts to think and rethink the practices of women. We embrace the experience of those who have ventured into representational politics, those who have developed alternative political practices in their daily lives in neighborhoods, communities or religious groups. We arrived at the conclusion that women have multiple and rich experiences of resistance yet they often lack reflexive processes and systematization that could enable individual and collective learning and enable them to transform their realities through these knowledges. We wanted to develop the space for such reflexive and systematizing practices. But we asked ourselves how do we ensure that we do not repeat hegemonic practices that like a form of banking education tends to divide subjects between those who know and those who do not know or, on the other hand, how do we avoid falling into the binary view that despises academic knowledge validating only the popular? How to create and nurture a real "ecology of knowledges"?[4]

In his epistemological reflections, Boaventura de Sousa Santos[5] states that what we call reality is impoverished by a politics of knowledge that interprets the world through normalizing and universalizing a fragment of reality as if it were everything that exists (Metonymic Reason). This he calls the contraction of the present and is the mechanism by which monocultures are built. De Sousa Santos continues that academic knowledge is considered the only valid knowledge, creating the notion of ignorance, illiteracy, subcultures. The author proposes a practice that opposes this monoculture of knowledge, in a way that does not seek to build an alternative monoculture, but rather an ecology of knowledges that establishes respectful dialogues and translations of each logic, where once there was only a hierarchical and disabling practice.

In the Pazíficas Women's Political School we are committed to fostering an ecology of knowledges building on the experiences, practices and knowledges of all women participants. Thus, both popular women and women from academia, artists, shamans, all can contribute with their experiences, knowledge and stories in a context in which we recognize their value to the lives of women as a whole, and try to make non-hegemonic translations across these differences

With all these questions, motivations, inspirations and intuitions, we decided it was worth spreading our wings and taking flight.

Water that Keeps Us in a State of Alert:
As Pirates We Embark

One of the first texts produced by our school said: "As rebel Penelopes, tired of waiting for wisdom in warriors, we put aside our tissues and we begin upon our own Odyssey."

Aware of the risks and uncertainties we would face in building an autonomous space for women's political formation, we embarked on the adventure, convinced that if we want to see changes in the landscape, we must move; if we want our dreams not to remain in the air (in our imaginations), we need to make them flow, meet with other streams and tributaries and begin to fertilize the land, our reality

Based on this analysis, we developed practices of systematization in which women in academia, human rights activists and leaders of popular processes participated. We checked the training programs offered to women from state institutions and human rights organizations and reflected on our own experiences. It became clear how some reinforced the traditional roles and stereotypes of women, offering, for example, training in arts and crafts such as clothing, cosmetics, food processing without any opening the possibility of questioning these roles or analyzing their political dimensions.

Moreover, many assumed a neutral political subject, which in reality is a patriarchal (masculinized) subjectivity. These programs do not ask questions or open possibilities to imagine and think the possibility of enacting another type of citizenship nor question the barriers for citizenship among women and specifically, among those women from popular sectors, from ethnic groups, disabled women, older women, etc.

Another result of our reflections was the identification that all training programs are directed to an individual subject, not one that transcends this toward a collective subject, toward an encounter with others, to think common realities and possible common agendas. By trying to differentiate ourselves from the limited offerings in terms of women's training programs, we built a school proposal with the following aims:

- To provide women's training opportunities that contribute to the full exercise of their citizenship and political participation with an active and effective gender perspective and to build opportunities for women's empowerment oriented to the development and strengthening of their leadership.
- To strengthen women's citizenship and participatory leadership in order to contribute to the consolidation of new organizational forms, raising awareness in other women and men, and promote the construction of new political proposals from feminist constructions and perspectives, incorporating multiple knowledges, traditional and new practices of women and the feminine.
- To contribute to the formation of women who aspire to positions of decision-making, including public officials, providing tools for an effective and participatory action with alternative proposals with a gender perspective.
- To facilitate tools for incorporating gender perspectives in the daily lives of women participants, promoting their empowerment.
- To encourage articulation processes and construction of alliances within the feminist and women's movement, and with other social and political sectors at local, national, regional and global levels.

In a profound dialogue with the women subjects of our processes, we tried to respond to the need for resistance against a patriarchy that assumes the primacy of reason over emotions, sustains the use of force over dialogue and compassion and privileges the homogenization of subjects.

Hence, the inputs for the construction of the School's guiding principles seek to practice counter-hegemony in the form and content of education:

- To promote nonviolence and the construction of peaceful methods of conflict resolution.
- To respect the ethnic and class diversity and the plurality of democratic and inclusive ideological positions.

- To incorporate training in sisterhood and other elements of feminine culture.
- To combine practice and theory at all levels of training, including both practical work and theoretical through the use of an inclusive and participatory approach.
- To integrate experiential and conceptual aspects, incorporating fun and enjoyment into academic work.
- To build pedagogically new ways of learning, of being in the public world and in the world of politics by inventing new meanings, perceptions and practices.
- To make visible the practices and experiences of women on the political agenda.
- To deconstruct patriarchal political practices, building other practices characterized by their resistance to the hegemonic paradigm.[6]

Navigations and Streams that Drive Our Boat

Inspired by all the above and with the commitment to feed other visions for the interpretation of the world and for constructing other possible worlds, we want to share our encounter between feminism, popular education and nonviolence, some counter-hegemonic currents that have helped to expand our present and to contract the future.[7]

For centuries, Colombia's history has been based on wars in which people have killed each other while wealth and political decisions are increasingly concentrated in fewer hands. In this context, women have been subalternized, even within the subalterns.

We are part of a political and economic regime characterized by the colonization and dictatorship of the market. In order to maintain this (dis)order, the cultural matrix composed by neoliberalism and patriarchy has been sustained on several pillars:

The installation of hierarchies (of class, gender and ethnicity) as something natural, the resolution of conflicts by the use of force and abuse of power, the destruction of nature and the commodification of life. Thus those powers and knowledges that come from subjects defined as "others" are despised, feared, distorted and made invisible by official knowledge and power.

Aware of this political, philosophical and epistemological context, we decided to make a counter-hegemonic intellectual craftwork woven with yarns from feminisms, nonviolence and popular education as currents of thought and action that feed, enhance and question these dominant articulations of power themselves. Sometimes these currents get stronger and sometimes they retreat but they always change after an encounter or fruitful dialogue.

The Feared World of Feminism

I will start with gender studies, because is a term that arouses less fear and allergic reaction than the term feminism.

Gender studies, daughter of the incursion of feminists into the social sciences, questions the sexual binary division understood as natural fact, by demonstrating that relationships between men and women, roles and identities, are cultural, historical and social constructions.

Preconceptions and rigid structures burst, showing that there are millions of ways of being a man, a woman, or none of the above. Within two decades, the binary and essentialist reading and explanation of gender and the power relations between them has led to complex and flexible understandings of gender and its intersection with the categories social class, ethnicity, generation, sexual orientation and other complexities.

Working with a gender perspective implies efforts to de-naturalize relations that appear as natural, interrogating how the sex-gender system in expressed in social and everyday relationships. This also implies revealing, enabling and enhancing the self-constitutive power of subjects in the construction of new masculine and feminine identities, new symbols, new meanings of being men and women.

Feminism as a theory has profound implications for the creation of an ecology of knowledges. To situate ourselves in a feminist perspective means to not only make visible the conditions and positions of women and men in society but also implies an intellectual and embodied commitment to transform those factors that place women in asymmetrical positions in terms of power, life opportunities, cultural valuations, discourses and practices and institutional and academic frameworks. It implies an attempt to reconfigure these relationships of power, hierarchy, asymmetry and alienation through the invention of other ways of relating and being embedded in commitments of recognition and reciprocity.

The social sciences understand epistemology as "a theory of knowledge which responds to questions such as who can know, which type of things can be known, how do we evaluate when beliefs can be recognised and legitimised as knowledge etc."[8] Feminism affirms that women can be knowers, that women's experiences are fonts of knowledge and that the evaluative frameworks used to judge what legitimate knowledge is should not be based only on the experiences and observations of men. The recognition of women as agents and subjects of knowledge implies a critique of an epistemology that represents itself as neutral but is thought and structured from the masculine.

At the political level, feminism is a diverse and plural movement that is committed to the democratization of life in all its spheres, denounces all forms of discrimination and creates actions to overcome these practices and representations. There are many differing currents and emphases within feminism and for this it must be named in the plural: feminisms.

In the Colombia context to take a feminist position is to take sides in the struggles for the redistribution of resources, democratization of political decisions, development of affirmative actions to overcome the historic exclusion of sectors of the population from development but above all it is to situate oneself radically on the side of care for life and rejection of the logics of war, violence and humiliation as methods of governing, accumulating power and sacrificing our daughters and sons' futures.

To be a feminist in Colombia and globally is also to build other ways of being and relating embedded in a redistribution of power and also practices of recognition and mutuality. This means not only making demands on the system but being part of an affirmative project of multiplicity, a project that attempts to decolonize our bodies and minds by building upon the powers and knowledges of subaltern subjects.

Feminism has been called the silent revolution of the twentieth century. This is because its arguments and methods have rejected the logics of violence. It is here that can be found its philosophical and political connection with traditions of nonviolence.

The Misunderstood World of Nonviolence

Even though the twentieth century is known as the century of great world wars, it is also a century in which a planetary movement of nonviolence created and generated great cultural changes.

The origins of this new concept are attributed to Aldo Capitini,[9] who wanted the semantics of the concept not to be dependent on the term and concept of violence, and above all would emphasize that Nonviolence would be identified as a humanist, spiritual and open conceptualization of human relations. For Capitini this concept went further than techniques and methods. It constituted an ethical, political, social, economic and ecological emancipatory project to reduce human suffering.

What Nonviolence Is Not

Maria Lopez (2006)[10] argues that it is as important to know what a concept isn't as much as what it is to avoid confusions, misunderstandings and misrepresentations.

According to Lopez the first element of what the concept is not is that it doesn't legitimize the taking of power with force, in counter-distinction to many revolutionary movements. This reimagines revolutionary counter-hegemony and is not, as it is often accused of, anti-revolutionary.

The second distinction the author makes is between nonviolence and passive resistance. According to Lopez this distinction itself comes from a bipolar framing that originates from the English context in which violence is classified as heroic if it comes from the English, but as terrorist if it comes from their enemies in which the term passive is used for strange things such as noncooperation, civil disobedience or boycott (none of which are actually passive). She also highlights that critics often equate nonviolence with naivety, silence, voluntary acceptance or social and ethical indifference.

Nonviolence has been conceptualized and theorized from a Latin American perspective. This affirms that power is a mobile force of all beings and in all relations. Power therefore circulates and exists in each person. In this way even though minorities have dominated the bodies and minds of majorities, resistances always emerge, not only or principally against dominating power but rather as an inherent way in which living beings affirm their aliveness.

As an affirmation of life, resistances are prior to domination, which attempt always to trap such affirmative being. Nonviolence therefore is not a reactive conceptualization whose object is to oppose violence but rather it aims to affirm life. Affirmative resistance does not therefore seek to destroy the other but rather paradoxically affirm the other. Nonviolence affirms our powers and creates lines of flight and trajectories that distance us from the logic of power and makes it difficult to capture our being in binary and bipolar logics.

In our practice to take up nonviolence as a philosophical and political framework has been an enormous struggle. It has meant learning to valorize the power of weakness, embracing the power of subtlety and developing gentle mechanisms that impact and transform ourselves, our lives and the lives of others. Additionally nonviolence has enabled us to make connections between women's micro and everyday actions and a planetary movement of emancipatory change.

The Misinterpreted World of Popular Education

According to Alfonso Torres, popular education can be defined as a group of social practices and discursive constructions in the field of education, whose intention is to contribute to the process of making the popular classes active subjects, which results in social transformation. Thus embracing popular education means recognition of its political nature, a commitment to strengthening popular movements, a practice that fosters the conditions of the subaltern's self-liberation and the development of pedagogies that can enable these.

Yet popular education is not singular rather it is comprised by a diversity of knowledges, practices and experiences. Some common features of popular education can however be identified.

The objectives of this framework are to develop a collective critical reading of the structures of power of Latin American societies that create the conditions of oppression, silencing and exclusion of the popular classes. This aims to enable participants to develop the tools and understanding to transform their lives and societies. The educator or facilitator is guided by a political commitment to fostering critical rereadings of the world.

The objectives and conceptualization of emancipatory politics are however multiple: for some the process of transformation must be made outside the state and the focus is rather on alternative organizational processes. For others there are attempts to occupy state spaces using the methods and practices of popular education for it is understood that the state is not monolithic but is populated by social and political actors that struggle over the power enacted by state institutions.

However, what are crucial are the ethical commitments of popular education, which is committed to the excluded, to others, to diversity, human rights, and active and participatory citizenship and transformation of an unjust reality. The political-pedagogical intention of popular education and its emancipatory character closely binds it to the problem/controversy of power, by seeking a power shift toward large majorities of society, facilitating their access to knowledge, life and power.

Popular education is a social practice that intentionally orientates its actions to the development and transformation of forms of representing, understanding and acting of the popular sectors. Popular subjectivity can express itself sometimes as social consciousness, other times as knowledges and understanding and at others in popular values and culture. The formation of social subjects with an emancipatory social agency is related to the creation of a system of representations, which includes images, ideas, meanings and symbols, which bring meaning to practise in the public sphere (and as feminism reminds us, in that considered the private sphere). This includes the valorization of the knowledges and understanding of participants, recognition of multiple forms of understanding and practices that develop the ability to reflect, analyse, pose and solve problems, synthesize and develop strategies etc. This is embedded in recognition of the diverse logics and forms of knowing that are involved in the process of constructing emancipatory knowledge and understanding.

Another great contribution of popular education is its commitment to generating criteria, methodological tools and strategies consistent with its critical and transformative intentions. This involves conscientization, dialogues of knowledge, active participant problematization, cultural negotiation and deconstruction that enrich not only the world of education but are cornerstones in the reconstruction of a pedagogic discourse for popular education. Generally this is embedded in a methodology of action-reflection, action-practice and theory-practice.

Popular education develops and is embedded in a diversity of methodological approaches and is based on recognition of diversity and questioning of homogenizing practices. The recognition of diversity does not necessarily lead to fragmentation and dislocation. Diversity is fruitful to the extent that it is socialized, systematized and opens spaces for building consensus and reasonable dissent. That is, it does not force agreement, rather, it recognizes that there are disagreements, that these need not divide us, but instead can become elements in our reflections about our daily lives

The recognition of such diversity and openness involves opening to the uncertainty of the process, the loss of control over the interpretations of reality developed and strategies of change generated. Therefore popular education breaks with the paradigm of instrumental rationality.

In our experience at the Escuela Política de Mujeres Pazíficas, popular education has given us a philosophy, ethics and a way of relating to multiple and diverse knowledges of women participants. We have gone through partnerships with public universities, experiencing the tensions between academic knowledge and popular knowledge, tensions between criteria of validity of what is knowledge and whose knowledge counts and we have made decisions that have put us on a path of autonomy, in which we have defended the possibility of constructing, deconstructing and reconstructing curricula and methodologies in dialogue with the changing context, and the recognition of women as subjects in the making of educational decisions. Thanks to the contribution of popular education and the other two perspectives discussed in this chapter, we also had the possibility of rethinking politics and democracy.

The River that Receives the Intersection of Worlds

Fuelled by these three powerful currents, the Escuela Política de Mujeres Pazíficas is a stage full of vitality, which raises the following question.

What happens when the legacies of feminism and gender studies are combined in the philosophical, ethical and political commitment of nonviolence and popular education? Many things.

I will return to Boaventura de Sousa Santos and his proposal of translations. "Translation is an intercultural and intersocial process. We use a transgressive metaphor of linguistic translation: to translate knowledge into other knowledge, to translate practices and subjects into each other, is to seek intelligibility without 'cannibalizing' without homogenization. In that sense, it attempts to translate in the opposite form than that of linguistic translation. It tries to find what there is in common between a movement of women and an indigenous movement between an indigenous movement and one of African descent, between the latter and urban or peasant movements, between a peasant movement in Africa with one in Asia, where are the distinctions and similarities. Why? Because you have to create intelligibility without destroying diversity." De Sousa Santos contributes in the sense to realizing a sociology of emergences. As he continues, "We try to see what are the signals, tracks, latencies, possibilities in the present which are signs of the future, which are emerging possibilities and they are without credibility (descredibilizadas) because they are embryos, because they are not very visible things."

So in the School we enact such a translating practice between the perspectives mentioned and their contributions to the world, running the risk that we pass as Kate Rushin,[11] African American feminist, has stated in one of her poems,

> I explain my mother to my father, my father to my little sister, my little sister to my brother, my brother to the white feminists, the white feminists to the Black church folks, the black church folks to the ex-hippies, the ex-hippies to the Black separatists, the Black separatists to the artists, the artists to my friends' parents.
> Then I've got to explain myself to everybody
> I do more translating than the gawdamn U.N.

So if here in Cali we keep trying to make bridges and translations, it is not because we have not been warned.

And then...What happens when we find in the same project the heritages of a world fear, such as feminism, of a world misunderstood, such as Nonviolence and of a world misinterpreted like popular education? Many things. Amongst these, are that we critique certain critical perspectives for the traces of hegemonic thinking and practice that they reproduce.

For example, nonviolence demonstrates and criticizes the construction of history as a succession of wars and not as a story of cooperation, resistances, or as the affirmation of life. Also it is a story that has been transmitted as a series of exceptional heroes who create history, masking collective history, the history of peoples and communities, the powers of the periphery. Thus the history of Colombia is a collection of heroes, usually on horseback, with sword in the hand or in their belt, who, we are told, fiercely and heroically gave their lives to build the motherland. We know that this story is a tangible example of the construction of absences.

However, when trying to do a sociology of absences, telling the story of nonviolence, how do we tell it? As a collection of heroes like Gandhi, David Thoreau, Mandela, Luther King, Walesa. They are of course diverse heroes, unarmed, peaceful, wise, very different from ones from our creole history, but they are exceptional individuals and of course, men. Does anyone remember the name of Gandhi's wife? Hardly anyone. And even though she appears in a few lines of biographies as Kasturba and in Gandhi´s interviews, we know that she was hit by Gandhi many times. From her Ghandi learned a key lesson not only in his life, but in the inspiration of the movement. Although he was never confronted by Kasturba, Gandhi never achieved her obedience by his force. Kasturba probably cultivated many other merits. Yet she like many others is left to silence and oblivion not only by the official historians, but in our own stories of the history of nonviolence. The task remains to not only examine Kasturba but also to try to change our monocle into a kaleidoscope, in which we can look at nuances, shades, multicolored figures and we can narrate these stories and transgress the official history.

This means that feminists demand the nonviolence movement makes radical changes in its languages, not just by saying "he and she," although we do also demand this, but by practicing an ecology of recognition and giving way to images, words and minor tones, as are sometimes the forms of knowing and being of the subaltern.

Feminisms sustain that the reenchantment of the world and the awakening of the powers of the periphery involves making visible, naming, recognizing and learning from diverse and multiple subjects. And these huge cultural changes do not occur in a neutral universe, but are configured by bodies and biographies of beings that house multiple differences that intersect in a context of patriarchal culture. For this reason, in addition to bringing the body as a strong reference point and presence in the pedagogical act, we ask questions to these bodies and to these subjectivities, trying to deconstruct the rigid system of allocation of rights, opportunities, roles and characteristics that depend on the sex of individuals. For feminisms emphasizes, on the one hand, the need to make present the history and experience of women as a source of knowledge, proposing also heroines, making visible stories and figures that can be a reference to the symbolic construction of lineage and female authority and on the other hand, in unlearning patriarchal culture, trying new relationships and agreements between women and between men and women.

The task is exciting: continuing with the construction of political subjects, rights and social transformations, but without carrying the weight of having to strengthen a struggle against a central power. But neither do we allow a masking of the effects of patriarchy that still circulate within the oppressed or subaltern, making women the subaltern of the subaltern (Spivak, 1997). So, all the power is at the service of the expansion of the present, making visible the absences and manifesting the emergences.

From the philosophy of nonviolence we are always called to remember to deconstruct bipolar categories, such as exploiter-exploited, oppressor-oppressed, perpetrator-victim, to prevent the dehumanization of the contenders and their conversion into enemies, a resource that has served all manner of fundamentalisms. That's why we question certain feminisms that do not break but rather reinforce bipolarity, building an enemy, the man, who becomes the holder of all patriarchal power, forgetting the perverse effects of this cultural matrix in the construction of masculinities.

Another criticism that emerges from nonviolence would be the building of oppositional discourses, which squander the opportunity to build affirmative knowledges, vital proposals, in the sense of an affirmation of life at the heart of nonviolence practice. Nonviolence also challenges the anthropocentrism of some feminist trends, as on many occasions these remain in the realm of the social and cultural and forget the larger system that hosts the other two: nature.

Popular education, for its part, questions the feminist elite's focus on achieving spaces in the same unquestioned patriarchal power scheme and masking their privileges and power, and also interrogates the gains of some group's rights, which are observed by other women as reinforcing discriminations that perpetuate inequality and lack of opportunities.

The same happens when nonviolence is enriched by the contributions of popular education. Here we learn to be vigilant in order that language and voice are not left in the hands of an intellectual elite, or circulate as an inventory of exceptional examples of heroines that changed history. Popular education provides a pedagogical and political point of view which ensures that the knowledges of feminism and nonviolence are inserted into the daily life of communities, with emphasis on those most in need, for having been historically excluded and oppressed.

With all these dialogues and translations, how do we translate these into the concrete space of educational journeys? Here is an example of how we have tried:

> In the School we run a diploma course. It begins with a ritual in circle orientated around fire, water, air, earth and spirit. We introduce ourselves. This is a moment in which we revere the word and the stories of women who coming from diverse roads and life paths, that have taken steps to this meeting place.

The dialogue of knowledges begins. One of the first questions to circulate in this encounter is: what is the learning that has been useful in your life that you would like to share with the group?

Through each woman's story we open the possibility of being co-educators. We break the two paradigms of ignorance and poverty. We affirm with conviction that there is no on who is so ignorant or so poor that they do not have something to share.

From the sharing of our stories we assemble them into themes and spend a number of weeks sharing them with the group.

So, for example, if a woman has learned to make a recipe with which she had fed her family well and cheaply, the group makes the dish, tastes it and discusses similar experiences. We then link this experience of making the recipe and the conditions of her life and learning to reflection on questions such as food sovereignty. We read texts, and watch videos about food sovereignty movements in Colombia and other places. We talk about the neoliberal crisis and how this increases the weight of labor on the shoulders of women. We explore alternative forms of economy such as the feminist economy.

We do the same with all the knowledges that are shared. Then we pass into another stage in the dialogue of knowledges in which we explore key thematics such as the history of women's human rights, the nonviolence movement, and concepts such as gender, sexual diversity, ethnicity. We explore alternative experiences of social and political change. Many of the topics are chosen by the participants as the educational journey progresses.

At the end of this stage we ask ourselves with the learning, understanding and emotions aroused by this experience how would we like to appear in the public sphere? Which aesthetics, which messages, proposals do we want to share with our society?

These are the questions that guide the final stage of our educational journey and constitute the graduation project in which we plan and develop a collective action that dialogues with the state, public opinion, other movements, our communities. From this we have developed many campaigns and actions from performances, marches, carnivals, urban games, linkages with global campaigns.

After more than ten journeys in our history, we have reflected, always bittersweet reflections, about our learning and transformation.

On the one hand the transformational capacity of this experience is clear. Some women for the first time have situated themselves in the mirror of the history of women and recognized the validity and courage of their life struggles. As Agripina a women from a popular-class community describes: "For me, as a shy person, it made me so happy to find other women who were so prepared yet so down to earth and with such human warmth. I loved all that I learnt and it gave me much support for my family, my life, my community. I never believed that these were political because I had such a narrow understanding of politics. So now when other women ask me what I have learnt I invite them to the next diploma, because of the wonderful things that happened for me in this process."

Others have connected and recognized their right to happiness and have decided to end unsatisfactory or abusive relationships of many years. Others have found friends for life and/or for adventures and projects. The only man to have graduated from the School became aware of the tenderness that he can hold in his masculinity and embraced joyfully his paternity. Some women have discovered or rediscovered their voices to speak, sing and protest. As Johana a student of social sciences recounts: "The school gave me the possibility to understand that in every space in which I participate, in the home, your work that I always have the right to declare myself as woman, to think differently, and to be in the process of change permanently." Others have decided that the fight to win a place in representative politics is worthwhile and they have prepared for this practice. Almost all participants agree that some of the most memorable moments were those of self-recognition and the creation of linkages with other women. As Aurora afro-Colombian wise woman grandmother describes: "In the School I found a family, which for has been a blessing. I learnt to love life, something I was losing. But thanks to this family I resuscitated this love."

What Is Cooked in the Fire: Themes Emerging from the Experience

Despite the complexities of translations and bridging, we are convinced that the encounter between feminisms, popular education and nonviolence enables all truths to be questioned, fertilized, transformed and strengthened. This contributes to the construction of education, ethical and political horizon. We want to share with travelers, nomads of resistances, some clues that have emerged from our experience and we wish to further explore to see where they lead us.

In the following website, you can find artwork and film that illustrate the campaigns and collective actions from which we have built these thematics: http://www.infogenero.net/sitio/

Diversity Celebrated

Sometimes we have to travel, as proposed by Carlos Eduardo Martinez, from "I tolerate your difference," through to "I recognize your difference" "I respect your difference" to "I need your difference." Like this we have attained altered states of consciousness, body and heart rejoicing in the full enjoyment of diversity. In the following website, you can find artwork and film which illustrate some campaigns and collective actions related to celebrating diversity: http://sites.google.com/site/despanfletizate/

Poetic Politics

We have concluded that politics lost its course when it distanced itself from poetry, philosophy and joy and focused on calculation, competitions and instrumentalization. So, returning to the legacy of feminism we have discovered the multiple dimensions of politics. We affirm that the personal is political. In our public interventions we celebrate that we are those who inherit the nonviolence lineage and reiterate that life is nurtured through resistances, in the moments when we take flight from central forms of power. The poetic is a space for this flight to occur. Therefore our incursions into the public space have sought time and time to return to such poetic politics.

Humor as Vehicle to Show that Other Gender Relations Are Possible

In the patriarchal cultural matrix everything becomes tragedy. We become serious, transcendentalists, we radicalize and we get wrinkles for worrying so much. We get entangled in fights, we complicate more than necessary. We repeat the arguments and strategies of a serious and boring culture that only feeds sad passions. Men killing and dying, imposing by force their unreason, running over even their own lives and plunging into a orgy of violence. Women unhappy, bitter, feeling like victims, with no end to their captivity. Squandering the possibilities of creation in repeating unsatisfactory roles and links without daring to challenge and reinvent their own history.

We have chosen to laugh a little at the established, demonstrating the ridiculousness of patriarchal power. We laughed at ourselves and our smallness. But we have also paid tribute to the efforts to build different women and men. We joined our steps to the progress of indigenous peoples. We are thrilled with Professor Moncayo, who walked and talked with a quena for his company, and was the first man who dared to assert his paternity as a public and political issue, as an urgent right, as a matter of unconditional love: http://paternidadsinviolencia. blogspot.com/2007/08/desde-cali-y-con-el-profe-moncayo-le.html.

We have invented symbols, redefined themes and concepts trapped for years in binary and exclusionary logics. We have enjoyed protesting, we have sung and danced, we disguised, we have protested crying, healing and we hope to help heal the country's history.

Incarnated Memory

> a Past that has not been tamed
> with words is not memory,
> it is stalking.
>
> Laura Restrepo

And we have declared ourselves women memory. Knowing that the memory of our mothers, grandmothers and our ancestors is tinged with pain and our bodies carry violations, humiliations and injustices that mark us like iron brands. We chose to tell the stories of resistances in audiovisual format for they deserve to be told in order that the official story does not continue dying from omission, fatalism and the silencing of our history.

We already have a diverse collection of stories in documentaries, filminutes, commercials, interviews and we are dabbling in argumentative videos. Our two websites: http://www.infogenero.net/sitio/ and http://aullemosmujeres.blogspot.com/ offer a sample of how life is defended, nurtured, reinvented and continues walking many paths of resistance.

With a decade of adventures, we are in a moment of reflexive interlude. We are creating Mingas of Feminist Thought and Action as a space in which we can recharge our ideas, hearts and energies with those of many minds and many reflections. We had a first meeting of feminists of Cali in March 2012, which brought together 120 women of different ages, conditions and trajectories to talk about what outrages us nowadays, what we hope, what moves us to action, what are the challenges we face.

These voices and these ideas will nourish our course from here on through creating sisterhood with the thousands of expressions that are emerging on the planet today and which are builders of hope and of the "buenvivir" (to live well) that we deserve.

Notes

1. Co-authored with Gloria Cecilia Pérez as part of a Masters of Education thesis. We developed a systematization of this experience with emphasis on popular education and community development.
2. S. C. Motta (2009), "Old Tools and New Movements in Latin America: Political Science as Gatekeeper or Intellectual Illuminator?" *Latin American Politics and Society* 51: pp. 31–56.
3. Inspired by a Vietnamese poem that mentions the idea of planting rice over US bomb craters.
4. See Boaventura de Sousa Santos (2005), *El milenio huérfano. Ensayos para una nueva cultura política*, Madrid: Editorial Trotta.
5. Ibid.
6. Promotional Brochure of the Pazíficas Women's Political School, June 2005.
7. The expansion of the present through a sociology of absence and a sociology of emergences is part of Boaventura de Sousa Santos' proposals (*El milenio huérfano*).
8. Sandra Harding (1998), "¿Existe un método feminista? Traducción de Patricia Prieto," Mimeo.
9. Giovanni Salio (2008), "La noviolencia política: Una alternativa en la era de la complejidad y de los problemas globales," *Cuadernos Alternativa Noviolencia* (1): pp. 1–18

10. Mario López (2006), *Política sin Violencia*, Bogotá: Corporación Universitaria Minuto de Dios.
11. Kate Rushin (2009) The Bridge Poem, http://katerushin.com/poem3 .html (accessed October 14, 2013).

References

López, Mario (2006), *Política sin Violencia*, Bogotá: Corporación Universitaria Minuto de Dios.

Santos, Boaventura de Sousa (2005), *El mileniohuérfano*, Ensayos para una nueva cultura política, Madrid: Editorial Trotta.

Gayathri Spivak (1997), "Estudios de la Subalternidad: Deconstruyendo Ia Historiografía," Rivera Cusicanqui, Silvia and Barragán, Rossana (eds.), *Debates Post Coloniales: Una introducción a los Estudios de la Subaltenidad*, trans. de Raquel Gutierrez, Alison Speeding, Ana Rebeca Prada and Silvia Rivera Cusicanqui, La Paz, Bolivia: SEPHIS; Ediciones Aruwiyiri; Editorial Historias.

Conclusion: The Current Crisis in Capitalism and the Role of Education

Mike Cole

Capitalism as a failed and thoroughly volatile and unstable social system is there for all to see, especially in its current crisis. That capitalism is inherently destabilizing was recognized by Marx and Engels a century and a half ago:

> The bourgeoisie cannot exist without constantly revolutionising the instruments of production, and thereby the relations of production, and with them the whole relations of society. Conservation of the old modes of production in unaltered form, was, on the contrary, the first condition of existence for all earlier industrial classes. Constant revolutionising of production, uninterrupted disturbance of all social conditions, everlasting uncertainty and agitation distinguish the bourgeois epoch from all earlier ones. All fixed, fast-frozen relations, with their train of ancient and venerable prejudices and opinions, are swept away, all new-formed ones become antiquated before they can ossify. All that is solid melts into air, all that is holy is profaned. (Marx and Engels, [1847]1977, p. 38)

Despite suggestions from a number of academics, politicians and media pundits that neoliberal capitalism or even capitalism itself was dealt mortal blows after the Lehman bank demise of September 2008, it is clear that the ruling capitalist classes of many American and European economies, and the international capitalist class as a whole, have not forsaken neoliberalism. Indeed, as Dave Hill (2012) argues, neoliberalism is being ruthlessly reinforced to make sure that first, the capitalist system is saved and, second, that workers pay for the current capitalist crisis. Ha-Joon Chang (cited in Hill, 2012) has highlighted the similarities between the Structural Adjustment Programmes (SAPs) imposed on governments in Latin America and Africa in the 1980s and 1990s by the IMF, and the infliction by European governments of old IMF-style programs on their own populations. The result of what Hill describes as "immiseration capitalism" is that welfare is slashed, the poor live more precariously, more unhealthily and die earlier. "The low paid strata of the working class are duped and failed by the ideological apparatuses of the state, and repressed and kept in line and in prison, and (in some cases) in the ghetto, by the repressive apparatuses of the state" (Hill, 2012). Moreover, capitalists and pro-capitalist politicians are using "austerity" capitalism to (attempt to) push through major structural changes, which they hope will be irreversible. In the United Kingdom, for example, we have the most right-wing and ideologically driven government since Thatcher, using the crisis to drive through a social counterrevolution: intent on drastically diminishing workers' rights and living standards, the latter having been pushed back 30 years (Shaoul, 2012), and on undermining the very basis of the welfare state.

As the University for Strategic Optimism (UfSO, 2012) puts it, our basic public services, we are told, are simply too expensive. Thus they must be "thrown under the wheels of the megalithic debt that bears down upon us. They must be privatised, corporatised and commodified." This is to ensure the continuation of a system that funnels wealth into the hands of a privileged few. "This failed and flailing market system we are told," they go on, is the only possibility, drastic cuts the only alternative, and the fairest thing we can do. "Any deviation from the path laid out for us," they conclude "will unleash the worst imaginable, a media-imagined Worst that threatens from our darkened skies."

This intensified assault on the working class has been met with mass demonstrations and riots on the streets of major cities in many parts of the world, with millions of workers and students protesting and taking part in general strikes. Such mass resistance is, of course, to be greatly welcomed by the Left, but this alone is not enough. Resistance needs to be accompanied by a program of action. Such a program, as has been demonstrated in this volume, is alive and kicking in Latin America.

There are, of course, massive barriers to be overcome in that continent. To take the case of Venezuela, as stressed in chapter 8, the country remains a capitalist state, but one that the late Hugo Chavez was, and millions of his supporters *are*, intent on overthrowing. The vision of twenty-first-century socialism (21 cs) advocated by Chavez has been echoed by his successor Nicholas Maduro. As Maduro put it, at Chavez's funeral:

We care for all and love all of the nations of our America, but we want relations marked by respect, cooperation, and true peace. We want, just as Commander Chavez wrote, "a world without empires," without hegemonic nations, a world of peace, a world in which international law is respected, a world of nations capable of coming together to cooperate, to live, to be just, in terms of equality. And why can't this be possible when all the will of one world is here, all of the strength of one world? And Latin America has the historic task of creating that new world, of unifying ourselves in our diversity and saying to the world: here is the Latin America of liberators; here we are standing up, together, [saying]: this world has to change.

At the time of writing, April 15, 2013, Maduro has just won the presidential election with 50.66 percent of the vote, against the right-wing candidate Henrique Capriles Radonski's 49.07 percent.

What Is to Be Done?
The Guiding Principles of the UfSO

The UfSO…sees…a magnificent opportunity, a multiplication of possibilities, the opening of a space in which we might think about, and bring about, a fairer and more fulfilling society for all. In short: Many good reasons for strategic optimism! We urge a rampant questioning of the ideological basis for the relentless privatisation and privation of our lives: Are these cuts incoherent, as some have said? Or is this a specific move/set of moves on the part of neoliberal capital? Are labour, education, healthcare, and the environment, mere commodities, to be consumed by those who will redeem them as more capital? Can the opposition to cuts begin moving towards a society 'fit for purpose'? Is it still easier to imagine The End-of-the-World than The End-of-Capitalism? (http://universityforstrategicoptimism. wordpress.com/)

The chapters of this book have *demonstrated* that societies "fit for purpose" are eminently possible and that the end of capitalism is firmly set in the minds and hearts of millions of companera/os in the global south, and that popular education for 21 cs is being tried and tested successfully in myriad forms and in a wide range of contexts.

The 1 percent and their allies in the ideological and repressive apparatuses of the state will continue to distort, misrepresent and vilify any counter-hegemonic challenges to their wealth, power and privilege, but the critique of world capitalism articulated by Karl Marx in *Das*

Kapital a century and a half ago has not gone away as its apologists would have us believe. Jean- Paul Sartre (1960) described Marxism as a "living philosophy" continually being adapted and adapting itself "by means of thousands of new efforts." To Sartre's observation, Crystal Bartolovich (2002, p. 20) added, Marxism is not "simply a discourse nor a body of (academic) knowledge" but a living project.

In various ways, the Left in the global north and the global south have much to learn from each other. The revolutionary teachers in the school in Mérida (see chapter 8, in this volume) have expressed a desire for open collaboration with revolutionary pedagogical scholars and theorists outside of Venezuela (personal correspondence). The United Kingdom has a history of working- class militancy, currently hindered by the ideological and repressive apparatuses of the British state, particularly since the advent of the Thatcher government, and accelerated under Tony Blair, and under the ConDem government. Blair's mantra "education, education, education," in essence creating a flexible workforce for capitalism, represents the antithesis of the forms of popular education advocated by the various contributors to this volume.

With respect to the United States, San Juan Jr. (2010, p. xiv) has suggested that among other factors, the lack of a viable labor-union tradition has distorted historical materialist principles there. Hence, among many leftist academics, "there is no mention of the working class as a significant force for over-throwing capitalism, much less initiating a socialist revolution" (p. xiv). Nevertheless, despite all this, revolutionary thought continues to exist among some key education- ists in the United States (see chapter 4 in Cole, 2011), and there is evidence of growing militancy among some schoolteachers.

San Juan Jr. (2010, p. xiv) shows awareness of how events in Venezuela may serve as a positive example to people in the United States, when he suggests that it is instructive to contrast the trend among those leftists in the United States who have abandoned the socialist cause with the revolutionary promotion of popular literacy in Venezuela, "a pedagogical experiment of historic significance for all anti-capitalist militants" (p. xiv).

As part of the more general process of conscientization for all workers, intercontinental collaboration between revolutionary teach- ers and revolutionary academics surely captures the key element in the spirit of this book.

Like all projects of social and political transformation, as indicated by the fine-grained analysis of the volume's contributors, these peda- gogical processes of social and political transformation are processes of struggle. Thus as our authors have demonstrated there are external barriers and threats (US intervention in Venezuela is a classic example) and internal contradictions such as the intentions of reform and the realities when they meet traditional institutions and subjects, for example, the teachers in the case of Bolivia (see chapter 5, in this volume) and the institutional structures in the case of Peru (see chapter 6, in this volume); or when there are projects being built from below, as in the case of Colombia (chapters 12 and 13, in this volume), but which face hostile states and social forces. There are also informal hierarchies in movements which reproduce inclusion and exclusions (see chapter 11, in this volume), and movements face states in the process of social transformation which are themselves caught between the old capitalist state and the new socialist state, in the case of CTUs in Venezuela (chapter 9, in this volume). It is however to the credit of popular educators, visionary politicians and community activists that the transformative pedagogical practices of Latin America's masses continue to contribute to the building of an alternative world.

In the barrios of Latin America, where "the people have awoken" (Martinez et al., 2010, p. 24), and everywhere else where the poor live and the spark of socialism has been lit, people are engaging with the possibility of a practical democratic socialism. It is the firm conviction of the contributors to this volume that current revolutionary movements in the Americas and their attendant educational practices as outlined throughout the book offer the world the most viable alternative to the unyielding ravages of neoliberal capitalism and imperialism.

References

Bartolovich, C. (2002), "Introduction," in Bartolovich C. and Lazarus, N. (eds.), *Marxism, Modernity and Postcolonial Studies*, Cambridge: Cambridge University Press.

Cole, M. (2011), *Racism and Education in the U.K. and the U.S.: Towards a Socialist Alternative*, New York and London: Palgrave Macmillan.

Hill, D. (2012), "Immiseration Capitalism, Activism and Education: Resistance, Revolt and Revenge," *Journal for Critical Education Policy Studies* 10(2), http://www.jceps.com/PDFs/10-2-01.pdf.

Martinez, C., Fox, M. and Farrell, J. (2010), *Venezuela Speaks: Voices from the Grassroots*, Oakland, CA: PM Press.

Marx, K. and Engels, F. ([1847]1977), "The Communist Manifesto," in Marx, K. and Engels, F., *Selected Works in One Volume*, London: Lawrence and Wishart.

San Juan Jr., E (2010), "Foreword" to Kelsh, D., Hill, D. and Macrine, S. (eds.), *Class in Education: Knowledge, Pedagogy, Subjectivity*, London and New York: Routledge.

Sartre, J. P. (1960), *The Search forMethod (1st Part). Introduction to Critique of Dialectical Reason*, http://www.marxists.org/reference/archive/sartre /works/critic/sartre1.htm.

Shaoul, J. (2012), "Cuts Push UK Workers' Living Standards Back 30 Years," World Socialist website, March 12, http://www.wsws.org/articles/2012 /mar2012/wage-m12.shtml.

Contributors

Lenin Valencia Arroyo is a Peruvian activist and researcher on educational and environmental issues. He obtained his BA in Sociology at the Pontifical Catholic University of Peru and since 2002 has been working on topics of higher education, development and inter-culturality. He has obtained an MA in development studies at the Institute of Social Studies (The Hague) and an MSc in Environmental Sciences at the Central European University (Budapest). Currently he is a researcher at the Peruvian Society of Environmental Law and professor in Peruvian universities.

Mieke Lopes Cardozo is currently employed as assistant professor at the Amsterdam Institute for Social Science Research of the University of Amsterdam. She is the coordinator of the "IS-Academie" co-funded research project of the University of Amsterdam and the Dutch Ministry of Foreign Affairs. Her work as lecturer and researcher is focused in the areas of Education and International Development, and more specifically on teacher agency, teacher education, critical and alternative forms of education and education in relation to conflict/peacebuilding.

Mike Cole is Professor in Education, University of East London, UK, and Emeritus Research Professor in Education and Equality, Bishop Grosseteste University, Lincoln, UK. His latest books are *Critical Race Theory and Education: A Marxist Response*, and *Racism and Education in the U.K. and the U.S.: Towards a Socialist Alternative* (both Palgrave Macmillan); *Education Equality and Human Rights* (3rd edition) (Routledge); and (with Curry Malott and John Elmore) *Teaching Marx: The Socialist Challenge* (Information Age Publishing). He is the co-author (with Sara C. Motta) of *Constructing Twenty-First Century Socialism in Latin America: The Role of Radical Education*, and the co-editor (also with Sara C. Motta) of *Education and Social Change in Latin America* (both Palgrave Macmillan, forthcoming).

Francisco Dominguez is Head of the Centre for Brazilian and Latin American Studies, Middlesex University. He has written extensively about contemporary Latin American affairs; his publications include: "Venezuela's Opposition: Desperately Seeking to Overthrow Chávez," in F. Dominguez, G. Lievesley and S. Ludlam (eds.), *Right-Wing Politics in the New Latin America* (2011); "The *Latinamericanization* of the Politics of Emancipation," in G. Lievesley and S. Ludlam (eds.), *Reclaiming Latin America: Experiments in Radical Social Democracy* (2009); "Violence, the Left and the Creation of *Un Nuevo Chile*," in W. Fowler and P. Lambert (eds.), *Political Violence and Identity in Latin America* (2008); "The Rise of the Private Sector in Cuba," in A. Gray and A. Kapcia (eds.), *The Changing Dynamics of Cuban Civil Society* (2008); and F. Dominguez and M. Guedes de Oliveira (eds.), *Mercosur: Between Integration and Democracy* (2003).

Angela Martinez Dy is a poet, writer, teaching artist and radical cyberfeminist femmecee. An original member of isangmahal arts kollective, seminal voice for the millennial Asian American spoken word movement, she later co-founded Youth Speaks Seattle and served as director from 2005 to 2009. She is the co-creator of the Sisters of Resistance blog (www.sistersofresistance.org). Raised in Seattle with her heart in Manila, Angela currently lives in the United Kingdom and is pursuing a PhD on intersectional entrepreneurship online.

Ana Margarida Esteves is a Portuguese-born scholar-activist who works with solidarity economy, participatory democracy and popular education. She holds a PhD and MA in Sociology from Brown University, an MSc in European Studies from the London School of Economics and a BA in International Relations from the Technical University of Lisbon. She is currently based at Tulane University, New Orleans. Besides, she collaborates with the solidarity economy movement in Brazil and the anti-austerity movement in Portugal. She is also a co-founder of "Interface: A Journal for and about Social Movements" and a member of its International Spokescouncil.

Ivette Hernandez Santibañez is a PhD student at the Institute of Education of University of London with a Master's in Education from University Autonoma of Barcelona. Her professional experience includes more than 17 years working in the educational sector in Chile in the context of poverty and social exclusion. She has taught courses on development and participation, and comparative education at postgraduate and undergraduate levels in Spain and in the United Kingdom. She has also served as a consultant and project advisor for Workers' Commision (CCOO) in Spain and NGOs working with indigenous rural communities in Guatemala. Between 2005 and 2008 she was involved in the human rights research group at the Universidad Politecnica de Cataluña (UPC). She has recently finished her field study on the Chilean student movement. This research was co-supervised by the National Award of History Professor Gabriel Salazar at the Faculty of Philosophy and Humanities at the Universidad de Chile. Since 2011 she has been involved in the London Occupy Movement and Peoples' Assemblies Network.

Liam Kane is a lecturer in modern languages and adult education in the Centre for Open Studies in the University of Glasgow. He is author of *Popular Education and Social Change in Latin America* (Latin American Bureau) and an elected *conselheiro* of the Brazilian NGO FREPOP (Popular Education Forum for the West of São Paulo Region).

Jon. L. Mansell is a doctoral candidate at the University of Nottingham; his research relates to the concept of Displacement in International Theory, as well as the history of ideas, the relationship of Critical Theory to the Working Classs and the Political Economy of Migration and De-Industrialisation in Europe.

Jennifer L. Martinez received her undergraduate degree from Stanford University and her doctoral degree from the School of Politics and International Relations at the University of Nottingham, UK. Her PhD thesis *Comites de Tierra Urbana (CTUs) and the "Right to the City"* won the 2011 British International Studies Association Michael Nicholson Thesis Prize. Jennifer is currently the executive director of a grassroots organization in California where she works on urban land and housing policy and immigration reform and continues to pursue research on global urban transformation

Sara C. Motta is Senior Lecturer in Politics at the University of Newcastle, NSW. Her research focus is the politics of subaltern resistance, with particular reference to Latin America and the reinvention of new forms of popular politics, political subjectivities and ways of life that seek to transcend neoliberal capitalism. This research has led her to explore the politics of knowledge and the linkages between knowledge, power and exclusion, as well as the ways in which new social movements are re-inventing democratic and participatory forms of knowledge creation that challenge the academic privilege of the academy. Methodologically she is therefore interested in developing movement relevant research and participatory research methods. As part of this she is also interested in the pedagogy of dissent, and the use of popular education and critical education in and outside of the University in the forging of struggles and practices of social justice.

Thomas Muhr is Lecturer at the Institute of Politics and Development Research at Johannes Kepler University (JKU), Linz (Austria), and visiting fellow in global development in the School of Geographical Sciences, University of Bristol (UK). Thomas works on the political sociology and geographies of globalization, regionalisms and development, and the themes of democracy, security and education therein, with a focus on Latin America and the Caribbean and its international and global relations. He is author of the book *Venezuela and the ALBA: Counter-Hegemony, Geographies of Integration and Development, and Higher Education for All* (VDM/Akademikerverlag, 2011), and editor of *Counter-Globalization and Socialism in the 21st Century: The Bolivarian Alliance for the Peoples of Our America* (Routledge, 2013). Over the past two decades, Thomas has worked as a teacher, lecturer, researcher and consultant in diverse settings in Latin America and the Caribbean and Europe.

Glory Rigueros Saavedra is Visiting Fellow at the School of Gender Studies Faculty of Human Sciences, Universidad Nacional de Colombia. She is a rural sociologist and equalities specialist with a PhD in Development Studies, an MA in Rural Development and an MSc in Science and Technology Policy. She has taught at Imperial College and at South Bank University, London. Her experience of research spans the United Kingdom, Mexico and Colombia, where she is also a social and human rights activist with trade unions, rural communities, ethnic minorities and women's groups.

Index

Printed and bound by CPI Group (UK) Ltd, Croydon, CR0 4YY